# THE SCHWARTZ
# STOCK MARKET HANDBOOK

# THE SCHWARTZ STOCK MARKET HANDBOOK

## Third Edition

by
**David Schwartz**

Burleigh Publishing Company

©Burleigh Publishing Company 1998

Compiled and edited by David Schwartz
Published by Burleigh Publishing Company Limited,
Burleigh Hall, Burleigh, Stroud, Gloucestershire GL5 2PF
First published 1994
Second edition 1995
Third edition 1998

ISBN 09523961 2 2

Printed in England by
Redwood Books, Trowbridge, Wiltshire

# CONTENTS

# INTRODUCTION

January profits
not random

Some stock market price fluctuations are random and unpredictable. Others are not. Take January for example. Over the long term, a hypothetical January investor who purchased a cross-section of shares every January, and switched to cash for the rest of the year, would have increased his capital by six-fold since World War 1. A June investor, following the same strategy, would see his start-up investment shrink by almost one half.

The example is artificial because all taxes and trading costs are conveniently overlooked but it makes an important point. Stock market gyrations are not always random.

No one can
explain why

Incidentally, strong Januarys are not unique to London. It is the best month of the year in Tokyo and second-best on Wall Street. Analysts have advanced many reasons for its strength including the availability of year-end results, frequent forecasts about the year ahead and floods of money pouring into pension-related investments. Although many theories proport to explain January's strength, no one knows for sure why shares rise so often in the year's opening month.

August profits

As Table 1 reveals, August is another superior month. If you wish to frustrate someone who claims to know why January investors do so well, point out that August also does well in most years without the benefit of year-end results, forecasts about the future and floods of new investment funds.

## LIKELIHOOD OF A PRICE RISE

| | Prices rise | Rank |
|---|---|---|
| January | 76% | 1 |
| February | 50% | 10 |
| March | 58% | 7 |
| April | 73% | 2 |
| May | 49% | 12 |
| June | 51% | 9 |
| July | 50% | 10 |
| August | 68% | 3 |
| September | 54% | 8 |
| October | 62% | 4 |
| November | 59% | 5 |
| December | 59% | 5 |

Table 1: The typical month rises 59% of the time. January, April and August, the year's three best months, each rise well above average. At the bottom of the pile are February, May, June and July. The chance of profit for these also-rans is strictly a 50:50 proposition. According to Efficient Market Theory, in the absence of new information, price changes are random occurrences. Over the long run, you would not expect to see such wide inter-month variations.

No one knows why January and August do so well, why June is so weak, or for that matter, the reasons behind hundreds of other trends discussed in the pages ahead. We can only report that many have been running for decades. Some involve specific months. Others involve specific weeks of the year and even individual days.

6 June

Here is an example. The odds of a price rise on any individual day of the year is around 52%. Yet some days are much better than average and have been for decades. Table 2 shows the year's most profitable days. The best of the best is 6 June which rises 77% of the time. No one

**THE YEAR'S BEST DAYS**

|  | Prices Rise |
|---|---|
| June 6 | 77% |
| December 27 | 76% |
| December 22 | 75% |
| August 5 | 73% |
| December 24 | 72% |
| January 4 | 70% |
| April 27 | 70% |
| December 23 | 70% |
| December 29 | 70% |
| August 3 | 70% |

Table 2: It's simply unbelievable. Five of the year's best days arrive in December. All occur after December 21.

knows why 6 June is so profitable but it has been since before World War 2.

26 September   At the bottom of the pile is 26 September which rises just 28% of the time, a truly terrible record *(see Table 3)*.

Trends like these are the focus of *The Schwartz Stock Market Handbook*, essentially a study of historical stock market trends. Our goal is to help investors to improve the odds of making profitable investment decisions by applying the lessons of the past to the future.

Free newsletter   The current edition is designed to carry readers through the year on a month-by-month basis. An important adjunct to the *Handbook* is a free quarterly newsletter to give readers up-to-the-minute advice of what to expect from the stock market in the months ahead. Details on how to receive your free copy can be found on page xv and on the token at the back of the book.

The *Schwartz Stock Market Handbook* contains many thousands of important facts. To our way of thinking,

## THE YEAR'S WORST DAYS

|  | Prices Rise |
|---|---|
| September 26 | 28% |
| February 21 | 32% |
| September 16 | 32% |
| September 23 | 32% |
| November 23 | 32% |
| February 4 | 33% |
| October 9 | 33% |
| March 11 | 34% |
| January 23 | 35% |
| October 10 | 35% |
| December 4 | 35% |

Table 3: Don't be too quick to believe that all short-term price fluctuations are a random occurrence. September is the only month to have three entries on the list of the year's worst days. The first few days of October have more two entires on the list. Five of the worst days of the year confined to a four week stretch is anything but random.

there is too much information to be digested at one sitting. So don't just read it once from cover to cover and then put it on the shelf and forget about it.

**Read it in a different way**

We suggest that you treat the *Handbook* as a reference book and use it constantly as a companion to all of your stock market decisions during the year. Near the beginning of each month, re-read the appropriate chapter. Even if you don't study every single individual trend, you should have a clear sense of how the month typically unfolds, whether the odds favour an up-move or a down-move, and which segments of the month are most likely to be strong or weak.

Most important of all, whenever you contemplate a

Nuances will
shift the odds

trade, you should re-read the relevant chapter, paying careful attention to the nuances as well as the big picture. This procedure will not put you on the winning side of every transaction, but over the long run, will shift the odds of being right a bit more in your favour.

As you will soon see, the *Schwartz Stock Market Handbook* contains many profit-enhancing trends to help you to maximise your investment performance. While reading and studying them, keep in mind the three guiding principles that underly every historical price trend analysis.

No guarantees

● No one can flawlessly forecast where share prices are heading. Historically-based probabilities define the odds of an up or down move based on past performance trends. They increase the likelihood that investors make the right choice but do not guarantee success. When we say prices rise eight out of 10 times after a given condition occurs, it also means they fall twice. By definition, every projection is periodically wrong

Fresh news
changes the
odds

● Although historical price trends often provide strong clues about the direction of future share price moves, fresh economic or political news makes hash of these probabilities. Witness the stock market's reaction to a possible change of government, sudden increase in the inflation rate or to rumours of an interest rate change.

Success breeds
failure

● Knowledge of a probable event often causes investor behaviour to change (perhaps buying shares in advance to catch an expected up-move). These behaviour changes alter the underlying pattern that created the trend in the first place. In a funny sort of way, success breeds failure when it comes to analysing stock market trends. Historical analysis is a never-ending process. Investors must keep studying the market to keep abreast of changing patterns.

### About our data sources

Monthly trend

A 78 year-long monthly price trend index was built from three sources: from 1919 to 1924, an index compiled by *British Banker Magazine*; from 1925 to March, 1962, the *Investors Chronicle* Industrial Index which was periodically changed and up-dated; from April, 1962 to the present, the FTSE All Share Index which also was periodically up-dated.

The *British Banker* and *Investors Chronicle* series' are both long out of print. They were located by researchers at Barclays deZoete Wedd Securities Limited. We are grateful to them, especially to Michael Hughes, Managing Director – Economics and Strategy for making this data available to *Schwartz Stock Market Handbook* readers.

Daily trend

Daily price trends have been running for a shorter period. They were first collected in a systematic fashion via the FT Ordinary Share Index (or FT-30) which began publication on 1 July 1935. For three decades, it was the only daily index available. All short-term (daily or partial month) price trends discussed in this book are based upon a combination of the FT Ordinary Share Index for the first 30 years, and the FTSE All Share Index for the balance of the period.

..and finally, the cartoons

Before moving on, a brief note about our cartoons. They are provided once again by Duncan Beedie, who I like to think of as my veteran cartoonist. Readers will be fascinated to learn that he is now a Grand Old Man of 20 years of age. Many will agree that his work speaks with a maturity far beyond his years.

*David Schwartz*
*November 1997*

# Free Quarterly Newsletter

Readers of the *Schwartz Stock Market Handbook* are invited to receive a free quarterly newsletter that we publish at the end of each quarter of the year – March, June, September, and December – using the token at the back of this book.

Each issue focuses on the three months ahead and contains our forecast of where the stock market is heading.

There are no gimmicks. It's absolutely free. To order, please tear out the token at the back of the book and submit it with four separate stamped, pre-addressed A4 sized envelopes (one for each issue) to:

Quarterly Newsletter
Schwartz Stock Market Handbook
Burleigh Publishing Company Ltd.
Burleigh Hall, Burleigh
Stroud, Gloucestershire GL5 2PF

For readers who find it more convenient for us to address and provide postage for the newsletter, we will send to you the next four issues, air mailed when appropriate, for a small fee to cover administration costs.

Please turn to the token at the back of the book for further details.

# DISCLAIMER

This book is essentially a review of past stock market trends. It is based upon an historical analysis of every closing price on the various share price indices available at the time this book was prepared.

Every statement we make about possible future price movements is a statistical projection derived from past trends. No one knows if any of these relationships will continue in the future. Our observations are not intended to be recommendations to buy or sell any particular stock or the market as a whole.

Statements about profits or losses associated with any buy or sell action are calculated before all fees and taxes of any kind.

Remember that the price of any stock market investment can go down as well as up. You can easily lose some or all of your investment. This is especially true of various derivatives which are very volatile.

Be sure to discuss the risk of any investment you are considering with a qualified advisor before making any investment decision.

# CHAPTER 1 – JANUARY

January is the best month of the year for UK investors. Prices rise 76% of the time.

At one time, the first and last quarters of the month were the two most profitable segments of the month. But the trend has changed in recent years. The stock market frequently runs out of fuel during the first half of the month, often a temporary setback after a good December rally.

But things soon improve. The third quarter of the month (15-23 January) has shown above-average strength in recent years and the final quarter continues to be as good to investors as it had been in the past. Prices have risen in 17 of the last 20 years.

History shows that the stock market is often very profitable in January in bull market years but disappointing during bear markets. The chance of a price rise is just 50:50, and if prices do rise, the rally is often weak. Given the difference in profit odds between bull and bear market Januarys, investors will be interested the guidelines on page 6 which will help them to determine which type of market is currently running.

Followers of Efficient Market Theory believe current share prices are a reflection of all past knowledge and future hopes. Without fresh news, future price changes are merely random gyrations.

According to EMT fans, the long-term odds of making money from the stock market in any single month are basically the same. Variations may emerge during any short stretch of course but over 50 or 100 years, no significant difference between months should exist.

**Do not believe EMT**

It is a fine theory but as far as the UK stock market is concerned, the theory does not fit the facts. History shows that the UK stock market does not fluctuate as randomly as EMT fans believe. There are wide differences in profitability from month to month. Take January for example, the year's most profitable month. Since 1919, when reliable stock market statistics were first compiled on a monthly basis, January prices rose 76% of the time. The average price rise was +2.48%, equal to about 100 points on an FTSE 100 in the area of 4000.

The long-term average is helped by January 1975's extraordinary rise of 53% which marked the end of the 1972–74 bear market, history's worst for UK investors. But even without 1975, January is a strong performer as Table 1.1 reveals.

**Consistently profitable**

No one knows why share prices rise so often in January. Some analysts guess that the large number of end-of-year company results and forecasts for the year ahead give investors more confidence to commit new funds. Others point to increased pension fund cash inflows. Whatever the cause, the only money-losing decade for the January investor was back in the 1930s, a period of generally poor stock market conditions. Since then, the month has been consistently profitable. The constant January investor may not have profited every year, but did so on a decade-by-decade basis in the 1940s to 1990s, six decades in a row.

## JANUARY PRICE RISES AND DECLINES: 1919–1996

|  | Average January price change | Up | Down/ No change |
|---|---|---|---|
| 1920–29 | 2.19% | 8 | 2 |
| 1930–39 | -0.29% | 5 | 5 |
| 1940–49 | 1.85% | 10 | 0 |
| 1950–59 | 0.91% | 6 | 4 |
| 1960–69 | 1.96% | 8 | 2 |
| 1970–79 | 5.93% | 7 | 3 |
| 1980–89 | 5.69% | 9 | 1 |
| 1990–96 | 0.57% | 5 | 2 |
| Average January change: 1919–96 | 2.48% | 76% | 24% |
| Rank (of 12) | 1 | 1 | |

*Source: BZW, Datastream/ICV*

Table 1.1: January investors last lost money during the 1930's. Since then, the month has been quite profitable. Investors did not profit every single year, but made money in every decade from the 1940s to the 1980s. Unfortunately, the size of the typical month's profit has dropped noticeably in recent years because of periodic bouts of weakness which often occur in the first half of the month.

**Short-run weakness**

January's performance has been very strong in recent decades. It was number one-ranked in the 1960s, '70s and '80s. But in one important respect, things have changed during the 1990s. Shares often suffer a very pronounced bout of weakness in the first half of the month, usually a temporary setback after a good December rally. In most cases, the weakness runs its course in a few days and prices then continue to climb.

3

• In 1994, the FTSE 100 temporarily peaked on 7 January and then fell 2.5% in the next four trading days. Once the selling wave ended on 13 January, prices resumed their upward march and hit a new all-time peak on 2 February, a gain of almost 5% in just 14 trading days.

• In 1996, the FTSE 100 fell about 2% in six trading days starting on 4 January. Shares then rallied, gaining 2% from 12 January to month-end.

• In 1997, the FTSE 100 fell 62 points in the year's first seven trading days before climbing to another all-time high by the end of the month.

On balance, recent evidence suggests January has not lost its magic. In most cases, the bout of weakness does not carry over to the month as a whole. In contrast, the last series of poor Januarys was in the 1930s when prices fell several years in a row. The pattern in those years was exemplified by continued weakness throughout the whole month. In our opinion, favourable January trading conditions are 'alive and kicking'. Investors will not make money every year but will do so most of the time. However, a short-term set-back now seems to be part of the January landscape.

The set-back is having an unfortunate side effect. The average annual January profit in recent years is noticeably lower than it had been in the preceding decades.

Bull market profits

Looking at the month as a whole, investors do especially well during bull market Januarys. Shares rise 86% of the time, the best performance of all 12 months. The average profit in bull market Januarys is +4.00%, also the best monthly performance *(see Table 1.2)*.

If prices happen to fall in bull market Januarys, the odds of a big loss are low. The average decline in losing months is just -1.60%, smaller than average, compared

4

## JANUARY PERFORMANCE IN BULL/BEAR MARKETS: 1919–1996

|                                    | Bull Markets | Bear Markets |
| ---------------------------------- | ------------ | ------------ |
| Average per cent price change      | *4.00%       | -1.37%       |
| Rank (of 12)                       | 1            | 3            |
| Per cent of time prices rise       | 86%          | 50%          |
| Rank (of 12)                       | 1            | 1            |
| Average per cent price change in:  |              |              |
| Rising years                       | **4.93%      | 1.81%        |
| Declining years                    | -1.60%       | -4.55%       |

```
*   3.20% without 1975
**  3.92% without 1975
```

*Source: BZW, Datastream/ICV*

Table 1.2: Investors do well in January during bull markets. It is the number-one-ranked month in terms of the likelihood of a price rise and the size of that rise. During bear markets, prices rise half the time. However, January bear market increases tend to be quite weak.

with other months. Since records began in 1919, there have been just eight losing bull market Januarys. Investors incurred losses of under two percent in six of those months. One of the two exceptions was a near-miss, -2.69% in January 1995. The sole major bull market exception occurred in 1964 when the stock market scented a base rate rise in response to an emerging balance of payments problem and January prices fell -5.47%.

The historical record sends a very clear message. The likelihood of profit is quite high in bull market Januarys. And if prices should fall, the odds of a big drop are low.

**Bear market blues**

The main risk for January investors occurs in bear market years when the odds of a price rise are 50:50. When prices do fall, the average price drop is -4.55%. On the other hand, if prices do rise, the size of the average increase is only +1.81%, the weakest profit record of all 12 months during bear market rallies. Since 1919, the stock market rose in January in 11 different bear market years. Eight of the rises were under two percent. Two of the three exceptions occurred more than 60 years ago. Once again, the message from the past is clear. In bear market years, the odds are low that January prices will rally strongly.

Given the drastically different profit opportunities for January in bull versus bear markets, it is critically important for investors to know if they are in a bull or bear market. Happily, the historical record provides a useful signal to help to answer this question.

**Spotting bull markets**

As Figure 1.1 reveals, small price shifts in December are virtually always associated with a bull market at the start of January. Since our records began, the UK stock market shifted within a range of -0.80% to +2.91% in 33 different Decembers. January enjoyed a bull market in 29 of those years, an 88% success rate. Furthermore, each of the four failures occurred in the first half of this century. Since 1950, this signal flashed 16 times. January enjoyed a bull market each time.

These figures do not tell you when the bull market started or when it will end. It is conceivable that the following month will see the start of a new bear market. Nevertheless, the lessons from the past send a strong message – bull market prospects for the month ahead generally look good following a moderate December shift.

**Spotting bear markets**

If the December price trend is weaker, with a decline in excess of -0.80%, the odds are slightly higher than 50:50 that the UK stock market is in a bear market as January begins. This is a useful warning signal to exercise caution in the weeks ahead until the situation

## ODDS OF BULL/BEAR MARKET TIPPED BY DECEMBER'S TREND

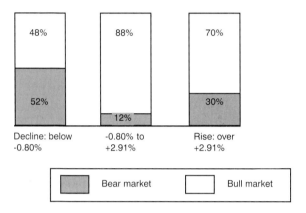

Source: BZW, Datastream/ICV

Figure 1.1: If the Stock Market shifts by a small amount in December, within a range of -0.80% to +2.91%, the likelihood is high that a bull market is in progress as January approaches. Since 1950, this signal flagged a bull market 16 times in a row.

becomes clarified.

**US Presidential cycle**

History also shows that the US Presidential cycle has a striking effect on the UK stock market in January. UK shares typically rise in a US Presidential election year. We first called attention to this relationship in an earlier edition of the *Schwartz Stock Market Handbook*. Since then, UK shares rose in January 1996 as expected. Since 1968, UK shares have risen eight election years in a row. The average level of profit is a whopping +5.61% per year. In the following two years, e.g., the first and second year of the next Presidential cycle, the chance of a January profit is not much higher than 50:50 *(see Table 1.3)*.

## JANUARY RECORD DURING THE US PRESIDENTIAL CYCLE: 1967–1996

|  | Year 1 | Year 2 | Year 3 | Year 4 |
|---|---|---|---|---|
| Prices rose | 4 | 4 | 6 | 8 |
| Prices fell | 3 | 3 | 2 | 0 |
| | | | | |
| Average price change | 2.83% | -0.01% | 7.85% | 5.61% |

*Based on FT Non-Financial Index. Source: Datastream/ICV*

UPDATE

Table 1.3: In recent years, US Presidential election years have been good to UK investors. 1996 proved to be more of the same with a January rise of +1.83%. Unfortunately, the magic does not carry over to Year One and Two of the new cycle. But Year Three (1999) is also usually profitable. Note though that Year Three's high average January price change is influenced by 1975's rally that increased prices by over 50%. Without it, the average Year Three increase is +1.63%.

### INCREASE YOUR PROFIT ODDS

Although prices frequently rise in January, it is possible to shift the odds of profiting with a January investment a bit more in your favour. There are a number of historical trends that often tip which way share prices will shift in January. Obviously, there are no guarantees they will continue to work as well in the future but they have been quite useful up until now.

Prior three-months signal

Since 1964, the FTSE All Share Index has risen by at least +5.60% in the previous three months (October–December) in 16 different years. January prices continued to rise in 15 of those years, a 94% success rate. The average January increase during those 16 years is +3.64%, about 146 points on an FTSE 100 in the area of 4000.

*Rose (15)*

*Fell (1)*

January's record after an October to December price rise of at least +5.60% (FTSE All Share Index since 1964)

---

**December signal No.1**

Another signal frequently associated with a January price rise is a large increase on the FT-Non-Financial Index or its predecessor index in December. Strong up-moves of at least +4.18% have taken place 14 times since 1921. The stock market continued to rise in January in 13 of those years, 93% of the time. The average January increase in years following a strong December up-move was +3.26%, around 130 points on an FTSE 100 in the area of 4000[1].

---

[1]Unless otherwise stated, all monthly calculations are based on the FTSE All Share Index or its predecessor index and all daily, quarterly, and bi-monthly calculations are based on the Ordinary Share Index, also known as the FT-30 from 1936–1968 and the FTSE All Share Index from 1969 to the present.

Most newspapers carry closing prices on the FTSE All Share Index but other indices like the FT-Non-Financial Index and FT Ordinary Share Index are less widely available. We will provide price trends on key indices for the last 12 months at no cost. Send a self-addressed, postage-paid envelope to:

Schwartz Stock Market Handbook Closing Price Offer
Burleigh Publishing Company
Burleigh Hall
Burleigh
Stroud
Gloucestershire GL5 2PF

*Rose (13)*

*Fell (1)*

January's record after a December price rise of at least +4.18%
(FT-Non-Financial Index since 1921)

The single exception occurred in January 1990 as
investors began to realise that 15% Base Rates were tak-
ing longer than expected to slow the economy, and that a
very serious recession was coming.

**December signal No.2**

A similar trend has run on the FTSE All Share Index
since 1964. During this period, there have been 11 occasions when December prices rose by at least +3.74%. The
stock market rose in January in 10 of those years.

*Rose (10)*

*Fell (1)*

January's record after a December price rise of at least +3.74%
(FTSE All Share Index since 1964)

**Prior 12-months signal**

Here is an up-date on a useful signal that has been
described in previous editions of the *Schwartz Stock
Market Handbook*. It is based upon the FT-
Non-Financial Index. Look for steadily rising prices
throughout the previous year including a price rise of
any size during the past month (December), a rise of at
least 2% in the past two months (November 1 to
December 31) and past three months, and a rise of any
size in the past six months and past 12 months. If the
necessary conditions are met, there is an 89% likelihood
that January prices will rise.

These conditions may seem onerous but, since 1920,

they have occurred 19 times. January prices rose in 17 of those years. The average January share price increase in the 19 years with a strong prior year up-trend was over 3%. This scenario occurred most recently in 1995 and prices rose as expected in January 1996.

*Rose (17)*

*Fell (2)*

January's record after steadily rising prices in the past 12 months (FT-Non-Financial Index since 1920)

The two exceptions are instructive and further support the rule. Prices fell in 1959, despite the positive price signal. However, the decline was a tiny -0.1%. In 1993, poor trading conditions at the beginning of the month were reversed with a late month rally that moved prices into positive territory on February 1st – one day late!

Prior six-months signal     Another trend worth monitoring is the direction of prices during the preceding six months. If they move moderately on the FT-Non-Financial Index, by no more than -0.85% on the down-side and +6.66% on the up-side, the odds of a January price increase improve considerably. Here's the evidence. Since 1923, share prices shifted within this range in the six-month run-up to January on 23 occasions. January prices rose in 20 of those years (87%). The average annual price increase was +2.19%.

*Rose (20)*

*Fell (3)*

January's record after a price shift of -0.85% to +6.66% in the past six months (FT-Non-Financial Index since 1923)

Although January is a good month in which to invest,

## QUARTERLY ODDS OF PRICE RISE IN JANUARY

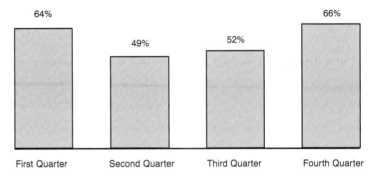

Source: Financial Times, Datastream/ICV

Figure 1.2: The first and fourth quarters have risen most often over the long-run. However, in recent years, there are signs of important trend changes in the first quarter (for the worse) and third quarter (for the better). Both of these issues will be discussed in the pages to follow.

Quarterly
differences

there are wide differences in profit potential in different segments of the month. To prove the point, January was divided into four quarters: January 1–8, 9–15, 16–23, and 24–31, and the price changes per quarter were analysed all the way back to 1936.

Over the long-term, the first and last quarters of the month have been January's two most profitable segments. Both have been consistent money-makers. Investing in the two middle quarters produced less profit. But in recent years, third-quarter share price trends have been getting stronger and persistent weakness has emerged for short periods during the first half of the month (see Figure 1.2).

Given the differences in profit potential between each quarter, and the recent trend changes, each segment will be examined separately.

# FIRST QUARTER OF JANUARY – JANUARY 2ND TO 8TH

> The first quarter used to be a steady money-spinner. But the likelihood of a price rise has declined in recent years to around 50%. There is also persistent weakness in the quarter to follow. On balance, the odds often favour holding back from any new investment at this point in the month.
>
> History reveals several pockets of profitability in the first quarter. A good example is the Friday profit trend. No one knows why but Fridays rise more than two-thirds of the time.

**Steady profits**    Historically, the first quarter of the year has been quite profitable. Between 1936 to the present, prices rose in 64% of all first quarters. A steady first-quarter investor made a profit in every single completed decade. Since records began, this part of the month has generated an average profit of +0.61% per year, equal to 24 points on an FTSE 100 in the area of 4000 *(see Table 1.4)*.

**Recent weakness**    Although the long-term trend is good, investors must not get too complacent. Prior to 1970, the first quarter was consistently ranked as the most profitable or second-most profitable quarter of the month. Since 1970, the first quarter slipped to a steady third place in quarterly profitability. Another point to consider is that the 1990s have not been good to first-quarter investors. Prices fell in four of the last seven years.

**Poor conditions soon improve**    In the past, first-quarter weakness was often followed by further weakness in the rest of the month. But the current bout of weakness is different. Prices tend to be weak for a week or two, usually after a good December rally, and then resume their upward climb in the second half or the month. What is the cause? No one knows for sure. We hypothesise that profitable January trading conditions have become so widely known that investors who planned to commit new funds to the market around

## PERCENTAGE PRICE CHANGE: JANUARY 1936–96

|  | Jan 1–8 | Jan 9–15 | Jan 16–23 | Jan 24–31 |
|---|---|---|---|---|
| Annual average |  |  |  |  |
| 1935–39 | -0.15% | -0.29% | -0.76% | 0.34% |
| 1940–49 | 0.52% | 0.49% | -0.39% | -0.01% |
| 1950–59 | 0.20% | -0.25% | -0.22% | 0.08% |
| 1960–69 | 0.69% | -0.12% | 0.36% | 0.97% |
| 1970–79 | 1.10% | 1.10% | 1.13% | 1.89% |
| 1980–89 | 1.17% | 0.46% | 1.59% | 1.53% |
| 1990–96 | -0.02% | -0.80% | -0.01% | 1.43% |
| | | | | |
| Average quarterly price change | 0.61% | 0.20% | 0.38% | 0.99% |
| | | | | |
| Per cent of time prices rise | 64% | 49% | 52% | 66% |

*Source: Financial Times, Datastream/ICV*

Table 1.4: The first quarter has been profitable in every completed decade since World War 2. Unfortunately, its share of total January profits is declining. In the 1930s–60s, it was typically the most profitable or second-most profitable quarter. Since 1970, it has become the third most profitable quarter. In contrast, the fourth-quarter record continues to be unbelievably strong. Prices have risen the last 10 years in a row.

the turn of the year now jump in a bit earlier to catch the expected rally. Such behaviour boosts shares in late December (precisely what has occurred recently) and hurts shares after the turn of the year due to a temporary reduction in demand.

Bull versus bear

This bout of recent first-quarter weakness is most noted during bull market years. Over the long run, shares rise in the first quarter in two out of three bull markets. But since

### JANUARY FIRST-QUARTER PERFORMANCE IN BULL/BEAR MARKETS: 1936–1996

|  | Total | Bull Markets | Bear Markets |
|---|---|---|---|
| Average price change | 0.61% | 0.81% | 0.08% |
| Rank (of 48) | 9 | 14 | 9 |
| Per cent of time prices rise | 64% | 68% | 53% |
| Rank (of 48) | 8 | 13 | 11 |

*Source: Financial Times, Datastream/ICV*

Table1.5: Prices rise in two out of three bull market years over the long-run. But the trend has weakened in recent years. Since 1980, the first quarter has risen just half the time in bull market years, just like the bear market trend.

1980, prices have risen just half the time in bull market first quarters which is similar to its bear market record *(see Table 1.5)*.

Daily differences  There are several daily price trends operating during this quarter that are worth monitoring. Over the long-run, prices tend to rise most often near the beginning of the quarter. In fact, the second and the fourth are the two most profitable trading days of the entire month on an historical basis *(see Figure 1.3)*. The price trend soon weakens. The final three trading days of the quarter rise about half the time.

First day of year  In the Good Old Days, the year's opening trading day was considered by many to be a guaranteed money-maker. From 1935, when daily price records were first systematically recorded, to 1964, share prices rose on the first trading day of the year, in 26 out of 29 years, regardless of whether the opener landed on January 1 (then a business day), 2, 3 or 4.

15

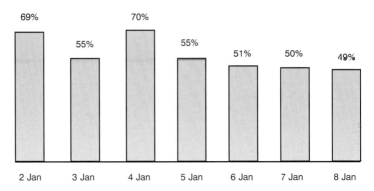

## PERCENTAGE OF TIME PRICES RISE EACH TRADING DAY IN JANUARY'S FIRST QUARTER

*Source: Financial Times, Datastream/ICV*

Figure 1.3: Over the long run, the likelihood of rising prices is high on 2 January and 4 January, the two most profitable days of the entire month. However, the January 2 trend has weakened a little in recent years.

Unfortunately, the strength at the year's opening bell has slipped in recent years, probably a victim of late-December's rally. Prices have risen just over half the time in the last three decades *(see Table 1.6)*. But note that 4 January continues to be a strong performer in years when it is not the opening trading day.

Pre-Christmas signal

It is not widely known but you can load the dice in your favour on the year's first trading day by monitoring the price trend on the final two trading days before Christmas. History shows that if share prices decline during this two-day stretch, they will probably also fall on the first trading day of the New Year, after investors forget the holiday spirit and settle down to some serious trading.

There have been 15 declines over the final two

## PERCENTAGE OF TIME PRICES RISE ON THE YEAR'S FIRST TRADING DAY: 1936–1996

|  | Prices rise |
|---|---|
| Total | 70% |
| 1936–1964 | 90% |
| 1965–present | 53% |

*Source: Financial Times, Datastream/ICV*

Table 1.6: The odds of a price rise on the year's opening trading day has weakened in recent years.

pre-Christmas trading days since 1935. On 10 of those occasions, the first trading day of the New Year also fell (67%). In the remaining 47 years, prices fell just nine times (19%) on the first trading day after New Years Day. In case you are wondering, the length of the New Year's holiday trading break has no effect on the market's likelihood of rising or falling. The market rises the same percentage of the time on the year's first trading day, regardless of the length of the holiday.

**Poor Monday and Tuesday**

One final trend worth monitoring is the correlation between day of week and profitability. Over the long-run, prices rise least often at the beginning of the week, and most often at the end of the week. No one can explain why this trend occurs but it has been running since 1935 *(see Figure 1.4)*. First-quarter Tuesdays are especially likely to disappoint investors, rising just 43% of the time, well below the typical Tuesday performance for the year as a whole. But things soon improve. First-quarter Thursdays rise 64% of the time, the fourth-best Thursday record in all 48 yearly quarters. The Friday record is even better. First-quarter Fridays rise 69% of time, the third-best Friday performance of the year.

## PERCENTAGE OF TIME PRICES RISE EACH DAY OF WEEK IN JANUARY'S FIRST QUARTER

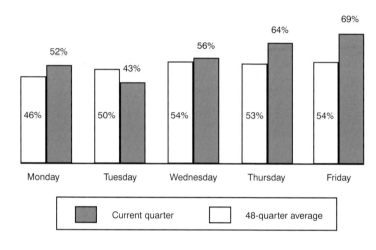

*Source: Financial Times, Datastream/ICV*

Figure 1.4: The chance of a price rise improves toward the end of the week. First-quarter Fridays are third-best, compared with all other quarters of the year. First-quarter Thursdays are ranked fourth-best.

### INCREASE YOUR PROFIT ODDS

Here are some useful statistically-based rules of thumb to help you to maximise your trading profits in this first quarter of the year. While they will not work every year, they will improve your track record over the long-run.

December signal No.1

Since 1970, there have been 12 occasions when the FTSE All Share Index rose steadily in the first and second halves of December. Prices continued to rise in January's first quarter in each of those years. During the remaining 15 years of this period, the first-quarter record was just five prices increases and 10 declines.

NEW

*Rose (12)*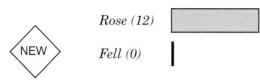

*Fell (0)* |

First-quarter record after a price rise in December's first half and second half (FTSE All Share Index since 1970).

December signal No.2

The following trend involves both the FT-Non-Financial Index and the FT Ordinary Share Index and has been running since 1938. During this period, there have been 15 years with a December shift within a range of -0.81% to +1.34% on the FT-Non-Financial Index or its predecessor index. Prices rose on the FT Ordinary Share Index 13 times.

UPDATE

*Rose (13)*

*Fell (2)*

First-quarter record after a December price shift of -0.81% to +1.34% (FT-Non-Financial Index since 1938)

December second-half signal No.1

Moderate price shifts on the FT Ordinary Share Index in the second half of December also do a good job of forecasting where first-quarter prices are heading. Since 1938, there have been 12 years when prices shifted within a narrow range of -0.42% to +0.92%. Prices rose in the first quarter of January in 11 of those years.

*Rose (11)*

*Fell (1)*

First-quarter record after a price shift of -0.42% to +0.92% in December's second half (FT Ordinary Share Index since 1938)

19

December
second-half
signal No.2

Since 1969, there have been 17 occasions when the FT-Non-Financial Index rose within a range of +1.65% to +3.95% in the second half of December. The first quarter rose in 15 of those years.

*Rose (15)*

*Fell (2)*

First-quarter record after a price rise of +1.65% to +3.95% in December's second half (FT-Non-Financial Index since 1969)

In the remaining 12 years of this period, the first quarter rose just four times and fell eight times.

December
fourth-quarter
signal

And finally, if prices rise by a small amount on the FT Ordinary Share Index in the fourth quarter of December, no more than +0.82%, a first-quarter increase usually follows. Since 1940, there have been 23 fourth-quarter price shifts within this range. January's first quarter rose in 20 of those years.

*Rose (20)*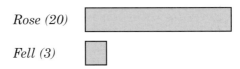

*Fell (3)*

First-quarter record after a price rise of up to +0.82% in December's fourth quarter (FT Ordinary Share Index since 1940)

## SECOND QUARTER OF JANUARY – JANUARY 9TH TO 15TH

Here comes the weakest quarter of the month. Prices used to rise about half of the time but the trend has been much weaker in recent years. The chance of a stock market drop is especially high following a large increase in the second half of December.

History reveals that the chance of a price rise is lowest in the first few days of the quarter, especially 11 January.

**Weakest quarter**

The second quarter has the questionable distinction of being January's worst-performing quarter. Although it is weak in a relative sense, share prices have risen about half the time and have produced a small average annual profit of +0.20% per year over the long-run.

**Bull versus bear**

There are wide differences in second-quarter profitability during bull versus bear markets. Over the long-run, prices rise more than half the time in bull markets but just one-third of the time in bear market years and typically produce a loss *(see Table 1.7)*.

During the 1980s, January's second quarter produced a reasonably sized average annual profit (+0.46% per year), causing some analysts to wonder if the underlying trend had improved. But under the surface, little had changed. In a decade that saw a consistent pattern of profitability for the entire month, during the greatest bull market of the century, second-quarter prices fell five times. In addition, the +0.46% average annual profit was the weakest (by far) of the month's four quarters.

**Weakness continues**

Recent years have brought more of the same, a continuation of weak first-quarter trading conditions. Since 1990, prices fell in the single bear market year and in five of six bull market years *(see Table 1.8)*.

**December warning**

In a previous edition of the *Schwartz Stock Market Handbook*, we warned of the emergence of a new trend which suggested that second-quarter prices are likely to fall in years following a big rally in December's second

## JANUARY SECOND-QUARTER PERFORMANCE IN BULL/BEAR MARKETS: 1936–1996

|  | Total | Bull Markets | Bear Markets |
|---|---|---|---|
| Average price change | 0.20% | 0.62% | -0.89% |
| Rank (of 48) | 20 | 19 | 32 |
|  |  |  |  |
| Per cent of time prices rise | 49% | 55% | 35% |
| Rank (of 48) | 31 | 33 | 33 |

*Source: Financial Times, Datastream/ICV*

Table 1.7: Prices rise more than half the time in bull market years over the long-term. But the bull market trend has weakened in recent years.

UPDATE

First four days

half. Here is an update. Since 1977, second-quarter prices have fallen in 11 out of 15 years following a second-half price increase of at least +1.72% on the FT-Ordinary Share Index.

Obviously, odds like this leave ample room for a second-quarter up-move following a December second-half rally. By the same token, they should cause investors to think long and hard about committing new funds following a December rally of sufficient size.

In timing your decision to buy or sell shares during this point of the month, note that the weak trend observed near the tail end of the first quarter continues through the middle of the second quarter. Three of the first four trading days rise less than half the time and are among the worst trading days of the month. Prices are most likely to rise at the very end of the quarter. If you are thinking of buying or selling around this part of the month, consider adjusting your timing based upon these daily trends *(see Figure 1.5)*.

## PERCENTAGE PRICE CHANGE: JANUARY 1985–96

|  | January 1–8 | January 9–15 | January 16–23 | January 24–31 |
|---|---|---|---|---|
| 1985 | 0.91% | -0.59% | 4.06% | -0.69% |
| 1986 | -0.42% | -1.18% | -0.33% | 3.98% |
| 1987 | 3.36% | 3.11% | 0.63% | 0.81% |
| 1988 | 3.93% | 0.55% | -0.42% | 1.14% |
| 1989 | 0.99% | 2.78% | 3.26% | 6.23% |
| 1990 | 0.92% | -2.60% | -2.81% | 1.41% |
| 1991 | -2.02% | -1.58% | 0.08% | 4.02% |
| 1992 | -0.81% | 2.55% | -0.06% | 1.70% |
| 1993 | -0.55% | -1.19% | 0.63% | 1.17% |
| 1994 | 1.42% | 0.86% | 3.09% | 0.13% |
| 1995 | -0.15% | -0.50% | -2.80% | 0.77% |
| 1996 | 1.03% | -1.42% | 1.78% | 0.81% |
| Average quarterly price change | 0.72% | -0.08% | 0.59% | 1.79% |
| Number of years in which prices | | | | |
| Rose | 7 | 4 | 7 | 11 |
| Fell | 5 | 8 | 5 | 1 |

*Source: Datastream/ICV*

Table 1.8: First- and second-quarter profitability have suffered in recent years. Since 1990, prices have fallen in four out of seven first quarters and six out of seven second quarters. The strong fourth-quarter trend continues unabated. Shares rose 11 times in a row since 1986.

**11 January**

11 January has been particularly poor recently. Following our warning a few years ago, prices fell in 1995 and 1996, right on cue. Here is an up-date of this day's

23

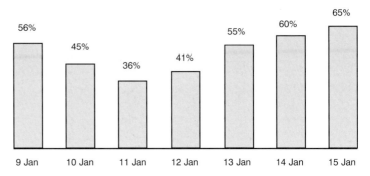

**PERCENTAGE OF TIME PRICES RISE EACH TRADING DAY IN JANUARY'S SECOND QUARTER**

*Source: Financial Times, Datastream/ICV*

Figure 1.5: The likelihood of profit is low on 10–12 January. Be especially cautious on 11 January which has fallen in 10 of the last 11 years.

UPDATE

recent performance. Since 1982, prices have risen once and fallen 10 times (weekends account for the other days) despite the fact that a bull market was running in 10 of those years. While no one can explain why prices are so consistently weak on this day nor predict if its poor performance will continue in the years ahead, it makes sense to invest with caution as the 11th rolls around.

Day of week

Analysis of price swings on by day of the week reveals a pattern of increasing strength as the week advances, just like the first quarter. But there is one very important difference. Compared to the first quarter, prices are less likely to rise on second-quarter Thursdays and Fridays. Thursdays rise 51% of the time in the second quarter compared to 64% in the first quarter. Fridays rise 58% of the time in the second quarter compared to 69% in the first quarter *(see Figure 1.6)*.

## PERCENTAGE OF TIME PRICES RISE EACH DAY OF WEEK IN JANUARY'S SECOND QUARTER

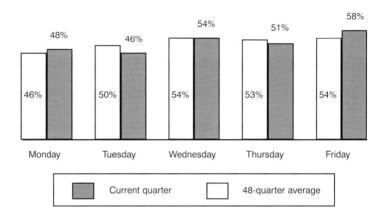

Source: Financial Times, Datastream/ICV

Figure 1.6: The profit odds improve as the week progresses. Monday and Tuesday each rise less than half the time. Friday is the best day of the week for second-quarter investors.

### INCREASE YOUR PROFIT ODDS

Despite this quarter's relatively weak performance, if you currently hold shares and are a long-term investor, in most years it pays to hold on to your position – given the good odds of a third- and fourth-quarter profit.

If you are contemplating making a purchase, you can improve the chance of catching an up-move or avoiding a drop by watching the direction of prices during the preceding few quarters.

Prior two-quarters signal No.1

On the up-side, the odds of a price rise on the FT-Non-Financial Index tend to be quite high when prices shift by a moderate amount in the preceding two quarters. Since 1969, there have been 10 occasions when shares shifted within a range of -0.06% to +2.17%.

25

Second-quarter prices rose nine times. In the remaining 18 years of this period, the second-quarter record was nine up and nine down.

*Rose (9)*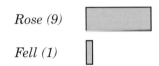

*Fell (1)*

Second-quarter record after a price shift of -0.06% to +2.17% in the preceding two quarters (FT-Non-Financial Index since 1969)

First quarter
signal No.1

Also on the up-side, there have been 15 occasions when the FT Ordinary Share Index shifted by a small amount in January's first quarter, dropping no more than -0.04% or gaining no more than +0.97%. Second-quarter prices rose each time.

*Rose (15)*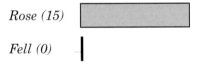

*Fell (0)*

Second-quarter record after a price shift of -0.04% to +0.97% in the first quarter (FT Ordinary Share Index since 1936)

On the down-side, here are two trends to help you to anticipate poor second quarters.

Prior two-
quarters signal
No.2

The first is an improved version of a correlation we first reported in an earlier edition of the *Schwartz Stock Market Handbook*. Since 1956, there have been 16 occasions when the FT Ordinary Share Index either fell by a small amount in the last quarter of December, no more than -0.03%, or rose by any amount, and rose by at least +1.05% in the first quarter of January. Second-quarter prices fell in 13 of those years.

26

IMPROVEMENT

*Rose (3)*

*Fell (13)*

Second-quarter record after a price rise (any amount) in December's fourth quarter or a fall no greater than -0.03% and a price rise of at least +1.05% in the first quarter (FT Ordinary Share Index since 1956)

First-quarter
signal No.2

This signal last flashed in 1996 and prices fell by a small amount in the second quarter, the only quarter of the month to show a loss in 1996.

If the FT Ordinary Share Index falls in the first quarter by -0.38% to -3.20%, the odds suggest the second quarter will also fall. Here is the evidence. First-quarter prices have fallen within this range 12 times since 1939. Second-quarter prices continued to fall in 10 of those years.

*Rose (2)*

*Fell (10)*

Second-quarter record after a price decline of -0.38% to -3.20% in the first quarter (FT Ordinary Share Index since 1939)

27

# Third Quarter of January – January 16th to 23rd

> At one time, the third quarter was a steady money-loser. But since 1980, the trend has considerably improved. Here is more good news. The quarter to follow has an even better record.
>
> But continue to be very cautious on 23 January which rises 35% of the time, the worst day of the month and the ninth-worst of the year.

**Poor historical record**

Over the long-term, the third-quarter record is not particularly impressive. Prices rise about half the time and produce an average annual profit of +0.38%, about 15 points on an FTSE 100 in the area of 4000. On this basis, it is the 16th-best quarter of the year (out of 48).

Investors lost money in the average year in the 1930s, '40s and '50s, and made a small amount in the 1960s by continuously investing during this segment of the month.

**1975 saved the decade**

The 1970s continued to be a poor time to invest during the third quarter. The apparent +1.13% increase in average annual third-quarter prices during this decade was entirely due to 1975's impressive rally when third-quarter prices rose by +16.76%. If not for 1975, the 1970s would have generated an average annual quarterly loss of -0.61% for those always invested in the third quarter.

Between 1936 and 1979, prices rose in the third quarter of January just 45% of the time.

**Recent trend change**

In 1980, a new third-quarter trend began. For the first time ever, the third quarter became January's most profitable segment. Share prices rose in eight of the decade's 10 years at an average annual rate of +1.59%, the best performance of all 48 quarters during the 1980s. The 1990s record of four up and three down is disappointing at first glance. But it is still the second-best quarter of the month, suggesting that the positive third-quarter trend continues. Even better, the quarter that follows is one of the best of the entire year, giving traders two consecutive

## JANUARY THIRD-QUARTER PERFORMANCE IN BULL/BEAR MARKETS: 1936–1996

|  | Total | Bull Markets | Bear Markets |
|---|---|---|---|
| Average price change | 0.38% | 1.01% | -1.13% |
| Rank (of 48) | 16 | 7 | 37 |
| Per cent of time prices rise | 52% | 58% | 39% |
| Rank (of 48) | 25 | 24 | 27 |

*Source: Financial Times, Datastream/ICV*

Table 1.9: The likelihood of a price rise in bull market years has improved recently. Prices have risen in 12 of the last 16 bull market third quarters. So far, the bear market trend shows no corresponding improvement.

periods of good profit potential.

**Bear market concern**

Despite the improved trend, there is still one source of concern, a poor performance during bear markets. Prices fall by more than 1% on average, during bear market years. And even though the recent overall trend improved, it seems to be a bull market phenomenon. By way of example, prices fell almost 3% in 1990, the last bear market to touch the third quarter *(see Table 1.9)*.

**23 January**

The main source of third-quarter weakness is at the end of the quarter. Prices rise on just 35% of all January 23rds, the worst day of the month and ninth-worst of the entire year *(see Figure 1.7)*. The problem spills over to the beginning of the fourth quarter of the month, January 24th, which rises just 45% of the time.

Note that January 23rd continued to be a drain on the quarter's performance during the 1980s and '90s when the overall third-quarter trend was improving. We don't know why, but the record since 1978 is three up and 11

## PERCENTAGE OF TIME PRICES RISE EACH TRADING DAY IN JANUARY'S THIRD QUARTER

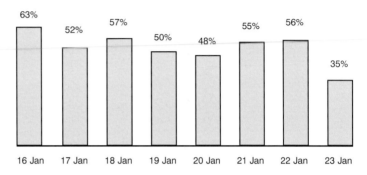

Source: Financial Times, Datastream/ICV

Figure 1.7: 23 January is the worst day of the month and ninth-worst of the year. The trend is more favourable on 19–20 January, especially when they land on Wednesday (see Table 1.10).

**Weak Monday and Tuesday**

down (weekends account for the missing days).

Analysis of price trends by day of week uncovers a pattern of generally rising prices as the week unfolds, like the first and second quarters. The chance of a price rise is quite low on Monday and Tuesday, especially Tuesday which rises just 41% of the time, the 45th-ranked Tuesday among all 48 quarters (see Figure 1.8). No one knows why the stock market does so poorly on third-quarter Tuesdays but it is a trend that has been steadily running since 1936.

In contrast, third-quarter Fridays rise 62% of the time, the fifth-best Friday performance of all 48 quarters.

**19–20 January**

An interesting exception to the pattern of late-week strength occurs on 19 and 20 January. Our research finds a strong tendency for shares to rise most often when these days land in mid-week. No one has explained why

## PERCENTAGE OF TIME PRICES RISE EACH DAY OF WEEK IN JANUARY'S THIRD QUARTER

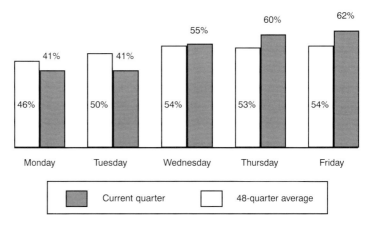

Source: Financial Times, Datastream/ICV

Figure 1.8: The chance of a price rise is lowest on Monday and Tuesday. The Tuesday record is especially weak, the 45th-ranked Tuesday of all 48 quarters.

prices act so atypically on 19–20 January but shares rise 78% of the time when either of these two days lands on Wednesday. It is a trend that has been running since 1936. The odds of a price rise are lower at the beginning and end of the week *(see Table 1.10).*

### INCREASE YOUR PROFIT ODDS

Second-quarter signal

There are several trends that help to improve the chance of making a third-quarter profit. Here is a new trend that first began in 1981. Since then, there have been nine occasions during bull markets when the FTSE All Share Index fell in the second quarter by -1.42% or more. Third-quarter prices rose in eight of those years.

31

**PERCENTAGE OF TIME PRICES RISE ON
19–20 JANUARY: 1936–1996**

|  | Prices rise |
|---|---|
| Total | 49% |
|  |  |
| Monday and Tuesday | 29% |
| Wednesday | 78% |
| Thursday and Friday | 53% |

*Source: Financial Times, Datastream/ICV*

Table 1.10: Shares often rise when 19–20 January land on Wednesday.

Third-quarter record in bull markets after prices drop in the second quarter by -1.42% or more (FTSE All Share Index since 1981)

First-half signal  An earlier edition of the *Schwartz Stock Market Handbook* suggested investors could improve the odds of correctly forecasting the direction of price shifts in the third quarter by monitoring prices in the first half of January.

If prices rise in both the first and second quarters of the month on the FT Ordinary Share Index, with the second quarter rising no more than +2.76%, the third quarter usually rises. Out of 12 such occasions since 1949, third-quarter prices rose 10 times. And one of the two exceptions was a minuscule -0.07% decline in the third quarter of 1954.

*Rose (10)*

*Fell (2)*

Third-quarter record after a price rise in the first quarter (any amount) and second quarter of up to +2.76% (FT Ordinary Share Index since 1949)

**December second-half signal**

When it comes to the stock market, too much good news makes us nervous, especially when it suddenly appears after decades of mediocrity. With this in mind, we located an indicator associated with falling third-quarter prices. Unfortunately, there are only nine observations on record, in part because it has not flashed since 1979.

The signal to watch for is a small price decline in the second half of December on the FT Ordinary Share Index. When such an event occurs, the third-quarter price trend tends to disappoint, regardless of what happens in the first half of January. Either the early January rally peters out or the December down-trend drags on to this point in the month.

Here is the evidence. Since 1938, there have been nine occasions with a small price drop in the second half of December, no greater than -2.10%. Third-quarter prices fell in seven of those years. Both exceptions saw very small price rises of about one-half of one percent. In other words, standing aside when this indicator flashed had little 'opportunity loss' even when the indicator was wrong.

*Rose (2)*

*Fell (7)*

Third-quarter record after a price drop in the second half of December of up to -2.10% (FT Ordinary Share Index since 1938)

33

# FOURTH QUARTER OF JANUARY – JANUARY 24TH TO 31ST

Here comes another fine money-making opportunity. Over the long term, it is the second-biggest profit-maker of all 48 quarters. Nothing has changed in recent years. Prices have risen in 17 of the last 20 years, the best quarterly performance of the year.

But be cautious on 24 January which rises less than half the time, a continuation of the weakness which often occurs at the very end of the third quarter.

January's best quarter

Investors frequently profit during the fourth quarter of January. Between 1936 and 1996, prices rose 66% of the time. The average annual gain was +0.99%, second highest of all 48 quarters of the year. Only the last quarter of December, with an average annual profit of +1.00%, has out-performed it.

The final segment of the month failed to produce a profit in just one decade, the 1940s, when it lost -0.01% per year, equivalent to less than one-half of a point on an FTSE 100 in the area of 4000.

Recent strength

The recent fourth-quarter record has been unbelievably strong. Prices have risen in 17 of the last 20 years, and all of the last 10, the year's best in both cases. The chance of a price rise is especially good during bull markets. Since daily records began, bull market fourth quarters rose in more than three out of four years at an average rate of +1.56%, the year's best bull market quarter on this dimension (see Table 1.11).

24 January

Analysis of daily price trends shows that the quarter starts off poorly, continuing the pattern of weakness observed at the very end of the third quarter. Prices rise just 45% of the time on 24 January (see Figure 1.9).

26–28 January

The trend is sporadically weak during the next few trading days as well. But under the surface a new trend is developing. Since 1979, 26 January has risen 10 out of

34

## JANUARY FOURTH-QUARTER PERFORMANCE IN BULL/BEAR MARKETS: 1936–1996

|  | Total | Bull Markets | Bear Markets |
|---|---|---|---|
| Average price change | 0.99% | 1.56% | -0.35% |
| Rank (of 48) | 2 | 1 | 18 |
| Per cent of time prices rise | 66% | 77% | 39% |
| Rank (of 48) | 5 | 4 | 27 |

*Source: Financial Times, Datastream/ICV*

Table 1.11: The fourth quarter is number one-ranked in profit during bull markets. The bear market record is close to average.

13 times, 27 January nine of 12 and 28 January, 10 of the last 14 opportunities. Grouping all three days together shows that there has been a three out of four chance of profit in recent years (roughly), quite an improvement from the 50:50 odds that were prevailing earlier.

**Weak Monday**   Despite the strong performance for the quarter as a whole, fourth-quarter Mondays tend to be poor. Prices rise just 44% of the time, the weakest day of the week during this time of year *(see Figure 1.10)*.

### INCREASE YOUR PROFIT ODDS

**Third-quarter signal No.1**   Here is a newly-discovered trend based upon the FTSE All Share Index. Since 1969, there were 10 occasions when shares shifted moderately in January's third quarter, within a range of -1.15% to +0.75%. Fourth-quarter prices rose each time. In the remaining 17 years of this period, the fourth-quarter record was slightly better than 50:50 with 10 rises and seven falls.

## PERCENTAGE OF TIME PRICES RISE EACH TRADING DAY IN JANUARY'S FOURTH QUARTER

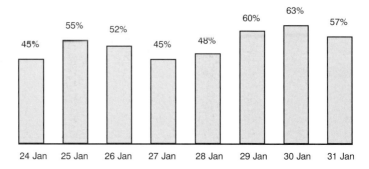

*Source: Financial Times, Datastream/ICV*

Figure 1.9: Since 1979, the likelihood of a price rise has increased on 26–28 January. Prices have risen in three out of four years on these three days. But no such improvement is noted on 24 January. It continues to fall in most years, a continuation of the weakness observed at the very end of the third quarter.

⟨NEW⟩

*Rose (10)*

*Fell (0)*    |

Fourth-quarter record after a price shift of -1.15% to +0.75% in the third quarter (FTSE All Share Index since 1969)

Third-quarter signal No.2

Another trend worth monitoring is based upon the FT Ordinary Share Index. Since 1936, a small price rise in the third quarter within a range of +0.41% to +0.97%, was generally followed by a further rise in the fourth quarter.

## PERCENTAGE OF TIME PRICES RISE EACH DAY OF WEEK IN JANUARY'S FOURTH QUARTER

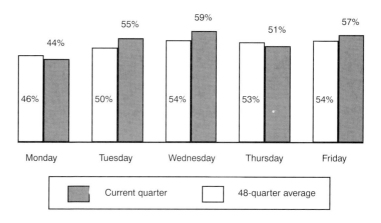

*Source: Financial Times, Datastream/ICV*

Figure 1.10: Once again, Monday is the weakest of all five week days.

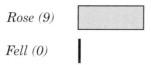

*Rose (9)*

*Fell (0)*

Fourth-quarter record after a price rise of +0.41% to +0.97% in the third quarter (FT Ordinary Share Index since 1936)

**Three prior-quarters signal**

Another statistical relationship on the FT Ordinary Share Index that signals increased odds of higher share prices is a rising trend in the first half of January that lifts prices by at least +0.23%, followed by a decline in the third quarter. There have been 11 'up then down' occasions since 1945 and fourth-quarter prices rose in 10 of them (91%).

| IMPROVEMENT | *Rose (10)* | |
|---|---|---|
| | *Fell (1)* | |

Fourth-quarter record after a price rise of at least +0.23% in the first half and fall in the third quarter (FT Ordinary Share Index since 1945)

## LOOKING AHEAD

Trying to forecast a week or month ahead is hard enough to do. Looking further ahead to the rest of the year is even harder. Too many unforeseen political and economic events, both domestic and international, easily confound even the most skilful and knowledgeable forecaster. Nevertheless, there are several historical trends involving January that have consistently tipped off the direction of prices in the months ahead.

Take February and March for example. They tend to be unexceptional months, not steady money-makers. Over the 78 years for which we have data, prices rose 42 times and fell 36 times during this two-month stretch. February is ranked eighth in monthly profitability, lower if 1975's extraordinary rally is omitted. March is ranked sixth. With a performance trend like this, it is particularly important to pick your time carefully if you plan to invest during this period. Fortunately, January price swings often tip off where shares are heading in the two months ahead which end on 31 March.

Rising prices by 31 March

Here is the evidence. There have been 14 years when January prices shifted by a tiny amount on the FTSE All Share Index or its predecessor index, no more than -0.10% on the down-side and no more than +1.10% on the up-side. This translates into a drop of up to four points on an FTSE 100 in the area of 4000, or a gain of up to 44 points. Shares rose in February–March in 13 of those years. The sole exception was in 1970.

Rose (13)

Fell (1)

Price shift to 31 March after a January price shift of -0.10% to +1.10% (FTSE All Share Index since 1923)

During the 1990s, this signal flashed in 1991 and 1993 and prices rose in the next two months as expected. The 1991 signal was particularly noteworthy as it came near the tail end of the 1990 bear market. A January price rise of just +0.20% was followed by a very large increase of over +15% in the next two months.

**Falling prices by 31 March**

On the other hand, if the stock market rallies strongly in December and January, producing a total two-month gain of +6.11% to +9.61%, history suggests low profit potential for February and March.

Since 1926, there have been 11 occasions when the FT-Non-Financial Index or its predecessor index rose within this range during December and January. Prices fell by 31 March in 10 of those years. The average price decline was -3.74%. The single exception to the rule occurred in 1984.

Rose (1)

Fell (10)

Price shift to 31 March after a December–January price rise of +6.11% to +9.61% (FT-Non-Financial Index since 1923)

**Falling prices by 31 May**

Another down-side indicator involving the FT-Non-Financial Index is a drop of -4.95% or more between November and January. History shows that a drop of this magnitude during the prior three months is often associated with further

39

drops in the four months that follow.

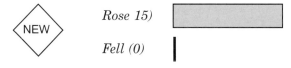

NEW

*Rose (2)*

*Fell (9)*

Price shift to 31 May after a November–January price drop of -4.95% or more (FT-Non-Financial Index since 1924)

**Rising prices by 30 June – signal No.1**

Looking a little further ahead to the end of June, the direction of prices in November to January provides a useful tip on where shares are heading. Since 1922, there have been 15 years with a small price rise on the FTSE All Share Index between 1 November and 31 January, no more than +3.06%. In each of those 15 years, prices rose still further in the next five months through June 30th. The average increase was a quite healthy +8.79%. Be warned that the trend was rarely a straight line. In some years, prices peaked before 30 June and began to fall. In other years, even more money could have been made by waiting until the end of February or March before committing funds.

NEW

*Rose 15)*

*Fell (0)*

Price shift to 30 June after a November–January price rise of up to +3.06% (FTSE All Share Index since 1922)

**Rising prices by 30 June – signal No.2**

A similar trend runs on the FT-Non-Financial Index. Since 1922. a November–January price rise of up to +3.07% was associated with 16 rises and one decline from 1 February to 30 June.

*Rose (16)*

*Fell (1)*

Price shift to 30 June after a November–January price rise of up to +3.07% (FT-Non-Financial Index since 1922)

### AS JANUARY GOES, SO GOES THE YEAR

Old saws about the future direction of share prices are comforting to recite. But as investment guides, most are not to be trusted.

If you 'Sell in May and go away, and don't come back 'til St Leger's Day', you would miss being invested in the stock market during August, on average the year's third best investment month.

Do 'Bull market bashes end with October crashes'? In fact, there have been more large increases in share prices during October than large decreases. Over the long-term, October has been profitable despite the headlines in 1929 and 1987.

The next 11 months

One exception: 'As January goes, so goes the year' has withstood the test of time for most of this century. When January share prices rise, further rises often occur in the rest of the year. Falling January prices are often associated with further declines in the remaining 11 months of the year. To monitor this trend, work with the FT-Non-Financial Index. It doesn't work as well on the FTSE All Share Index.

Unfortunately, a lot of what is written about this trend is either misleading or out-and-out wrong. Here are two major problem areas.

● Some analysts include January's performance in their yearly total, thereby loading the dice in favour of their conclusion. Predicting a full year price rise after a January price rise of 8% provides an 8% head start

41

toward being right. It may be great for your predictive accuracy but painful for the investor who commits new funds on February 1st, based upon that advice. A better approach is to use the January price shift to forecast the direction of prices during the 11 months that follow.

- The relationship between January and the rest of the year is complex. It is not simply a case of January up – rest-of-year up, or January down – rest-of-year down, as some commentators seem to suggest.

**Big drops**

It is true that big January price declines are invariably associated with further losses in the remainder of the year. If January's prices fall by -3.15% or more, there is only a 22% chance that prices will be higher on 31 December, well below average. To put this figure into perspective, over the long-run, prices rise 64% of the time in February to December.

**Small gains or losses okay**

On the other hand, a moderate or small January loss is a good sign for investors, as is a small gain. History shows that prices rise in the next 11 months 74% of the time following a January price shift within a range of -3.14% to +3.86%.

The trend changes for the worse if January prices rise any higher. The odds are a little over 50:50 (55% to be exact) that share prices will rise still further in the next 11 months if January prices rise between +3.87% and +9.24%. (January 1994 rose by +3.90% and the market turned down soon after.) Furthermore, the average level of profit for the 11 months that follow a big January price increase is just +1.45% per year, less than the level of interest provided by a Building Society.

There were only three years since 1919 with larger January price rises. That is not enough data for us to make a proper forecast but we note that each of the three saw very strong further rises in the 11 months that followed.

# CHAPTER 2 – FEBRUARY

February often disappoints bulls as well as bears. Prices rise half the time, quite a come down from January's strong performance.

There is a 65% chance of profiting with a February investment during bull market years, about average compared with other months. But the size of the typical bull market profit is well below average, once the unique rally of 1975 is factored out of the way.

February's bear market record is simply terrible. Prices rise just 17% of the time, the worst bear market record of all 12 months.

Over the long-term, most of February's weakness has occurred in the first three quarters of the month. Each declines more than half of the time. In contrast, the last quarter is often profitable.

History's verdict on a February investment is quite clear-cut. Investors who hold shares every February, for the entire month, are making a poor investment decision.

**1980s were a temporary exception**

Although profits were earned in some years, the long-term February investor lost money in the 1930s, '40s, '50s, and '60s. The large average annual increase of the 1970s was almost entirely due to the explosive rally of 1975 which signalled the end of the 1973–74 bear market, when February gained +24%. In the 1980s' bull market, February performed better than its long-term average, as did most other months, producing an average annual monthly gain of +1.89%. But since October 1987, February has reverted to traditional form with a record of four ups and five downs. Two of the four recent increases were well under one-half of one per cent (see Table 2.1).

Between 1919 and 1996, the stock market rose 50% of the time in February. In contrast, January rose 76% of the time which in relative terms, is 52% more often.

**Losses without 1975**

During this period, the average February share price rise was just +0.25% per year, equal to 10 points on an FTSE 100 of 4000. A hypothetical investor who only invested in February, from 1919 to 1996, would have run up his £1,000 to about £1,100. If the rally of 1975 was eliminated from these computations, that investor would have registered a loss after 78 years of steady investing. Historically, February is ranked eighth on monthly profitability. Without 1975, its rank would drop to tenth position.

**Small bull market profits**

There is a light-hearted expression often heard in City dealing rooms. Shares do poorly in February in just two types of markets – bull markets and bear markets! This humorous comment is remarkably accurate. During bull markets, prices rise 65% of the time, about average compared to other months. But when the stock market does manage a rise during bull-market Februarys, those increases are well below average compared to other

## FEBRUARY PRICE RISES AND DECLINES: 1919–1996

|  | Average February price change | Up | Down/ No change |
|---|---|---|---|
| 1920–29 | 1.06% | 7 | 3 |
| 1930–39 | -0.11% | 4 | 6 |
| 1940–49 | -1.93% | 4 | 6 |
| 1950–59 | -0.80% | 6 | 4 |
| 1960–69 | -0.83% | 4 | 6 |
| 1970–79 | 2.39% | 5 | 5 |
| 1980–89 | 1.89% | 5 | 5 |
| 1990–96 | 0.86% | 4 | 3 |
| | | | |
| Average February change: 1919–96 | 0.25% | 50% | 50% |
| | | | |
| Rank (of 12) | 8 | 10 | |

*Source: BZW, Datastream/ICV*

Table 2.1: City dealers like to tell their clients that February is profitable over the long term except in bull markets and bear markets! If not for the +23.80% gain in 1975 which marked the end of the 1972–74 bear market, the 78-year average would be in the red. The apparent improvement in the 1980s was a bull market phenomenon. Since the 1987 crash, the February record was four up and five down.

months, once the effect of the unique rally of 1975 is factored out. The typical increase during bull market February up-moves is just +1.14% excluding 1975.

**Down months are painful**

During bull market down months, February's performance is also quite poor. Prices fall by an average rate of -2.66% during the average down month which makes February 10th-ranked on this dimension *(see Table 2.2)*.

In bear market years, February prices rise just 17% of

## FEBRUARY PERFORMANCE IN BULL/BEAR MARKETS: 1919–1996

|  | Bull Markets | Bear Markets |
|---|---|---|
| Average per cent price change | *1.56% | -2.68% |
| Rank (of 12) | 8 | 9 |
|  |  |  |
| Per cent of time prices rise | 65% | 17% |
| Rank (of 12) | 7 | 12 |
|  |  |  |
| Average per cent price change in: |  |  |
| Rising years | **3.85% | 4.83% |
| Declining years | -2.66% | -4.18% |

\*  Without 1975, 1.14%
\*\* Without 1975, 3.26%

*Source: BZW, Datastream/ICV*

Table 2.2: During bull markets, prices rise 65% of the time, about average compared with other bull market months. But when prices do rise in bull market Februarys, the typical rise is just +1.14% once the unique performance of 1975 is factored out. And when prices fall during bull market Februarys, the typical decline is -2.66%, quite steep compared with other months. During bear markets, the February record is horrid. Prices rise just 17% of the time.

Large bear market losses

the time, the year's worst bear market performance on this dimension. To help to put things into perspective, bear market Januarys rise 48% of the time, bear market Aprils, 50%. Clearly, the chance of making money in February during bear markets is poor.

Given the drastically different profit odds in bull versus bear market Februarys, it is critically important for investors to know if they are in a bull or bear market.

## ODDS OF BULL/BEAR MARKET TIPPED BY JANUARY'S TREND

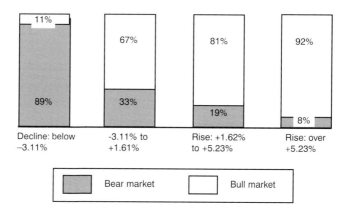

Source: BZW, Datastream/ICV

Figure 2.1: If prices drop by more than -3.11% in January, the chance is quite high that UK shares are in a bear market. On the up-side, a rise in January of over +5.23% is virtually always associated with a bull market.

**Spotting bear markets**

Happily, the January historical record provides some useful clues to help to answer this question. As Figure 2.1 reveals, a price decline in January of more than -3.11% is associated with a bear market 89% of the time. There are exceptions to every rule of course but if shares drop sharply in January, the odds strongly suggest investing with extreme caution in the months ahead.

Keep in mind that this figure does not tell you when the bear market started or when it will end. It is conceivable that the following month will see the start of a new bull market. However, every bear market in our historical record fell by at least 15%. So if January's fall, plus any preceding fall, is much smaller than 15%, history says there are high odds that the bear market has much further to go.

**Spotting bull markets**

On the up-side, history shows that large January rallies that raise prices in excess of +5.23% are virtually always associated with bull market advances. Here too, Figure 2.1 does not tell us when the bull market started or when it will end. It is conceivable that the following month will see the start of a new bear market. Still, as a bull market confirmation signal, a strong January price serves a useful purpose.

**No sign of improvement**

As far as the future is concerned, we see no sign of improvement in the February trend. The best-ever stretch of time for the February investor was back in 1922–5 when shares rose in value in four consecutive years. Since then there have been three occasions when prices rose three years in a row: 1944–6, 1979–81 and 1991–93. Each time, they fell the following year. In the most recent assault on the Three-Year rule, share prices rose to new peaks in December, 1993 and January, 1994 as commentators repeatedly warned that the stock market was over-extended and ripe for a fall. But prices kept rising until the start of February when they suddenly ran out of steam with a -4.04% setback, the start of the 1994 bear market.

It seems safe to assume that any long-term change in the February trend will be associated with a successful attack on the Three-Year rule. Until then, invest in February with caution.

**No one knows why**

Why is the stock market so disappointing in February? No one knows with any certainty. Obviously, no market can continue to rise forever. Prices must rest or occasionally react against a rising up-trend even in the best bull market. But why does it happen so consistently in February? Why not in January? Why not in December? The most likely reason is that start-of-year money flows and optimism about the year ahead which often powers

## QUARTERLY ODDS OF PRICE RISE IN FEBRUARY

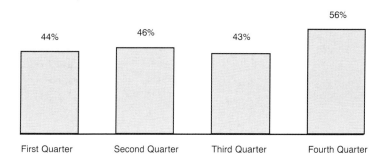

Source: *Financial Times, Datastream/ICV*

Figure 2.2: Prices fall more than half of the time in the first three quarters of the year. The third-quarter record is especially poor, the 45th-ranked quarter of the year. Happily, the odds improve by a small amount in the final quarter of the month.

a January price advance peter out in February, causing shares to give back some of their January gains.

Another possible reason is that short-term investors take a position in January in advance of the February reporting season, and take profits in February when companies announce good news or sell out to lick their wounds when the February news is bad. Either way, it creates more down-side pressure on shares in February.

**Fourth quarter is best**

Despite the poor overall trend, there are a number of ways to profit with a February investment. Take, for example, the pattern of profit and loss during different parts of the month. Over the long term, most of February's profits have been realised in the last quarter of the month which rises 56% of the time. For many decades, the last quarter has often been either the best or second-best quarter of the month. In contrast, the other three quarters each rise less than half of the time *(see Figure 2.2)*.

49

### Increase Your Profit Odds[1]

**Bear market signal**

There are several ways to increase the likelihood of correctly forecasting which way share prices will shift in February. We have already touched upon the following relationship that operates in bear market years. Since 1919, the UK has been in a bear market during February in 24 separate years. Shares rose in February in just four of those years (17%). Two of the four were during World War 2 and a third was in 1974 during the run-up to an election that many investors thought would be won by the Tories. Clearly, it takes very unique circumstances for prices to rise in February during bear markets.

*Rose (4)*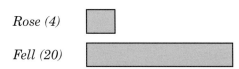

*Fell (20)*

February record during bear market years (FTSE All Share Index since 1919)

**January fourth-quarter signal**

Another way to anticipate falling share prices in February is to watch the FT Ordinary Share Index during the last quarter of January. Since 1936, there have been 15 occasions when prices shifted by a small amount in the fourth quarter, either dropping no more than -0.57% on the down-side or rising no more than +0.41% on the up-side. February prices fell 14 times.

*Rose (1)*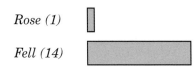

*Fell (14)*

February record after prices shifted within a range of -0.57% to +0.41% in January's fourth quarter (FT Ordinary Share Index since 1936)

---

[1]We will provide closing price trends on key indices for the last 12 months at no cost (see page 9).

January signal
No.1

It is also worth monitoring the size of the advance for the total month of January. History shows that strong January advances are often followed by partial February pull-backs e.g. declines that are smaller than the preceding January advance. Here is the evidence.

Since records began in 1919, there have been 11 occasions when the UK stock market rose significantly during the month of January by +4.52% to +8.33% on the FT-Non-Financial Index or its predecessor index. February share prices fell in 10 of those years. Nine of those 10 falls were merely partial retractions of the January rise.

There was only one occasion, over 30 years ago, when a strong January rise was followed by a February advance.

*Rose (1)*

*Fell (10)*

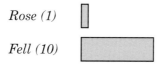

February record if January prices rose by +4.52% to +8.33% (FT-Non-Financial Index since 1919)

Information like this has considerable value for investors who are looking to avoid February losses as well as those who wish to move into shares after a healthy January advance. Since the odds favour a partial pullback after a strong January advance, any price plateau after a decline which eats up much of the January advance can be regarded as being near February's low point and serve as useful buy signal.

January signal
No.2

Since 1964, a similar trend has been running on the FTSE All Share Index. During this period, there have been nine occasions when prices rose in January within a range of +3.48% to +6.60%. February prices fell in eight of those years.

51

*Rose (1)*

*Fell (8)*

February record if January prices rose by +3.48% to +6.60% (FTSE All Share Index since 1964)

**Prior 11-months signal**

On the up-side, here is a newly discovered signal involving the FTSE All Share Index and its predecessor index which, historically, has done a good job of anticipating rising February prices in bull markets. Since 1941, there have been 19 occasions when a bull market was running at the start of February and prices had shifted in the 11 preceding months within a range of -3.04% to +15.64%. February prices rose in 18 of those years.

*Rose (18)*

*Fell (1)*

February record in bull markets if the preceding 11 months shifted -3.04% to +15.64% (FTSE All Share Index since 1941)

In all other bull market Februarys since 1941, prices rose eight times and fell 14 times.

**Prior 12-months signal**

Another useful indicator to monitor is the price trend in the past year. We discussed this trend in a previous edition of the *Schwartz Stock Market Handbook*. Here is an improved version. If each of the following shifts occur, a February profit is likely.

| | |
|---|---|
| Previous 12 months: | prices shift -4.40% to +13.37% |
| Previous 6 months: | prices shift -6.17% to +11.79% |
| Previous 3 months: | prices rise by any amount |
| Previous month: | prices rise by any amount |

Since 1927, there have been 14 years with appropriate price shifts within each one of these four ranges in the run-up to February on the FTSE All Share Index or its predecessor index. February prices rose in 13 of those years. The single exception was back in 1929.

*Rose (13)*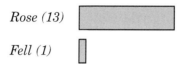

*Fell (1)*

February record if prices shift within defined limits (FTSE All Share Index since 1927)

Be sure to watch the size of the past 12 month up-move very carefully. Since 1933, if prices rise by +14.52% or more, the odds of a decline in February are 67%. A excessively large rise in the previous 12 months was recently observed in 1994 and 1996. Shares fell in February in both years.

Prior three-months signal

It also pays to keep an eye on the direction of prices in November to January. There have been 11 instances when the FTSE All Share Index or its predecessor index rose in the past three months between +1.72% and +3.06%. February prices rose in all 11 years. The average annual increase was over three per cent.

UPDATE

*Rose (11)*

*Fell (0)*

February record after a price rise of +1.72% to +3.06% in November to January (FTSE All Share Index since 1922)

Volatility signal

Although its long-term record is poor, February prices are not particularly volatile. Shifts of ±3% are about average compared with other months. But if prices have dropped in the past 12 months by at least -3.54%, be alert for volatile trading conditions.

Since 1920, there have been 23 years in which share prices declined by at least -3.54% in the 12 months preceding February. February's prices rose or fell by at least 2.5% in 18 of those years. With moves of this magnitude, it is important to know the direction of the shift so that you can either step aside or commit more funds for a short-term investment. The price signals discussed earlier in this section should be of some help in this regard.

| UPDATE |

## FIRST QUARTER OF FEBRUARY – FEBRUARY 1ST TO 7TH

Over the long run, the stock market rises less than half of the time during the first quarter. Even during bull markets, the profit odds are just 50:50.

The recent bear market record has been very poor. Prices have fallen 10 times in a row.

Investors should be especially cautious on first-quarter Mondays which rise 30% of the time, one of the worst Monday performances of the entire year. Another day to watch out for is 4 February which rises 33% of the time, the sixth-worst trading day of the entire year.

Favourable late-January trading conditions often come to a sudden end during the first quarter of February. History shows that it is hard to turn a profit in the first quarter by steadily holding shares year-in and year-out.

Recent poor record

Over the long-run, first-quarter prices rise less than half the time. The average increase in share prices is just +0.13% per year. If we eliminate all profits from 1975's rally, an annual investment in February's first quarter would be very close to break-even after six decades of effort. Profits seem to have improved since 1980 but this is a function of the bull market which saw many other segments of the year perform better than their long-term average as well. Since the 1987 crash, the first-quarter record has reverted to form – four up and five down *(see Table 2.3)*.

**Bull and bear market weakness**

As Table 2.4 shows, the first-quarter record is lacklustre in bull market years, as well as bear markets. During bull markets, prices rise half the time, quite low compared with the likelihood of profit in other bull market quarters.

During bear markets, prices have risen one-third of the time over the long-run. But the record has worsened in recent years. Since 1965, prices have fallen 10 times in a row during bear markets.

**Avoid Mondays**

Analysis of price trends for each day of the week during the first quarter finds nothing out of the ordinary on Tuesday to Friday. Prices rise about half the time, close to average when compared to other quarters. Mondays are a different matter. The profit odds are simply horrid. First-quarter Mondays are ranked in 47th position of all 48 quarters. Prices rise just 30% of the time. The only worse Monday performance is in the fourth quarter of May which rises 29% of the time *(see Figure 2.3)*. It is an important point to keep in mind if you are thinking about buying or selling shares during this part of the year. While no one knows for sure what will happen this coming year, one thing is certain. If you buy shares at the close of business on the previous Friday to catch an expected Monday rally, history says you are betting on a long-shot.

Monday's weakness is most apparent on 3–4 February which, between them, have risen just twice on Monday out of 17 attempts since our records began in 1936 *(see Table 2.5)*.

**4 February**

Looking at price trends on a day-by-day basis shows

## PERCENTAGE PRICE CHANGE: FEBRUARY 1936–96

| | Feb 1–7 | Feb 8–14 | Feb 15–21 | Feb 22–29 |
|---|---|---|---|---|
| Annual average | | | | |
| 1935–39 | 0.30% | -0.43% | 0.07% | 1.51% |
| 1940–49 | -0.74% | -1.17% | -0.30% | 0.39% |
| 1950–59 | 0.81% | -0.83% | -0.73% | 0.01% |
| 1960–69 | -0.22% | 0.25% | -0.95% | -0.34% |
| 1970–79 | -0.06% | -0.20% | 0.12% | 2.45% |
| 1980–89 | 0.48% | 1.07% | 0.14% | 0.50% |
| 1990–96 | 0.44% | 0.13% | -0.22% | 0.44% |
| | | | | |
| Average quarterly price change | 0.13% | -0.19% | -0.29% | 0.60% |
| | | | | |
| Per cent of time prices rise | 44% | 46% | 43% | 56% |

*Source: Financial Times, Datastream/ICV*

Table 2.3: It is difficult to profit consistently in the first three quarters of February. The first quarter appears to be an exception but it was helped by the strong rally of 1975.

that the first two days are profitable over the long-run, a continuation of January's end-of-month strength. It is the trading days to follow that tend to lose money in most years and help to create the weak first-quarter record *(see Figure 2.4)*. Prices fall more than half the time from 3 February to the end of the quarter. Be especially cautious on 4 February which rises just 33% of the time, the sixth-worst day of the entire year.

1 February

Unfortunately, things may be changing for the worse on the first day of the month. Since 1980, 1 February has been persistently weak, rising just four times in 13 tries. No one knows if this is a short-term blip or a more permanent

## FEBRUARY FIRST-QUARTER PERFORMANCE IN BULL/BEAR MARKETS: 1936–1996

|  | Total | Bull Markets | Bear Markets |
|---|---|---|---|
| Average price change | 0.13% | 0.58% | -0.71% |
| Rank (of 48) | 23 | 22 | 29 |
|  |  |  |  |
| Per cent of time prices rise | 44% | 50% | 33% |
| Rank (of 48) | 42 | 42 | 35 |

*Source: Financial Times, Datastream/ICV*

Table 2.4: The bull market record is poor. Prices rise just 50% of the time, well below average compared with other quarters of the year. The bear market record is even worse than it looks. Since 1965, shares have fallen 10 times in a row during bear market first quarters.

trend change but once again, it is a point worth considering if you are a short-term trader or are thinking about selling a longer-term position at this point in the year.

### INCREASE YOUR PROFIT ODDS

January second-half signal No.1

Despite the generally poor trading conditions, it is possible to increase the likelihood of profit in this difficult segment of the year by investing selectively.

A good starting point is to monitor the direction in which the stock market moves in the second half of January. Since 1969, the FTSE All Share Index rose during this period by +3.34% or more on nine occasions. The rise was followed by a further rise in February's first quarter in eight of those years. During the other 19 years of this period, the FTSE All Share Index rose just four times.

57

## PERCENTAGE OF TIME PRICES RISE EACH DAY OF WEEK IN FEBRUARY'S FIRST QUARTER

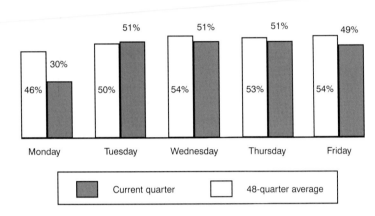

*Source: Financial Times, Datastream/ICV*

Figure 2.3: Mondays are painful to first-quarter investors. Prices rise just 30% of the time, the 47th-ranked Monday of all 48 quarters.

First-quarter record after a price rise of +3.34% or more in January's second half (FTSE All Share Index since 1969)

January
second-half
signal No.2

A similar trend has been running on the FT Ordinary Share Index since 1936. During this period, if second-half prices increased by +1.38% to +2.63%, there was a very good chance of a price rise in the first quarter of

## PERCENTAGE OF TIME PRICES RISE ON FEBRUARY 3–4: 1936–1996

|  | Prices rise |
| --- | --- |
| Total | 40% |
| Monday | 12% |
| Rest of week | 47% |

*Source: Financial Times, Datastream/ICV*

Table 2.5: Shares rise less than half of the time on 3–4 February. The record is especially poor when either of these two days land on a Monday.

February. Out of 10 increases within this range, the first quarter rose nine times.

IMPROVEMENT

*Rose (9)*

*Fell (1)*

First-quarter record after a price rise of +1.38% to +2.63% in January's second half (FT Ordinary Share Index since 1936)

January
second-half
signal No.3

On the down-side, a drop on the FT Ordinary Share Index in the last half of January or a rise by no more than +1.37% is often associated with share price weakness in the first quarter of February.

Since 1969, the FT Ordinary Share index has shifted within the defined range in 12 different years. Prices continued to disappoint investors in the first quarter of February in 11 of those years. Short-term traders would have found that betting against the market or simply pulling out completely was the most profitable course of action to take each time. Long-term investors also would

59

## PERCENTAGE OF TIME PRICES RISE EACH TRADING DAY IN FEBRUARY'S FIRST QUARTER

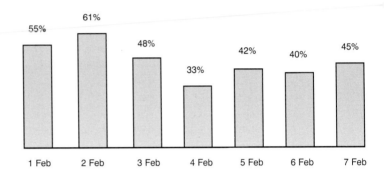

*Source: Financial Times, Datastream/ICV*

Figure 2.4: The first two days are the best days of the quarter. If you are planning to sell shares around this point of the year, the odds suggest holding on during these two days. But things soon change, especially 4 February which is the sixth-worst day of the year.

have done well to adjust their buy/sell schedule.

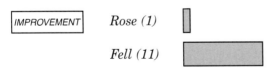

First-quarter record after a price decline in January's second half, or a rise of up to +1.37% (FT Ordinary Share Index since 1969)

January third-quarter signal

There is a strange correlation between the third quarter of January and February's first quarter. It seems that a price drop during January's third quarter is often followed by a further decline in the first quarter of

February, regardless of how prices move in January's fourth quarter. Apparently, market forces and money flows during January's fourth quarter (one of the best quarters of the entire year) are sufficiently powerful to overwhelm the negative trend for a short period of time. But, as soon as the fourth quarter ends, the negative trend comes back into effect at the beginning of February.

Since 1960, the FT Ordinary Share Index fell in January's third quarter by -0.87% or more in 11 different years. Prices continued to decline in 10 of those years in the first quarter of February, regardless of how they moved in January's fourth quarter.

UPDATE

*Rose (1)*

*Fell (10)*

First-quarter record after a price fall of -0.87% or more in January's third quarter (FT Ordinary Share Index since 1960)

January signal No.1

Another trend worth watching is the direction of prices in the whole month of January. Since 1965, each time January's prices rose by +3.65% to +8.33% on the FT-Non-Financial Index, they fell in the first quarter of February.

This signal flashed most recently in 1994 when a strong January rise was promptly followed with a decline of -1.64% in February's opening quarter.

*Rose (0)*

*Fell (10)*

First-quarter record after a price rise of +3.65% to +8.33% in January (FT-Non-Financial Index since 1965)

61

| January signal No.2 | A similar trend runs on the FTSE All Share Index and the FT Ordinary Share Index. Since 1965, there have been 10 occasions when January prices rose +3.38% to +6.60% on the FTSE All Share Index. February's first quarter fell in nine of those years. |
|---|---|
| January signal No.3 | Since 1957, there have been 10 occasions when January prices rose +4.03% to +9.31% on the FT Ordinary Share Index. February's first quarter fell nine times. |

## Second Quarter of February – February 8th to 14th

Like the first quarter, the second quarter offers investors poor profit potential. Prices rise less than half the time. History shows that the chance of a price rise is below average in bull markets and bear markets alike.

The likelihood of a rise is lowest on second-quarter Mondays and Tuesdays.

Here is a bit of good news. The likelihood of a price rise on 13 February is quite good in years when it does not land on a Monday.

| Money loser | February's second quarter is also a tough period in which to make money in the stock market. Prices fall 54% of the time, the 40th-ranked quarter of the year, and produce an average annual loss of -0.19%. The quarter performs poorly in bull and bear markets alike *(see Table 2.6)*. |
|---|---|
| | At first glance, the investment climate seems to have improved in the 1980s. Prices rose six times, fell four times, and increased at an average rate of +1.07%. But here again, the improvement was a temporary bull market phenomenon. The trend since 1987 has reverted to form with a record of three up and six down *(see Table 2.7)*. |

## FEBRUARY SECOND-QUARTER PERFORMANCE IN BULL/BEAR MARKETS: 1936–1996

|  | Total | Bull Markets | Bear Markets |
|---|---|---|---|
| Average price change | -0.19% | 0.34% | -1.19% |
| Rank (of 48) | 37 | 31 | 39 |
|  |  |  |  |
| Per cent of time prices rise | 46% | 53% | 33% |
| Rank (of 48) | 40 | 38 | 35 |

*Source: Financial Times, Datastream/ICV*

Table 2.6: The second quarter is another money loser in most years. The chance of a price rise is just over 50:50 in bull market years, well below average compared with other quarters of the year.

**Monday and Tuesday weakness**

As you execute your trades, keep in mind that the most profitable days of the week during this quarter are Wednesday to Friday. Mondays and Tuesdays are quite weak. Both are among the five worst Monday/Tuesday performers of all 48 quarters *(see Figure 2.5)*.

**11–14 February**

The Tuesday problem is especially acute on 11–12 February. Prices have risen just three out of 17 times when Tuesdays landed on 11 or 12 February since our records began in 1936. Likewise, the record has been poor on 13–14 February when either day landed on Monday. Prices have risen just three times in 18 attempts *(see Table 2.8)*.

**13 February**

A special note about 13 February. Despite its Monday weakness, it is the best day of the quarter. Prices rise 56% of the time *(see Figure 2.6)*. Even better, the profit odds seem to be improving. Since 1974, prices have been especially strong on this day, rising in 13 out of 17 years (Saturdays and Sundays account for the missing days).

## PERCENTAGE PRICE CHANGE: FEBRUARY 1985–96

|  | February 1–7 | February 8–14 | February 15–21 | February 22–29 |
|---|---|---|---|---|
| 1985 | 1.20% | -0.46% | -0.69% | -1.10% |
| 1986 | 0.83% | 2.40% | 2.58% | 1.80% |
| 1987 | 4.19% | 0.29% | 3.22% | 0.90% |
| 1988 | -2.56% | -0.31% | -0.05% | 2.12% |
| 1989 | 1.50% | -0.92% | 0.68% | -2.38% |
| 1990 | -1.08% | -0.47% | -1.85% | -0.49% |
| 1991 | 3.40% | 3.00% | 1.09% | 3.08% |
| 1992 | -1.68% | -0.14% | 1.14% | 0.86% |
| 1993 | 2.30% | -0.82% | 0.24% | 0.65% |
| 1994 | -1.52% | -1.48% | -0.41% | -0.68% |
| 1995 | 2.19% | 0.34% | -1.46% | -0.60% |
| 1996 | -0.52% | 0.47% | -0.27% | 0.25% |
| Average quarterly price change | 0.69% | 0.16% | 0.35% | 0.37% |
| Number of years in which prices | | | | |
| Rose | 7 | 5 | 6 | 7 |
| Fell | 5 | 7 | 6 | 5 |

*Source: Datastream/ICV*

Table 2.7: Since the 1987 crash, the first to third quarters have reverted to form with prices down in most years.

14 February

In case you are wondering, three of those four failures occurred on a Monday.

In contrast, 14 February, St. Valentine's Day, disappoints investors, even when it does not land on a Monday. On average, prices rise just 41% of the time, the 25th-ranked day of the month. If you have ever wondered why

## PERCENTAGE OF TIME PRICES RISE EACH DAY OF WEEK IN FEBRUARY'S SECOND QUARTER

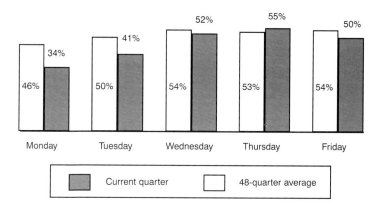

*Source: Financial Times, Datastream/ICV*

Figure 2.5: The chance of a price rise on Monday is well below average. It is one of the five worst Mondays of all 48 quarters. Tuesday's record is slightly better but it too is one of the five worst Tuesdays of the year.

Cupid is always shooting arrows at people, perhaps it is because he's a frustrated investor!

### INCREASE YOUR PROFIT ODDS

Fortunately, the stock market sends several key signals to help nimble investors to profit or to avoid losses during these very difficult trading conditions.

First-quarter signal No.1

Here is a new signal for readers of the *Schwartz Stock Market Handbook* based upon the FTSE All Share Index and its predecessor index. There have been 14 years since 1941 with a large January up-move, at least +2.26%, followed by a price drop in February's first quarter no

## PERCENTAGE OF TIME PRICES RISE ON FEBRUARY 11–14: 1936–1996

|  | Prices rise |
|---|---|
| Total February 11–12 | 39% |
| Tuesday | 18% |
| Rest of week | 45% |
| | |
| Total February 13–14 | 48% |
| Monday | 17% |
| Rest of week | 56% |

*Source: Financial Times, Datastream/ICV*

Table 2.8: It pays to invest with extreme caution when either 11 or 12 February lands on Tuesday or when either 13 or 14 February lands on Monday. The likelihood of a price rise is less than one in five on either occasion.

greater than -3.05%. Prices continued to fall in the second quarter in 13 of those years.

IMPROVEMENT

*Rose (1)*  ▮

*Fell (13)*  ▭

Second-quarter record after a January price rise of at least +2.26% and a price decline in February's first quarter no greater than -3.05% (FTSE All Share Index since 1941)

The signal last flashed in 1994. After a strong January rally, the stock market reached its all-time peak on February 2nd. By the end of the first quarter, shares had fallen by a small amount, and second-quarter prices fell by an additional -1.48%.

## PERCENTAGE OF TIME PRICES RISE EACH TRADING DAY IN FEBRUARY'S SECOND QUARTER

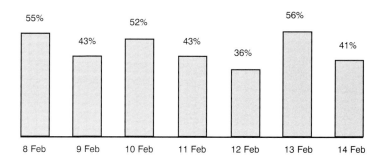

*Source: Financial Times, Datastream/ICV*

Figure 2.6: The stock market rises just one-third of the time on 12 February, the worst day of the quarter. Prices are especially likely to fall when 12 February lands on Tuesday. 13 February is the quarter's best day.

**First-quarter signal No.2**

A second signal to monitor is the direction of prices in February's first quarter, regardless of what happened in January. If they fall slightly on the FT Ordinary Share Index, by -0.29% to -1.01%, share prices will probably also drop in the second quarter. Out of 11 declines of this magnitude in the first quarter since 1941, second-quarter prices dropped 10 times. The average decline was -0.98% per year, about 39 points on an FTSE 100 in the area of 4000.

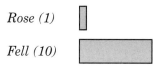

*Rose (1)*

*Fell (10)*

Second-quarter record after a price fall of -0.29% to -1.01% in the first quarter (FT Ordinary Share Index since 1941)

January third-
quarter signal

Another signal to watch for is a flat price trend in January's third quarter. History shows that tiny moves in mid-January are usually followed by declines in mid-February, regardless of what happens in the two intervening quarters. By a 'flat' price trend, we mean any small shift within a range of -0.52% to +0.43%.

Since 1937, there were 14 years with small third-quarter price shifts within this range. February's second quarter fell in 12 of those years (86% of the time) and generated an average loss of -1.51% per year.

*Rose (2)*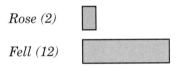

*Fell (12)*

Second-quarter record after a price shift of -0.52% to +0.43% in January's third quarter (FT Ordinary Share Index since 1937)

First-quarter
signal No.3

The previous three trends help investors to forecast when the second quarter is likely to fall. On the up-side, there have been 10 years since 1939 when the FT Ordinary Share Index rose in the first quarter of February by +2.12% or more. Second-quarter prices rose in nine of those years. The last time this signal flashed was in 1995 and prices rose as expected.

*Rose (9)*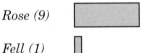

*Fell (1)*

Second-quarter record after a price rise of +2.12% or more in February's first quarter (FT Ordinary Share Index since 1939)

# THIRD QUARTER OF FEBRUARY – FEBRUARY 15TH TO 21ST

Here comes the month's worst quarter. Prices rise just 43% of the time.

The red ink is quite likely to flow in bear markets. Shares fell in 13 of the last 15 bear market years. Even during bull markets, the profit odds are just 50:50.

Be especially cautious on 21 February which rise 32% of the time, the worst day of the month and second-worst day of the year.

Another money loser

The third quarter of February has been a steady money-loser over the years. The stock market slips -0.29% during the average year. The typical share price fell 57% of the time between 1936 and 1996, the month's worst performance and fourth-worst of all 48 quarters of the year. Even during the early 1980s when the third quarter turned a small profit, as did other so-so segments of the year, it rose just four times and fell six times.

The trend is weak in bull and bear markets alike. During bull markets, third-quarter prices fall by -0.07% during the average year, the fifth-worst performance of all 48 quarters (see Table 2.9).

Poor bear market record

Prices rise 29% of the time during bear markets but many of those rises occurred before 1948. Since 1948, the third-quarter record during bear markets has been two rises and 13 drops, a 13% 'success' rate.

Thursday profits

Over the long-run, history shows that the odds of making money are low on most days of the week. Thursday is a notable exception. Prices rise 57% of the time on Thursday, the only day of the week that rises at an above-average rate. No one can explain why mid-month Thursdays are consistently more profitable than the rest of the week but it is a trend that has been running since 1936 (see Figure 2.7).

15 and 21 February

History also shows a pattern of relative strength at the start of the third quarter followed by extreme weakness

## FEBRUARY THIRD-QUARTER PERFORMANCE IN BULL/BEAR MARKETS: 1936–1996

|  | Total | Bull Markets | Bear Markets |
|---|---|---|---|
| Average price change | -0.29% | -0.07% | -0.72% |
| Rank (of 48) | 41 | 44 | 30 |
| | | | |
| Per cent of time prices rise | 43% | 50% | 29% |
| Rank (of 48) | 45 | 42 | 42 |

*Source: Financial Times, Datastream/ICV*

Table 2.9: The third-quarter record is poor in bull and bear markets alike. Be especially cautious in bear markets. The record has weakened in recent years. Prices have fallen in 13 of the last 15 bear market years.

toward the end of the quarter. The best day of the quarter is at the very beginning, the 15th, the fourth-best day of the month. The worst is 21 February where prices rise just 32% of the time, the worst day of the month and second-worst day of the entire year *(see Figure 2.8)*. Prices are especially likely to fall on the 21st when it lands on Monday. Since our records began, the 21st landed on Monday nine times. Shares fell every time.

### INCREASE YOUR PROFIT ODDS

The direction of prices in the first half of February provides several good clues on the likely direction of third-quarter share prices.

First-half signal No.1

If you choose to bet on a rising market, a small shift during the first half of the month has often signalled that third-quarter prices will rise. Since our records began in 1936, there were 11 occasions with a small first-half

## PERCENTAGE OF TIME PRICES RISE EACH DAY OF WEEK IN FEBRUARY'S THIRD QUARTER

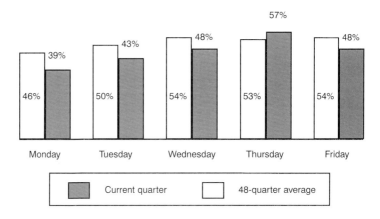

*Source: Financial Times, Datastream/ICV*

Figure 2.7: Thursday is the only weekday in the third quarter that rises more than half the time.

price shift on the FT Ordinary Share Index of -0.14% to +1.15%. Third-quarter prices rose in 10 of those years. The single exception to the rule occurred in 1967.

*Rose (10)*

*Fell (1)*

Third-quarter record after a price shift of -0.14% to +1.15% in the first half (FT Ordinary Share Index since 1936)

First-half signal No.2

On the down-side, there have been 15 occasions since 1937 with a first-half price drop of -0.24% to -2.23%. Third-quarter prices rose in just 2 of those years.

71

## PERCENTAGE OF TIME PRICES RISE EACH TRADING DAY IN FEBRUARY'S THIRD QUARTER

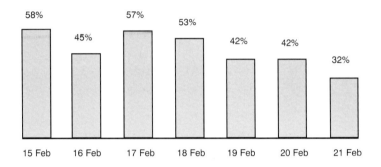

*Source: Financial Times, Datastream/ICV*

Figure 2.8: The best day of the quarter is 15 February. The trend steadily drops over the next six days until the end of the quarter. 21 February rises one-third of the time, the worst day of the month and one of the worst trading days of the entire year. The chance of a decline on 21 February is especially high on Monday where it fell nine times in a row in the past six decades.

NEW

*Rose (2)*

*Fell (12)*

*No change (1)*

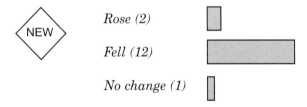

Third-quarter record after a price shift of -0.24% to -2.23% in the first half (FT Ordinary Share Index since 1937)

First-half signal No.3

There were another 10 occasions since 1938 when the FT Ordinary Share Index fell in the first half within a range of -2.85% to -6.09%. Third-quarter prices fell in nine of those years.

*Rose (1)*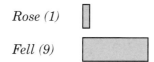

*Fell (9)*

Third-quarter record after a price shift of -2.85% to -6.09% in the first half (FT Ordinary Share Index since 1938)

**First-half signal No.4**

The following trend overlaps the previous two but also spots some third-quarter declines that the other two miss. If the FT Ordinary Share Index rises during the first quarter by no more than +0.61%, or falls by any amount, and the second quarter falls by -0.74% to -2.62%, the third quarter is especially likely to fall. The average annual decline during these years is -1.79%. This signal last flashed in 1994 and third-quarter prices fell on cue.

*Rose (0)*

*Fell (11)*

Third-quarter record after a price shift of +0.61% or less in the first quarter and a decline of -0.74% to -2.62% in the second quarter (FT Ordinary Share Index since 1936)

**Prior four-quarters signal**

The best early warning signal of all is a weak price trend in January's second half and February's first half. If prices decline in February's first half and either rise by no more than +0.33% or decline in January's second half, the odds favour a decline in the third quarter. Since 1936, there were 19 years that fit this profile. The third quarter of February declined in 18 of those years (95%), with an average decline of -1.41% per year. The single exception was back in 1947.

*Rose (1)*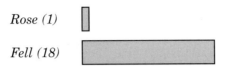

*Fell (18)*

Third-quarter record after a price shift of +0.33% or less in January's second half and a decline in February's first half (FT Ordinary Share Index since 1938)

Here is a newly discovered trend that does a good job of spotting third-quarter declines during bear markets. It is based on the FTSE All Share Index and its predecessor index.

**Second-quarter signal No.1**

In years that a bear market is running at this point of the year, a decline in the second quarter or a small rise, no more than +0.52%, is typically associated with a third-quarter price drop. There have been 13 times with a price shift within the target range. Third-quarter prices dropped each time.

*Rose (0)*

*Fell (13)*

Third-quarter record after a price shift of +0.52% or less in the second quarter during bear markets (FTSE All Share Index since 1948)

**Second-quarter signal No.2**

A new trend seems to have developed on the FT Ordinary Share Index since 1984. We originally called attention to it in a previous edition of the *Schwartz Stock Market Handbook*. With several years of additional data now available, we have been able to refine it.

Although it is still too early to call it a definite trend because of the low number of observations, we note the following events with great interest. Prices have risen on the FT Ordinary Share Index in the second quarter by +0.30% or more five times since 1984. Third-quarter prices rose each time. During the other eight years of this period, the third-quarter record is four up and four down.

## FOURTH QUARTER OF FEBRUARY – FEBRUARY 22ND TO 29TH

Here comes the only profitable quarter of February. No guarantees for any one year of course, but shares rise in most years, a welcome change to the record of the three preceding months.

The likelihood of a price rise is especially good in a leap year. No one knows why but since 1956, fourth-quarter prices have risen in every single leap year, 11 times in a row.

The daily price trend starts off weakly. 23 February is the quarter's weakest link. Prices rise just 45% of the time. But the trend steadily improves as the quarter unfolds. The two most profitable trading days in the quarter are near the end.

The fourth quarter is February's best segment. Prices rise 56% of the time. It is February's only quarterly segment that rises in most years. Between 1936 and 1996, the average annual gain was +0.60%.

**Profitable in bull and bear markets**

As Table 2.10 shows, the fourth quarter is February's only quarter that produces an average annual profit over the long-run in bear markets as well as bull markets. Buried in Table 2.10 is an important clue about the behaviour of share prices during this quarter. In bear markets, prices rise 40% of the time which places this quarter right in the middle of the pack on the quarterly performance rankings. But at the same time, prices rise by +0.18% during the average bear market year which is sixth-best of all 48 quarters.

## FEBRUARY FOURTH-QUARTER PERFORMANCE IN BULL/BEAR MARKETS: 1936–1996

|  | Total | Bull Markets | Bear Markets |
|---|---|---|---|
| Average price change | 0.60% | 0.80% | 0.18% |
| Rank (of 48) | 11 | 15 | 6 |
| Per cent of time prices rise | 56% | 63% | 40% |
| Rank (of 48) | 21 | 20 | 25 |

*Source: Financial Times, Datastream/ICV*

Table 2.10: The fourth quarter is February's best segment. Prices rise 40% of the time in bear markets, right in the middle of the pack. Even better, the typical price rise is +0.18% in bear market years, well above average. The reason is that the typical decline in bear market *down* years is much smaller than average. Half are less than 1%.

The reason for this apparent inconsistency is that the typical rise during bear market up-years is much higher than average, and more important, the typical decline during bear market down years is much smaller than average. Half are drops of under 1%.

No one can explain why the fourth quarter behaves so atypically during bear markets but the historical record tells a clear story. While you can easily lose money during bear markets, the odds of being smashed badly by a big drop is small.

23 February    The daily price trend shows a steady improvement as the quarter unfolds. 23 February is the quarter's weakest link. Prices rise just 45% of the time since 1936. The recent trend shows no sign of improvement. Since 1980, the 23 February record is four up and eight down.

27–28 February    The trend soon improves. The two most profitable

## PERCENTAGE OF TIME PRICES RISE EACH TRADING DAY IN FEBRUARY'S FOURTH QUARTER

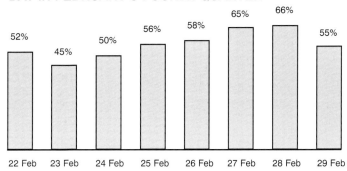

*Source: Financial Times, Datastream/ICV*

Figure 2.9:  27 and 28 February are the best days of the month. If you plan to sell shares near the end of the month, holding on until the very end will move profits a bit more in your favour in most years.

trading days in the quarter are at the end. In fact, 27 February is the second-best day of the month and 28 February is the best day – prices rise 66% of the time. So if you are planning to sell shares late in the month, the odds favour holding on until the very end of the month *(see Figure 2.9)*.

**Wednesday profits**

The fourth quarter is the only segment of the month with good profit odds on every trading day of the week, especially on Wednesdays which rise 60% of the time, the year's sixth-ranked Wednesday *(see Figure 2.10)*. Not surprisingly, the likelihood of profit on 26–28 February is best on Wednesday. Since our records began in 1936, one of these days landed on Wednesday 26 times. The stock market rose 21 times (81%) and fell five times.

February 28 is a very safe day in which to hold shares for one other very important reason as well. In addition

## PERCENTAGE OF TIME PRICES RISE EACH DAY OF WEEK IN FEBRUARY'S FOURTH QUARTER

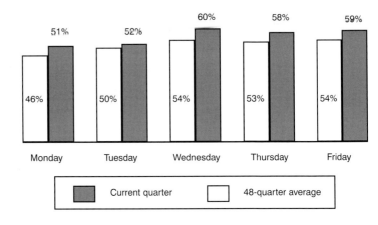

*Source: Financial Times, Datastream/ICV*

Figure 2.10: Each weekday rises more than half of the time. Fourth-quarter Wednesdays are the sixth-best of all 48 quarters. The chance of a Wednesday price rise is especially high on 26–28 February.

to the high percentage of time that prices rise, it is one of the few days in the entire year in which prices have never fallen by over 1%.

### INCREASE YOUR PROFIT ODDS

Prior two-quarters signal No.1

To improve the chance of profiting in the fourth quarter, watch the behaviour of prices in the two preceding quarters.

Between 1936 and 1996 there were 15 occasions when the FT Ordinary Share Index rose by at least +1.69% in total in the second and third quarters. Prices continued to rise in the fourth quarter in 13 of those years (87%).

The average increase was +2.52%.

*Rose (13)*

*Fell (2)*

Fourth-quarter record after a total price rise of at least +1.69% in the second and third quarters (FT Ordinary Share Index since 1936)

Prior two-quarters signal No.2

A similar trend runs on the FTSE All Share Index, where a rise in the previous two quarters of +1.00% or more is likely to be followed by a fourth-quarter increase. Since 1969, there have been 12 years with a sufficient rise in the preceding two quarters. Fourth-quarter prices rose 10 times. One of the two exceptions was a decline of just -0.24% in 1984.

*Rose (10)*

*Fell (2)*

Fourth-quarter record after a price rise of at least +1.00% in the second and third quarters (FTSE All Share Index since 1969)

Prior four-quarters signal

Here is a new trend in the process of developing. During bear markets, a drop of -2.02% or more on the FT-Non-Financial Index in the four preceding quarters is likely to be followed by a fourth-quarter decline.

Since 1969, there have been six occasions with a bear market fall of this magnitude. Fourth-quarter prices fell five times. The single exception, in the midst of the 1973–4 bear market, saw a fourth-quarter rise of just +0.04%, the equivalent of less than two points on an FTSE 100 in the area of 4000.

◇ NEW

*Rose (1)*

*Fell (5)*

Fourth-quarter record after a price drop of -2.02% or more in the preceding four quarters during bear markets (FT-Non-Financial Index since 1969)

February first-half signal No.1

There is also an interesting relationship between the first half of February and the fourth quarter, regardless of which direction prices move in the third quarter. Solid moves, either up or down, are often associated with fourth-quarter price increases. But small shifts are often associated with fourth-quarter price declines. Here is the evidence. Since 1939, first-half prices rose by at least +1.15% 19 times. Fourth-quarter prices also rose in 16 of those years.

UPDATE

*Rose (16)*

*Fell (3)*

Fourth-quarter record after a price rise of at least +1.15% in the first half (FT Ordinary Share Index since 1939)

February first-half signal No.2

During this same period, there were 13 additional years with a first half decline of -2.29% to -5.10%. Fourth-quarter prices rose in 11 of those years.

*Rose (11)*

*Fell (2)*

Fourth-quarter record after a price drop of -2.29% to -5.10% in the first half (FT Ordinary Share Index since 1939)

80

There were an additional 26 years with a smaller first-half price shift, no more than +1.14% on the up-side and -2.28% on the down-side. Fourth-quarter prices rose just eight times.

Here are two final statistical relationships to help you to make money in February. They both operate on a four-year cycle. We offer no rationale to explain why they work. But they do work.

**Leap year signal**

Since 1956, there have been 11 leap years. Fourth-quarter prices on the FT Ordinary Share Index have risen in every single one of them. The average annual price increase was +1.52%. In the other 30 years since 1956, fourth-quarter prices rose just 43% of the time.

| UPDATE |

*Rose (11)*

*Fell (0)*

Fourth-quarter record in leap years (FT Ordinary Share Index since 1956)

Surprisingly, February 29th itself is not consistently profitable. Since 1956, its record is four up and four down (the missing three days fell on weekends).

**Even-numbered year signal**

During even-number years that are not leap years (like 1990, 1994 and 1998 for example), shares often fall. Since 1958, there have been 10 even-numbered, non-leap years. FT Ordinary Share Index prices fell in eight of those years.

*Rose (2)*

*Fell (8)*

Fourth-quarter record in even numbered, non-leap years (FT Ordinary Share Index since 1958)

## LOOKING AHEAD

Rising prices by
31 May

History shows that a rise on the FTSE All Share Index or its predecessor index in the last eight months within a range of +8.26% to +27.38% is often associated with further rises in the three months ahead.

Since 1941, prices rose within the defined range in 23 different years. The stock market rose still higher in the three months ahead 21 times. In the remaining 33 years of this period, the March-May record was 20 rises and 13 declines.

*Rose (21)*

*Fell (2)*

Trend to 31 May after a price rise of +8.26% to +27.38% in the past eight months (FTSE All Share Index since 1941)

As you use this data, remember that shares will not necessarily peak at the end of May. It is theoretically possible for prices to peak near the beginning of March, drift downward for the rest of the three month period yet still show a profit at the end of May.

Rising prices by
31 December

A related trend has been running on the FT-Non-Financial Index and its predecessor index since 1925. During this period, history shows that if prices rise in the six month period between September 1 to February 28/29 by +4.08% to +20.47%, the odds are very good that prices will rise still higher in the 10 months ahead, that is, through the rest of the year to December 31.

Since 1925, there have been 31 years with a September–February price rise within the designated range. Prices rose still further in the next 10 months in 28 of those years. One of the three failures was a drop of just -0.68% in 1961.

*Rose (28)*

*Fell (3)*

Trend to December 31 after a September-February price shift of +4.08% to +20.47% (FT-Non-Financial Index since 1925)

**Rising prices by 31 October**

The FT-Non-Financial Index and its predecessor index also shows an uncanny ability to forecast where prices are heading eight months ahead, that is, to the end of October. Here is an up-date on a trend that has been running since 1923. During this period, there have been 25 years with a February price rise of up to +3.29% or a tiny fall, no greater than -0.55%. In 24 of those years, prices rose in the eight months to 31 October. The average increase was +8.9%. This signal flashed most recently in 1993, 1995 and 1996. Prices rose in the next eight months each time.

A single exception to the rule occurred in 1957 and even then, the February up-move was followed with rising prices in March, April, May and June, stimulated by falling Bank Rates and an expanding economy. The party came to an end with a July rise in Bank Rates to 7%, their highest level in four decades. Equities fell sharply from their early summer peak for the next four months.

*Rose (24)*

*Fell (1)*

Trend to 31 October after a February price shift of -0.55% to +3.29% (FT-Non-Financial Index since 1923)

# CHAPTER 3 – MARCH

The March story is heavily influenced by the former Spring Budget. History suggests that the recently announced return to a Spring Budget will have an enormous effect upon the March trend. But much depends upon the precise date which had not been announced at press time.

To understand why, consider this. Up until the 1940s, Spring Budgets were a late-April or May event, and March was a money-loser in most years. The trend began to improve as budget schedules were steadily advanced. By the 1980s, when Budget Day typically landed in mid-March, shares rose in value in eight out of 10 years.

The return to a Spring Budget will also affect the pattern of price shifts within the month. In the 1940s to 1960s when many budgets landed in late March and April, first-half prices rose much less than half of the time. Once budgets began to appear in early- and mid-March, the profit trend changed dramatically. First- and second-quarter prices both rose 68% of the time in the last few decades.

The price trend during the second half of March was directly opposite. When budgets were an April event, prices rose about two-thirds of the time. But in recent decades, its performance slipped badly with prices rising less than half of the time in both quarters as shares gave back some of their budget-induced first half advance.

The future March trend is likely to be affected by the actual day that the budget is presented.

Unimpressive record

Investors who held shares every March made very little money over the long term. Between 1919 and 1996, March prices rose 58% of the time. The average price rise was just 0.62%, equal to 25 points on an FTSE 100 in the area of 4000. Historically, March has been the sixth-best month to invest in shares *(see Table 3.1)*. A 1919 investment of £1,000, held in shares each March and in cash for the other 11 months of the year, would now be worth just £1,464 after 78 years of steady investing.

Bull markets

The price trend in bull market years shows the same tendency toward 'averageness'. Prices rise 67% of the time during bull markets, at an average rate of +1.76% each month, both in the middle of the pack on the monthly league tables. When prices rise during March bull markets, the size of the typical rise is close to the norm for the 12 months as a whole. During bull market down months, the typical drop is also close to average *(see Table 3.2)*.

Bear markets

At first glance, the bear market trend looks to be another average performer. But beneath the surface, March's bear market record is much better than it appears to be at first glance. The confusion is caused by a -20.74% decline in March 1974 during our worst-ever bear market. Investors who anticipated a Tory win in late-February's election panicked following Labour's surprise win and dumped shares all at once. It was the worst monthly drop in the entire 1973–4 bear market, and the third-worst month of all time. Only October 1987 (-26.59%) and June 1940 (-22.10%), when investors feared we might lose the war, were associated with bigger falls.

If 1974 is eliminated from this analysis, a different underlying trend becomes apparent. March causes less pain to investors in bear markets, compared to other months. It typically returns a loss of -1.13%, less than most other months.

Without 1974, prices fall -3.47% in the typical bear market down month, the best performance of all 12

**MARCH PRICE RISES AND DECLINES: 1919–1996**

|  | Average March price change | Up | Down/ No change |
|---|---|---|---|
| 1920–29 | 0.59% | 4 | 6 |
| 1930–39 | -0.40% | 4 | 6 |
| 1940–49 | -0.62% | 3 | 7 |
| 1950–59 | 0.40% | 7 | 3 |
| 1960–69 | 1.86% | 7 | 3 |
| 1970–79 | 0.33% | 7 | 3 |
| 1980–89 | 1.84% | 8 | 2 |
| 1990–96 | -0.56% | 4 | 3 |
| Average March change: 1919–96 | 0.62% | 58% | 42% |
| Rank (of 12) | 6 | 7 | |

*Source: BZW, Datastream/ICV*

Table 3.1: Prior to 1950, prices rose just over one-third of the time. But in the second half of this century, the March record steadily improved. Budget Day played an important role in this improvement.

months. To put this figure into context, the typical decline in September during bear market down months is over 6%. In other words, history shows that you will lose less money in March during bear market down months, than any other month.

Spotting bull markets

Despite the fact that bear markets are not as bloody for March investors as they are in other months, it still pays to hold shares in March during bull markets and avoid them during bear markets. The long-term trend contains a useful signal which increases the odds of spotting bull and bear markets. As Figure 3.1 reveals,

## MARCH PERFORMANCE IN BULL/BEAR MARKETS: 1919–1996

|  | Bull Markets | Bear Markets |
|---|---|---|
| Average per cent price change | 1.76% | *-1.95% |
| Rank (of 12) | 6 | 5 |
|  |  |  |
| Per cent of time prices rise | 67% | 38% |
| Rank (of 12) | 5 | 6 |
|  |  |  |
| Average per cent price change in: |  |  |
| Rising years | 3.89% | 2.51% |
| Declining years | -2.51% | **-4.63% |

\*  -1.13% without 1974
\*\*  3.47% without 1974

*Source: BZW, Datastream/ICV*

Table 3.2: March's record is average compared to other months in bull and bear markets. But the bear market record is much better than it appears to be at first glance. Prices fell by almost 21% in 1974, the third-worst monthly drop of all time as investors panicked following Labour's surprise win. If not for 1974, the March bear market record would be much better than average.

February price increases of up to +3.29% are usually associated with bull markets. Since our records began in 1919, February prices rose by this amount in 23 different years. All but one occurred in bull markets. The single exception was back in 1932.

Remember that Figure 3.1 does not tell you when the bull market will end. It is conceivable that the following month will see the start of a new bear market. Still, as a bull market confirmation signal, a February price rise serves a useful purpose.

## ODDS OF BULL/BEAR MARKET TIPPED BY FEBRUARY'S TREND

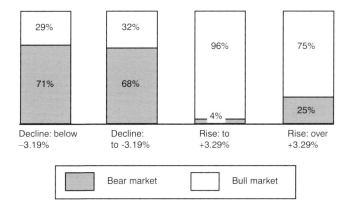

Source: BZW, Datastream/ICV

Figure 3.1: A small February price increase of up to +3.29% is a very strong signal that a bull market is running.

**Spotting bear markets**

At the other end of the continuum, February declines of any size are associated with bear markets in two out of three years.

**Budget Day's big shadow**

For bull and bear markets alike, Budget Day seems to play a role in March's long-term performance *(see Figure 3.2)*. From 1919–43, the first 25 years of our historical record, March prices rose just 10 times. During this money-losing period, 21 out of 25 budgets were presented in late April. In the next 25 years, from 1944–1968, Budget Day was often scheduled in early/mid-April, and March prices rose 15 times. From 1969–93, 19 budgets were presented in March and the number of March price rises improved once again, despite 1974's drop following a surprise Labour victory.

## NUMBER OF TIMES MARCH PRICES ROSE: 1919–1993

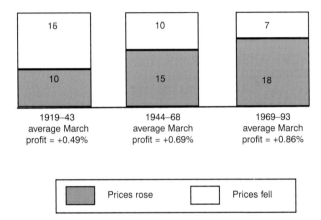

| 1919–43 average March profit = +0.49% | 1944–68 average March profit = +0.69% | 1969–93 average March profit = +0.86% |

Prices rose    Prices fell

*Source: BZW, Datastream/ICV*

Figure 3.2: March prices rose more frequently in successive 25-year periods as budgets were presented earlier in the spring. Profitability also steadily improved. The average annual profit of +0.86% in 1969–93 would have been even higher if not for 1974.

There is no way to prove conclusively that Budget Day caused this improvement. There are too many other issues that also influence share price movements. However, we believe the parallels between Budget Day and the March profit trend are not a coincidence. For this reason, we thought it very fitting that prices fell by -6.78% in 1994, the first spring without a Spring Budget. We did not expect big drops like this every year. The 1994 drop was triggered by concerns over further interest rate rises on both sides of the Atlantic. But as a symbol of the 'new' March or perhaps, a return to the 'old' March, the decline was very appropriate.

As we go to press, the government has announced a return to Spring Budgets. Depending on the specific date that is eventually selected, investors should be ready for either a re-run of poor conditions as in the 1920s and 1930s, or very good conditions as in the 1980s.

**Budget Day affects intra-month trends as well**

Not only did Budget Day affect the month's overall performance, it also had an impact on the point in the month when most profits were accumulated. Prior to 1969 when budgets often landed in April, second-half prices rose much more often compared with the first half *(see Figure 3.3)*. Although the third and fourth quarters rose roughly the same amount of time during this period, the fourth quarter, one week closer to Budget Day and to the beginning of the new tax year, tended to generate bigger increases.

Since 1969, as budgets were increasingly more likely to be presented in the first half of March, the profit pattern abruptly changed. Between 1969–93, the third and fourth quarters rose about half of the time. Meanwhile, the strength formerly associated with the second half shifted to the first half. Between 1969–93 when early-March budgets were the norm, the first two quarters each rose 68% of the time *(see Figure 3.4)*.

**Specific date is important**

How will the intra-month profit trend behave with the return of Spring Budgets? No one knows for sure. Much depends upon the specific date of Budget Day. Figures 3.3 and 3.4 will provide a useful perspective of what to expect once the exact date is announced.

### INCREASE YOUR PROFIT ODDS

As with other months, historical price trends help to identify specific years when the stock market is most likely to rise or decline. Unfortunately, the effect of constant Budget Day shifts adds an unknown dimension to these forecasts. Nevertheless, here are several trends which, historically, have done a good job of anticipating

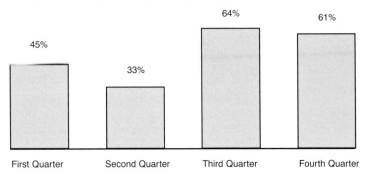

**ODDS OF A PRICE RISE IN MARCH: 1936–68**

45%

33%

64%

61%

First Quarter       Second Quarter       Third Quarter       Fourth Quarter

*Source: Financial Times, Datastream/ICV*

Figure 3.3: In the 1930s to 1960s, late-spring budgets were associated with a better chance of making money in the second half of the month. Things changed when budgets became an early-spring event (see Figure 3.4 opposite).

**Prior 12-month signal No.1**

the direction of March price shifts and which we believe are not dependent on Budget Day.

One long-running trend worth monitoring is the tendency for shares to rise in March if they have risen very sharply in the past 12 months. What we like about this trend is that it ran in the 1920s to 1960s when Budgets landed in April as well as the 1970s and 1980s when they landed in March. It also flashed in 1996 after Budgets had been shifted to November and prices rose as expected. Here is the trend.

Since 1923, there have been 17 occasions when the FTSE All Share Index[1] or its predecessor index rose +22.83% or more in the preceding 12 months. March prices rose in 16 of those years.

---

[1]We will provide closing price trends on key indices for the last 12 months at no cost (see page 9).

## ODDS OF A PRICE RISE IN MARCH:1969–93

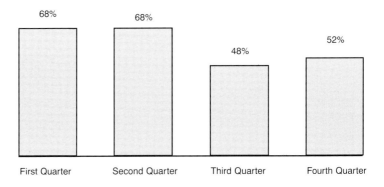

*Source: Financial Times, Datastream/ICV*

Figure 3.4: When budgets began to appear in the first half of March, the intra-month profit trend changed. It was a sharp reversal of the trend illustrated in Figure 3.3 (opposite). Prices immediately began to rise much more often in the first two quarters of the month. Making money in the second half of the month became a 50:50 proposition. The approach of profitable April trading conditions failed to help the fourth-quarter trend.

IMPROVEMENT

*Rose (16)*

*Fell (1)*

March record after a price rise of +22.83% or more in the 12 preceding months (FTSE All Share Index since 1923)

Prior 12-months signal No.2

Here is an up-date on a related trend involving the FT-Non-Financial Index and its predecessor index. Since 1923, there have been 13 years in which prices rose between +21.04% to +35.45% in the preceding 12 months. March shares rose each time.

*Rose (13)*

*Fell (0)*

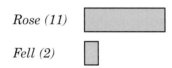

March record after a price rise of +21.04% to +35.45% in the 12
preceding months (FT-Non-Financial Index since 1923)

**Prior three-
months signal
No.1**

It also pays to watch the price trend during December to
February. A large price decline in this three-month period
is often associated with a rise in March. A small decline is
often associated with further declines in March.

Here is the evidence. Since 1930, there have been 13
years when prices dropped on the FTSE All Share Index
or its predecessor index by -2.69% to -14.99% in the past
three months. March prices rose 11 times. One exception
was due to Labour's surprise win in 1974.

NEW

*Rose (11)*

*Fell (2)*

March record after a price fall of -2.69% to -14.99% in the past
three months (FTSE All Share Index since 1930)

**Prior three-
months signal
No.2**

A similar trend runs on the FT-Non-Financial Index and
its predecessor index. Since 1930, there have been 12 years
where prices fell in the past three months within a range
of -3.30% and -13.71%. March rose 10 times.

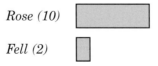

*Rose (10)*

*Fell (2)*

March record after a price fall of -3.30% to -13.71% in the three
preceding months (FT-Non-Financial Index since 1930)

**Prior three-months signal No.3**

In contrast, small drops between December and February are often followed by March declines. There were 11 years since 1925 with smaller declines in the preceding three months, -2.68% or less. March prices fell in 10 of those years.

| IMPROVEMENT |
| --- |

*Rose (1)*

*Fell (10)*

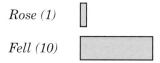

March record after a price decline of -2.68% or less in the past three months (FTSE All Share Index since 1925)

**Prior three-months signal No.4**

On the FT Ordinary Share Index, moderate rises between December and February are often followed by further advances in March.

Since 1943, there have been 12 occasions when prices rose +1.77% to +3.90% in the prior three months. March fell just once. This signal last flashed in 1996 and March rose as expected.

◇ NEW ◇

*Rose (11)*

*Fell (1)*

March record after a price rise of +1.77% to +3.90% in the three preceding months (FT Ordinary Share Index since 1943)

**February fourth-quarter signal No.1**

A shorter-term indicator worth watching is the direction of prices in the fourth quarter of February. History shows that a small fourth-quarter rise on the FT-Non-Financial Index and its predecessor index, within a range of +0.44% to +2.08%, often precedes an increase in March. Since 1945, there have been 12 quarterly shifts of that size. March prices rose 11 times.

UPDATE

Rose (11)

Fell (1)

March record after a price rise of +0.44% to +2.08% in February's fourth quarter (FT-Non-Financial Index since 1945)

February
fourth-quarter
signal No.2

A similar trend has run on the FTSE All Share Index and its predecessor index since 1945. During this period, there have been 11 quarterly shifts of +0.44% to +1.80%. March prices rose in 10 of those years.

Rose (10)

Fell (1)

March record after a price rise of +0.44% to +1.80% in February's fourth quarter (FTSE All Share Index since 1945)

Bear market
signal

All preceding trends have run in bull and bear markets alike. The next one functions only during bear markets. Since 1920, there were 15 occasions when a bear market was running at the beginning of March and the FTSE All Share Index or its predecessor index had risen in the last 12 months or had fallen by up to -10.66%. March prices fell in 14 of those years. This signal last flashed in 1994 and shares fell in March as expected.

Rose (1)

Fell (14)

March record during bear markets after a price rise in the 12 preceding months or a decline of up to -10.66% (FTSE All Share Index since 1920)

## FIRST QUARTER OF MARCH – MARCH 1ST TO 8TH

Profit prospects for the first quarter are highly dependent upon the precise date of the Spring Budget.

The best years for first quarter investors were in the 1980s when prices rose eight out of 10 times, helped by an early or mid-March budget. But April budgets provided little help to the first-quarter investor in the 1930s to 1960s when prices usually fell.

Invest with care on first-quarter Mondays, regardless of when the budget is presented. Prices rise just 40% of the time.

Over the long-run, investors gained very little by steadily investing in every first quarter of March. During the 61 years for which we have quarterly data, the first quarter rose 49% of the time and produced a +0.12% average price increase, the equivalent of less than five points a year on a 4000 FTSE 100.

**Bull versus bear markets**

There are interesting performance differences during bull versus bear markets. Prices rise 57% of the time during bull market years, about average compared to other quarters. But the bear market record is disappointing. Prices rise just 32% of the time, below average when compared to other quarters *(see Table 3.3)*.

**Helped by a March budget**

A decade-by-decade analysis finds small losses during the 1930s and '40s, when budgets were often presented in late April, and tiny profits in the 1950s and '60s, when budgets were in early or mid-April. Once budgets were moved to March, there was a marked improvement in the first-quarter trend. The relatively large annual decline of -0.48% in the 1970s was mainly due to a -12.36% decline in the 1974 bear market, immediately following the Labour party's surprise election win. Prices rose throughout the remainder of the decade and continued to do so in the 1980s with increases in eight out of ten years and an average annual gain of +1.13% *(see Table 3.4)*.

## MARCH FIRST-QUARTER PERFORMANCE IN
## BULL/BEAR MARKETS: 1936–1996

|  | Total | Bull Markets | Bear Markets |
|---|---|---|---|
| Average price change | 0.12% | 0.77% | -1.31% |
| Rank (of 48) | 24 | 16 | 40 |
|  |  |  |  |
| Per cent of time prices rise | 49% | 57% | 32% |
| Rank (of 48) | 31 | 27 | 37 |

*Source: Financial Times, Datastream/ICV*

Table 3.3: The likelihood of a price rise in bull market years is about average, compared to other quarters of the year. But prices rise in one out of three years during bear markets, below average compared to other quarters.

Up-coming budgets

Now that Spring Budgets are back, first-quarter expectations will be influenced by the exact date of the budget, unknown as we go to press. One view of the future is quite visible in the unshaded bars of Figure 3.5 which shows the pre-1974 daily price trend, without the stimulus of an early-March budget. Clearly, the daily price trend was decidedly weaker.

Weak Mondays

Analysis of price trends by day of week shows that the profit odds are below average on each week day with the odds lowest on Monday when prices rise just 40% of the time *(see Figure 3.6)*.

4–5 March

Monday's weakness is especially acute on 4–5 March. Since 1936, both days have done poorly when they landed on Monday, with a record of 4 up and 13 down, a success rate of just 24%. Prices rose much more often (57% of the time) when these two days landed on Tuesday to Friday. Even more telling, prior to 1974 when budgets often landed in late-Spring, prices fell on Monday 10

## PERCENTAGE PRICE CHANGE: MARCH 1936–96

|  | Mar 1–8 | Mar 9–15 | Mar 16–23 | Mar 24–31 |
|---|---|---|---|---|
| Annual average | | | | |
| 1935–39 | -0.57% | -2.89% | 0.24% | -0.96% |
| 1940–49 | -0.40% | -0.63% | 0.12% | 0.43% |
| 1950–59 | 0.02% | -0.76% | 0.67% | 0.61% |
| 1960–69 | 0.17% | 0.43% | 0.36% | 0.82% |
| 1970–79 | -0.48% | 1.47% | -0.87% | 0.08% |
| 1980–89 | 1.13% | 0.74% | 0.69% | -0.90% |
| 1990–96 | 0.36% | -0.22% | -0.31% | -0.41% |
| | | | | |
| Average quarterly price change | 0.12% | 0.00% | 0.08% | 0.09% |
| | | | | |
| Per cent of time prices rise | 49% | 48% | 57% | 56% |

*Source: Financial Times, Datastream/ICV*

Table 3.4: The first- and second-quarter record improved in the 1970s and 1980s when Budgets were often scheduled in early March. The average annual first quarter loss in the 1970s was due to a very large price drop of -12.36% in 1974 following the Labour Party's surprise win.

times in a row on 4–5 March. History clearly warns investors to be cautious around this point of the month.

### INCREASE YOUR PROFIT ODDS

February signal No.1

The constant Budget Day shifts of the past makes trend-spotting especially hazardous during this part of the year. But several trends have been in effect since before World War II, pre-dating the effects of March Budget Days, and have continued to operate right up to the present. One

## PERCENTAGE OF TIME PRICES RISE EACH TRADING DAY IN MARCH'S FIRST QUARTER

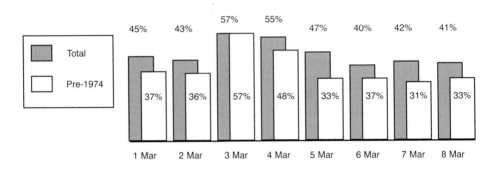

*Source: Financial Times, Datastream/ICV*

Figure 3.5: Prior to 1974, prices fell most of the time in the first quarter. The only day that rose more than half of the time was 3 March.

worth watching is the direction of prices on the FTSE All Share Index or its predecessor index during February. When shares drop within a range of -2.41% to -4.04% in February, the odds of a first-quarter drop are quite high. Since 1941, there were 12 falls of this magnitude. The first quarter fell 11 times.

*Rose (1)*

*Fell (11)*

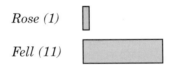

First-quarter record after a February price drop of -2.41% to -4.04% (FTSE All Share Index since 1941)

Another newly-discovered trend is the tendency for first-

## PERCENTAGE OF TIME PRICES RISE EACH DAY OF WEEK IN MARCH'S FIRST QUARTER

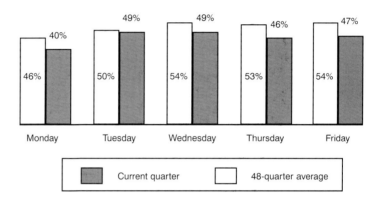

*Source: Financial Times, Datastream/ICV*

Figure 3.6: Monday weakness is especially apparent on 4 or 5 March which rise on just one out of four Mondays. In contrast, the stock market rises 57% of the time when these two days land between Tuesday and Friday.

February signal No.2

quarter prices to fall following a February rise of +3.48% to +5.26% on the FTSE All Share Index or its predecessor index. Since 1940, first quarter prices have fallen eight consecutive times following a February price rise in the defined range.

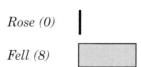

*Rose (0)*

*Fell (8)*

First-quarter record after a February price rise of +3.48% to +5.26% (FTSE All Share Index since 1940)

February signal No.3

It also pays to monitor prices on the FT-Non-Financial Index during the month of February. If they fluctuate by a small amount, from -1.35% to +1.15%, it is likely that first-quarter prices will rise. Since 1943, there have been 13 years with a small February move within this range. First-quarter prices on the FT-Non-Financial Index or its predecessor index rose in 11 of them (85%).

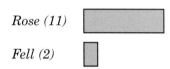

*Rose (11)*

*Fell (2)*

First-quarter record after a price shift of -1.35% to +1.15% in February (FT-Non-Financial Index since 1943)

February signal No.4

During this same period, the FT Ordinary Share Index rose in 12 out of 13 years following the same small February shift of -1.35% to +1.15% on the FT-Non-Financial Index

February fourth-quarter signal No.1

The direction that prices move in February's fourth quarter also helps investors to anticipate the first-quarter trend.

If the FT Ordinary Share Index declines in February's fourth quarter within a range of -0.97% to -2.71%, the chances are good it will rise strongly in the first quarter of March. Between 1936 and 1996, February's fourth quarter declined 13 times within this range. March's first quarter rose in 11 of those years (85%) at an average annual rate of +1.24%.

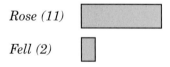

*Rose (11)*

*Fell (2)*

First-quarter record after a price fall of -0.97% to -2.71% in February's fourth quarter (FT Ordinary Share Index since 1936)

**February fourth-quarter signal No.2**

A similar trend runs on the FT-Non-Financial Index and its predecessor index. Since 1944, a drop of -1.05% to -2.95% in the fourth quarter has occurred 11 times. First-quarter prices rose nine times. One of the two exceptions was a tiny decline of just -0.03% in 1970.

*Rose (9)*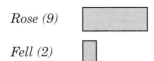

*Fell (2)* ▯

First-quarter record after a price fall of -1.05% to -2.95% in February's fourth quarter (FT-Non-Financial Index since 1944)

**February fourth-quarter signal No.3**

Small price rises in February's fourth quarter on the FT Ordinary Share Index often forecasts a price drop in the first quarter. Out of 11 years with small February fourth-quarter price rises in the range of +0.42% to +1.34%, March first-quarter prices fell nine times.

UPDATE

*Rose (2)* ▯

*Fell (9)* ▭

First-quarter record after a price rise of +0.42% to +1.34% in February's fourth quarter (FT Ordinary Share Index since 1937)

## Second Quarter of March – March 9th to 15th

Here comes a re-run of the first quarter. Profit prospects are highly dependent upon the precise date that the Spring Budget is presented.

The best years for second-quarter investors were in the 1980s when prices rose in most years. But further back in the 1930s to 1960s, when budgets were much later in the spring and had little effect on the second quarter, prices rose in just one year out of three.

Regardless of the date of the budget, look for trouble on 11 March, the worst trading day of the month and one of the worst of the entire year. Profit prospects are also often poor on second-quarter Fridays.

Zero profits

The second-quarter profit trend is lacklustre. Prices rose 48% of the time between 1936 and 1996. The average annual price change was precisely zero. This profit level is very close to average, compared with other quarters of the year *(see Table 3.5)*.

Budget Day correlation

As in the first quarter, the long-term second-quarter trend is correlated with the budget presentation schedule. From 1936 to 1959, when most Budget Days were in April, the second-quarter record was dismal: six up, 17 down and one quarter unchanged.

During the next three decades, the price trend strengthened in line with earlier budgets. The 1960s saw an average annual increase of +0.43%. Prices rose nine times in the 1970s at an average rate of +1.47%, equal to 59 points on a 4000 FTSE 100. Unfortunately, the trend has weakened since budgets were switched to November in 1993. Prices fell in three of the last four years *(see Table 3.6)*.

11 March

An examination of the daily price trend reveals a pattern of mid-quarter weakness with prices especially likely to be weak on 11 March, the worst day of the month and eighth-weakest of the entire year.

14 March

The best day of the quarter, and best of the month as

## MARCH SECOND-QUARTER PERFORMANCE IN BULL/BEAR MARKETS: 1936–1996

|  | Total | Bull Markets | Bear Markets |
|---|---|---|---|
| Average price change | 0.00% | 0.25% | -0.54% |
| Rank (of 48) | 28 | 35 | 23 |
|  |  |  |  |
| Per cent of time prices rise | 48% | 52% | 37% |
| Rank (of 48) | 38 | 39 | 23 |

*Source: Financial Times, Datastream/ICV*

Table 3.5: After six decades, the first quarter investor was still at the starting point with a 0.00% level of profit.

well, is 14 March with a 63% likelihood of a price rise. But note that 14 March has been helped by an exceptionally strong performance in recent years. Since 1980, when many budgets were presented in early March, prices have risen in 11 out of 12 occasions on this day. Prior to 1974, when budgets landed later in the year, the 14 March record was much weaker *(see Figure 3.7)*. For this reason, we expect that future profit odds on this day will be affected by the specific day upon which the Spring Budget is presented.

Friday troubles   Analysis of price trends by day of week shows that shares behave normally on most days with one glaring exception. Second-quarter Fridays rise just 38% of the time. It is the worst Friday performance of all 48 quarters of the year. No one can explain why the stock market is so weak on Friday at this point of the year but it is a trend that has been running since 1935. Not surprisingly, 11 March has been especially weak when it lands on Friday, steadily falling nine times in a row since 1936 *(see Figure 3.8)*.

## PERCENTAGE PRICE CHANGE: MARCH 1985–96

|  | March 1–8 | March 9–15 | March 16–23 | March 24–31 |
|---|---|---|---|---|
| 1985 | 1.85% | 1.74% | -0.59% | -1.63% |
| 1986 | 1.72% | 3.58% | 3.68% | -1.18% |
| 1987 | 1.04% | 0.39% | 1.75% | -1.44% |
| 1988 | 2.54% | 1.08% | 0.05% | -4.77% |
| 1989 | 3.80% | 1.61% | -2.81% | 0.70% |
| 1990 | -0.49% | -0.44% | 1.56% | -1.25% |
| 1991 | 3.66% | 1.89% | -2.10% | 0.35% |
| 1992 | -0.94% | -2.15% | -1.56% | -0.15% |
| 1993 | 2.99% | -0.92% | -1.33% | 0.14% |
| 1994 | -1.63% | -0.10% | -3.00% | -2.21% |
| 1995 | -0.96% | 1.59% | 2.57% | 0.26% |
| 1996 | -0.09% | -1.41% | 1.67% | 0.00% |
| Average quarterly price change | 1.12% | 0.57% | -0.01% | -0.93% |
| Number of years in which prices |  |  |  |  |
| Rose | 7 | 7 | 6 | 5 |
| Fell | 5 | 5 | 6 | 7 |

*Source: Datastream/ICV*

Table 3.6: The likelihood of profit has been poor in the first and second quarters in recent years. Since 1990, the record for each has been two rises and five declines.

### INCREASE YOUR PROFIT ODDS

As in the case of first-quarter historical relationships, constant past Budget Day shifts makes trend-spotting hazardous during this point in the year. But here are some trends that have been in effect since the 1930s,

## PERCENTAGE OF TIME PRICES RISE EACH TRADING DAY IN MARCH'S SECOND QUARTER

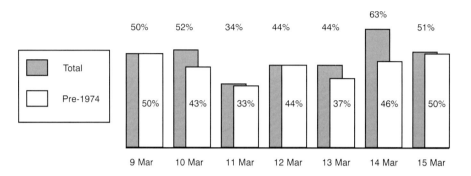

*Source: Financial Times, Datastream/ICV*

Figure 3.7: Prior to 1974, the price trend was noticeably weaker throughout the second quarter. Be cautious on 11 March, the weakest day of the month and one of the weakest of the entire year.

pre-dating the effect of March budgets

**First-quarter signal No.1**

To help improve the odds of avoiding a poor second quarter, watch for a small decline in share prices during the first quarter. Since 1937, prices on the FTSE All Share Index or its predecessor index dropped in the previous quarter by -0.49% to -1.08% 11 times. The stock market continued to fall in the second quarter in 10 of those years.

*Rose (1)*

*Fell (10)*

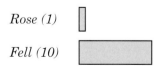

Second-quarter record after a price fall of -0.49% to -1.08% in the first quarter (FTSE All Share Index since 1937)

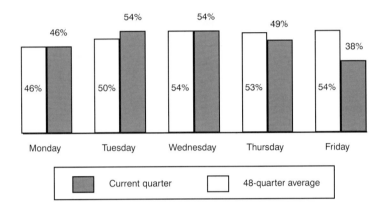

**PERCENTAGE OF TIME PRICES RISE EACH DAY OF WEEK IN MARCH'S SECOND QUARTER**

*Source: Financial Times, Datastream/ICV*

Figure 3.8: Second-quarter Fridays are the worst of the entire year. Be especially careful if 11 March lands on a Friday.

First-quarter signal No.2

A similar trend runs on the FT Ordinary Share Index. Since 1936, first-quarter prices fell by -0.52% to -1.08% on the FT Ordinary Share Index in nine different years. Second-quarter prices continued to decline each time.

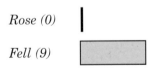

*Rose (0)*

*Fell (9)*

Second-quarter record after a price fall of -0.52% to -1.08% in the first quarter (FT Ordinary Share Index since 1936)

First-quarter signal No.3

Another trend involving the FT Ordinary Share Index emerged in 1978. Since then, the FT Ordinary Share

Index rose in the first quarter by at least +0.71% 11 times and the second quarter continued to rise in 10 of those years. The single exception was in 1993 when a large first-quarter gain of almost 4% was followed by a partial reversal in the second quarter. We suspect that Budget Day had a role in this relationship. Depending on when future budgets are scheduled, this relationship may continue to operate in the future.

*Rose (10)*

*Fell (1)*

Second-quarter record after a price rise of at least +0.71% in the first quarter (FT Ordinary Share Index since 1978)

Prior two-quarters signal No.1

It also pays to watch the trend over the two preceding quarters. Since 1964, a price rise on the FTSE All Share Index during the previous two quarters of +1.17% to +10.40% has been associated with a second-quarter price rise in 13 out of 14 years. During the remaining 19 years of this period, the odds of a second-quarter price rise on the All Shares Index was less than 50:50, eight rises and 11 declines.

*Rose (13)*

*Fell (1)*

Second-quarter record after a price rise in the preceding two quarters of +1.17% to +10.40% (FTSE All Share Index since 1964)

A similar trend has run on the FT-Non-Financial Index since 1964. During this period, there have been 14 occasions

109

Prior two-
quarters signal
No.2

when the FT-Non-Financial Index rose in the last two
quarters within a range of +1.57% to +10.54%. Second-
quarter prices rose in 13 of those years.

*Rose (13)*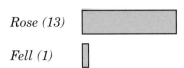

*Fell (1)* ▯

Second-quarter record after a price rise in the preceding two
quarters of +1.57% to +10.54% (FT-Non-Financial Index since
1964)

## THIRD QUARTER OF MARCH – MARCH 16TH TO 23RD

Budget Day has a major effect upon the third-quarter trend. Future
prospects are highly dependent upon precise date that the Spring
Budget is presented.

In the 1930s to 1960s, when budgets typically landed in late spring,
this quarter rose in most years. More recently, the trend weakened in
lock-step with a move toward earlier Spring Budgets.

Early-March
budgets hurt

Over the long-term, the third quarter has produced
middle-of-the-pack returns for investors in bull and bear
markets alike *(see Table 3.7).*

Unlike the first two quarters of March, whose performance was helped by early March budgets, the third
quarter was hurt by these shifts. The record for pre-
1970s third quarters looks better than the more recent
record.

During the 1930s to 1960s, a constant third-quarter
investor would have made steady profits by being fully
invested during the third quarter of March. Things

## MARCH THIRD-QUARTER PERFORMANCE IN BULL/BEAR MARKETS: 1936–1996

|  | Total | Bull Markets | Bear Markets |
|---|---|---|---|
| Average price change | 0.08% | 0.39% | -0.58% |
| Rank (of 48) | 26 | 28 | 25 |
| Per cent of time prices rise | 57% | 64% | 42% |
| Rank (of 48) | 19 | 18 | 30 |

*Source: Financial Times, Datastream/ICV*

Table 3.7: The likelihood of a price rise is about average compared to other quarters of the year in bull and bear markets. However, the trend has weakened since 1970.

changed in the 1970s, the first losing decade on record. At first glance, the problem looks to be caused by the events of 1975. After an extraordinary rally during the first few months of that year, prices dropped -7.79% in the third quarter, a temporary and long-overdue correction. But the rest of the decade wasn't that good either. The remaining nine years showed a small average annual third-quarter loss as well.

Temporary improvement

The trend did strengthen in the bull market 1980s as did other quarters, but since the October 1987 crash, the record to 1993 (before the switch to a November budget) weakened to three up and four down. Prospects for the future depend upon when Spring Budgets are scheduled. Late March or April might trigger a return to the strength of the 1930s–'60s. Early March could be associated with future third-quarter weakness.

19 and 21 March

Analysis of price trends on a day-by-day basis shows that the odds of profit are best in mid-quarter, especially on 19 and 21 March *(see Figure 3.9).*

111

## PERCENTAGE OF TIME PRICES RISE EACH TRADING DAY IN MARCH'S THIRD QUARTER

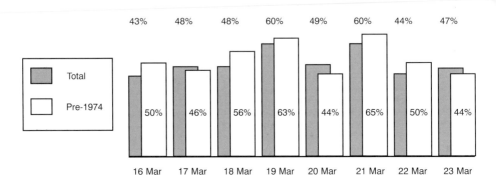

*Source: Financial Times, Datastream/ICV*

Figure 3.9: It is difficult to make money consistently during the third quarter. However, 19 and 21 March are two notable exceptions.

18 and 23 March

The trend by day of the week shows a familiar pattern of Monday weakness with the odds of a rise just 36%, well below average *(see Figure 3.10)*. The problem is especially severe on 18 and 23 March. Since our daily records began in 1936, 18 March has landed on a Monday in 9 different years. Prices rose just once. The record for 23 March is marginally better – two rises out of nine tries.

At the other extreme, the profit odds on Thursday are better than average during this quarter.

### INCREASE YOUR PROFIT ODDS

Prior three-quarters signal

Here is an interesting trend that used to be associated with third-quarter price rises. It ran for over three decades but stopped working after 1973, once the budget was moved to mid-March. If Spring Budgets are returned

## PERCENTAGE OF TIME PRICES RISE EACH DAY OF WEEK IN MARCH'S THIRD QUARTER

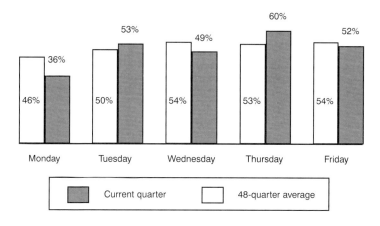

*Source: Financial Times, Datastream/ICV*

Figure 3.10: Monday weakness is most apparent on 18 and 23 March.

to late March or April, it could come alive once again. Between 1936 and 1973, prices fell in the preceding three quarters on the FTSE All Share Index or its predecessor index by -0.71% to -5.73% on 14 occasions. Third-quarter prices rose in 13 of those years.

*Rose (13)*

*Fell (1)*

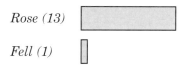

Third-quarter record after a price drop in three prior quarters of -0.71% to -5.73% (FTSE All Share Index, 1936–1973)

# Fourth Quarter of March – March 24th to 31st

Once, again, Budget Day has a major effect upon the likelihood of prof-iting. Future prospects for the fourth quarter are highly dependent upon the precise date that the Spring Budget is presented.

Prices often rose during the 1930s to 1960s, when budgets typically landed in late spring. More recently, the profit odds fell in conjunction with a move toward earlier Spring Budgets.

Be especially cautious on 24 March, historically the worst day in the quarter.

Here comes another middle-of-the-pack quarter during bull markets. But during bear market years, the fourth quarter is a bit better than the norm. Prices fall about half the time and the average annual bear market loss is smaller than average *(see Table 3.11)*.

The averages hide some interesting differences. At one time, the fourth quarter was a good time to hold shares. From 1940 to 1969, when the quarter was helped by an imminent April budget, prices rose 67% of the time. The average annual increase in share prices during this stretch was +0.62%.

**Early-March Budgets hurt**

Unfortunately, the trend began to change in the 1970s with a weak average annual profit of +0.08%. The trend weakened still further during the 1980s. Prices fell six times including 1984, 1985, 1986 and 1987, the heart of the best bull market of the century. (In each of these four years, March as a whole was quite profitable.)

The last minute rush into PEPs has not helped share prices. Since their 1987 introduction, the record is four up, five down and one year unchanged.

Now that budgets are returning to the spring, the trend might change once again. The precise nature of the trend depends on the exact date of the budget.

**24 March**

History shows that the worst day of the quarter is 24

114

## MARCH FOURTH-QUARTER PERFORMANCE IN BULL/BEAR MARKETS: 1936–1996

|  | Total | Bull Markets | Bear Markets |
|---|---|---|---|
| Average price change | 0.09% | 0.25% | -0.27% |
| Rank (of 48) | 25 | 35 | 16 |
| Per cent of time prices rise | 56% | 57% | 53% |
| Rank (of 48) | 21 | 27 | 13 |

*Source: Financial Times, Datastream/ICV*

Table 3.11: This quarter has produced a middle-of-the-road record in bull market years. But in bear markets, the record is above average compared with other quarters.

March which rises just 41% of the time. The odds of a price rise on 24 March are especially poor when it lands on a Monday. It is a trend that has been running since 1936 and was operating when Budget Day landed before this day as well as when it landed later. There has been just one Monday rise out of eight attempts since 1936, continuing the pattern of Monday weakness that also affects 23 March, which was reported in the preceding section *(see Figure 3.12)*.

Monday blues      The Monday problem is not confined to 24 March. Monday is the weakest day of the week for the rest of the fourth quarter as well, continuing the pattern of Monday weakness that affects many other quarters of the year as well *(see Figure 3.13)*.

### INCREASE YOUR PROFIT ODDS

Here are two statistical correlations that may help investors to predict profitable fourth quarters if budgets

## PERCENTAGE OF TIME PRICES RISE EACH TRADING DAY IN MARCH'S FOURTH QUARTER

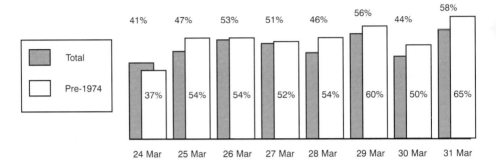

*Source: Financial Times, Datastream/ICV*

Figure 3.12: Fourth-quarter prices frequently rise, especially on 29 March. But be careful on 24 March, the worst of the quarter.

are presented in late spring.

**Prior four-quarters signal**

Prior to 1970, a rise on the FT Ordinary Share Index during the preceding four quarters by +0.93% to +4.79% occurred 10 times. Fourth-quarter prices rose each time.

*Rose (10)*

*Fell (0)*

Fourth-quarter record after a rise of +0.93% to +4.79% in the preceding four quarters (FT Ordinary Share Index: 1936–1969)

**Third-quarter signal**

Between 1936 and 1971, the FT Ordinary Share Index shifted during the third quarter by a small amount in 10 different years, no more than -0.78% on the down-side and +0.56% on the up-side. Fourth-quarter prices rose all 10 times. Since the mid-1970s shift to a mid-March budget, this price signal stopped working. We shall wait to

## PERCENTAGE OF TIME PRICES RISE EACH DAY OF WEEK IN MARCH'S FOURTH QUARTER

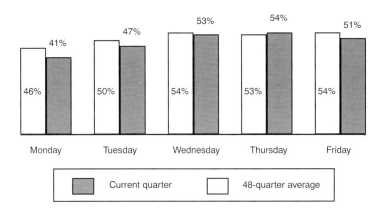

*Source: Financial Times, Datastream/ICV*

Figure 3.13: The Monday record is a weak one, especially on 24 March which has risen just once out of eight attempts since 1936.

see if it comes alive again if budgets are presented in late spring.

*Rose (9)*

*Fell (2)*

Fourth-quarter record after a price shift of -0.78% to +0.56% in the third quarter (FT Ordinary Share Index: 1936–71)

## LOOKING AHEAD

Rising prices by
31 December –
signal No.1

The price trend over the first three months of the year offers investors some interesting clues about where shares are heading in the next nine months, that is, to the end of the year.

Since 1941, there have been 26 years when the FT-Non-Financial Index or its predecessor index shifted by a small amount in the first three months of the year, no more than -1.96% on the down-side and no more than +5.77% on the up-side. Prices rose still further by the end of the year in 25 of those years. The average increase was over 14%.

The sole exception was in 1966 when a small first-quarter increase was followed by rising prices until July when an announcement of higher taxes caught the markets by surprise. Prices fell over 20% in the next two months, and then plateaued for the rest of the year.

UPDATE

*Rose (25)*

*Fell (1)*

Trend to December 31 after a price shift of -1.96% to +5.77% in the first three months of the year (FT-Non-Financial Index since 1941)

We first called attention to this trend in an earlier edition of the *Schwartz Stock Market Handbook*. Since then prices shifted within the designated range in the first three months of 1995 and 1996 and prices continued to rise in the next nine months as expected.

Rising prices by
31 December –
signal No.2

Since 1932, there have been 20 years with a March price rise of +1.77% to +9.66% on the FT-Non-Financial Index. Prices rose still higher in the nine months that followed, until year end, 19 times. The average increase was almost 13 %.

UPDATE

*Rose (19)*

*Fell (1)*

Trend to December 31 after a March price rise of +1.77% to +9.66% (FT-Non-Financial Index since 1932)

Since 1941, there have been 37 years touched by one or both of these signals. Prices rose still higher in the next nine months in 35 of those years. In the remaining 19 years during this period of time, the record for the next nine months was four up and 15 down. It would take a brave soul to hold shares in the months ahead if neither of these two March signals flash.

Rising prices by 30 September

Turning to the FTSE All Share Index, there have been 23 occasions since 1936 when the FTSE All Share Index or its predecessor index rose +2.59% to +15.29% in the preceding four months – that is, from 1 December to 31 March. Shares rose in the next six months in 22 of those years.

NEW

*Rose (22)*

*Fell (1)*

Trend to September 30 after a rise of +2.59% to +15.29% in the prior four months (FTSE All Share Index since 1936)

# Chapter 4 – April

April has had a superb record for many decades. Since 1940, prices have risen 48 times and fallen just nine times, by far the best monthly performance of the year during this period.

Over the long run, each quarter of the month rises more than 60% of the time, the only month in the year to exhibit such powerful across-the-board strength. The stock market typically turns in a very strong record during bull and bear markets alike.

Steady shifts to ever-earlier Spring Budgets during the 1960s to 1980s and a brief switch to a late-November Budget have failed to dampen April's strength.

We forecast a continued above-average likelihood of profit in the years ahead for the full month.

However, in one important respect, there have been some signs of change. The second half of the month has produced a disappointing profit trend in recent years. Most profits were gained in the first half of the month.

**Fabulous record**

April is the year's second-best month over the long run. A hypothetical £1,000 April investment in 1919 (moved into cash in the other 11 months) would have grown to £3,936 by 1996. Prices rise by +1.87% during the average April, a fabulous record only exceeded by January.

As we pointed out earlier, January's superiority is helped greatly by a 53% rise in 1975, marking the end of the 1972–74 bear market. If not for this extraordinary price rise, the best one-month rally in history, April would be quite close to January on the monthly performance rankings.

**Spring Budgets help**

April was not always such a strong performer. Back in the 1920s and 1930s when budgets were often a late-April event, prices rose less than half the time. But things soon improved in parallel with a steadily advancing Budget Day schedule. In the next 50 years when most budgets were presented in March to mid-April, prices rose 43 times and fell just seven times. During this period, April's worst performance was in the 1940s when it was fourth-best month and produced an average annual profit of +1.70%. In the four decades that followed, it was ranked either number one or two. Its performance peaked in the 1980s when prices rose all 10 years, a rare event that has occurred just one other time, in January 1940–49 *(see Table 4.1)*.

**All four quarters profitable**

Over the long run, the April trend looks good throughout the month. Prices rise more than 60% of the time in each quarter of the month. It is the only month in the year that can make this claim. The 'worst' period is the third quarter which rises 62% of the time *(see Figure 4.1)*.

**Bull and bear market strength**

History shows the April trend to be strong in both bull and bear markets. During bull markets, prices rise 83% of the time, close to January and August (86% each). When prices occasionally do fall during bull markets, the typical April drop is just -1.09%, the smallest drop of all 12 months. During bear markets, the odds of an April

## APRIL PRICE RISES AND DECLINES: 1919–1996

|  | Average April price change | Up | Down/ No change |
|---|---|---|---|
| 1920–29 | -0.50% | 4 | 6 |
| 1930–39 | -0.93% | 5 | 5 |
| 1940–49 | 1.70% | 8 | 2 |
| 1950–59 | 4.17% | 9 | 1 |
| 1960–69 | 1.93% | 7 | 3 |
| 1970–79 | 4.44% | 9 | 1 |
| 1980–89 | 2.90% | 10 | 0 |
| 1990–96 | 1.44% | 5 | 2 |
| | | | |
| Average April change: 1919–96 | 1.87% | 73% | 27% |
| | | | |
| Rank (of 12) | 2 | 2 | |

*Source: BZW, Datastream/ICV*

Table 4.1: April has been the second-best month over the long-run. From 1940 to 1989, prices rose in at least seven out of every 10 years, usually more, a fabulous record. Many thought the Spring Budget helped to create this fine record. But prices rose steadily in 1994–96 without the help of a Spring Budget.

up-move are 50:50, the best bear market performance of all 12 month. *(see Table 4.2).*

Given this strong performance, is it any surprise that many investors think April is the closest thing to a one-way bet that the stock market offers?

And what about the future? We once guessed that the shift to a November Budget would hurt the April trend. But April prices continued to rise steadily in the last few years with no sign of any weakness. Now that budgets are returning to the spring, we expect a further

## QUARTERLY ODDS OF PRICE RISE IN APRIL

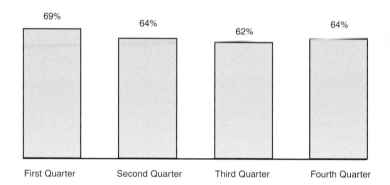

Source: Financial Times, Datastream/ICV

Figure 4.1: The long-term record has been strong throughout the month.

Expectation of profit

continuation of these favourable trading conditions.

One thing that does concern us about the future is the expectation of profit which is so rampant in April. Knowledge of April's profitability is wide-spread. Investors have come to expect a profitable stretch during this part of the year and make their investment decisions accordingly. History shows that the expectation of profit can cause a trend to change as investors become aware of a likely event, and try to take advantage of this knowledge. (If you thought you knew which way prices were likely to move tomorrow, wouldn't you act on that information today?) Perhaps money is committed to the market earlier, thereby reducing the concentrated buying pressure which drove up prices in the first place. Perhaps a sale toward the end of the previous month gets deferred, thereby reducing the extent of the temporary decline that often served as a springboard for the April rally.

## APRIL PERFORMANCE IN BULL/BEAR MARKETS: 1919–1996

|  | Bull Markets | Bear Markets |
|---|---|---|
| Average per cent price change | 2.96% | -0.58% |
| Rank (of 12) | 3 | 2 |
|  |  |  |
| Per cent of time prices rise | 83% | 50% |
| Rank (of 12) | 3 | 1 |
|  |  |  |
| Average per cent price change in: |  |  |
| Rising years | 3.77% | 4.01% |
| Declining years | -1.09% | -5.16% |

*Source: BZW, Datastream/ICV*

Table 4.2: The April trend is strong in bull markets and bear markets. When prices happen to drop in bull market years, the typical decline is just -1.09%, the smallest average decline of all 12 months in bull market down years.

We hasten to add that we see no sign of any weakness due to changing investor expectations or behaviour. We raise our concern merely as a point to watch out for in the years ahead.

**Bear market signal**

So much for the future. As far as current trading conditions are concerned, history shows that it is quite easy to lose money during bear markets in every month of the year, including April. For this reason, it is critically important for investors to know if we are in a bear market.

Happily, the March historical record provides a useful clue to help to answer this question *(see Figure 4.2)*. Over the long run, large March price declines that reduce shares by -4.12% or more are usually associated with bear markets.

At the other end of the continuum, bull market odds

## ODDS OF BULL/BEAR MARKET TIPPED BY MARCH'S TREND

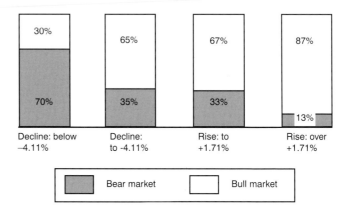

Source: *BZW, Datastream/ICV*

Figure 4.2: A March decline of more than -4.11% is a yellow flag warning signal that a bear market may be in progress. A March rise in excess of +1.71% is a good sign that a bull market is running.

Bull market
signal

are especially high if the stock market rises by +1.72% or more during March. There have been 30 increases of this magnitude since our records began in 1919. Bull market conditions reigned in 26 of those years (87%). The last exception to the rule occurred in 1948, half a century ago.

We remind investors that these figures say nothing about when the bull market will end. It is conceivable that the following month will see the start of a new bear market. Nevertheless, the lessons from the past send a strong message – bull market prospects are generally good following a strong March advance.

### INCREASE YOUR PROFIT ODDS[1]

There are a number of historic price trends that do a good job of forecasting which way April prices are most likely to move. Each has been in effect for many decades, and is based on price shifts over the past several months or the past year, not on what just happened in March (which could be budget-related).

Prior five-months signal

Since 1940, all nine April drops have been preceded by a small price rise on the FTSE All Share Index or its predecessor index in the five month run-up to April, within a range of +0.50% to +12.05%. A five-month advance of this magnitude preceded a large number of April price rises as well so we can not use it as a sell signal. Nevertheless, it is a useful indicator to monitor for one very important reason. There were 27 years with price shifts outside of this range in the five preceding months and April rose each and every time.

*Rose (27)*

*Fell (0)*

April record after a price shift below +0.50% or above +12.05% in the past five months (FTSE All Share Index since 1940)

Prior seven-months signal

Since 1943, the FT Ordinary Share Index has risen in the seven month run-up to April within a range of +6.00% to +23.98% in 21 different years. April rose in 20 of those years. The single exception was in 1991 when the FT Ordinary Share Index fell from 1953.9 to 1953.7, a miniscule drop of -0.01%.

---

[1]We will provide closing price trends on key indices for the last 12 months at no cost (see page 9).

*Rose (20)*

*Fell (1)*

April record after a price shift of +6.00% to +23.98% in the past seven months (FT Ordinary Share Index since 1940)

Prior 12-months signal No.1

It also pays to monitor the direction of prices in the past 12 months, April 1st to March 31st, on the FT-Non-Financial Index or its predecessor index. A sharp up-move often tips rising April prices. Since 1923, there have been 20 years when prices rose in the preceding 12 months by +19.26% or more. April share prices rose 19 times. The single exception to the rule occurred back in 1960.

*Rose (19)*

*Fell (1)*

April record after a price rise of at least +19.26% in the past 12 months (FT-Non-Financial Index since 1923)

Prior 12-months signal No.2

Another trend associated with rising April prices is a decline in the last 12 months of -10.79% or less. Since 1949, the FTSE All Share Index or its predecessor index has fallen by an amount within this range in 14 different years. April prices rose each time.

*Rose (14)*

*Fell (0)*

April record after a price fall of -10.79% or less in the past 12 months (FTSE All Share Index since 1949)

Prior 12-months
signal No.3

A similar trend has run on the FT-Non-Financial Index since 1948. During this period, a drop of -4.93% to -12.53% occurred 13 times. April prices rose every time.

*Rose (13)*

*Fell (0)*

April record after a price fall of -4.93% to -12.53% in the past 12 months (FT-Non-Financial Index since 1948)

Prior three-
months signal
No.1

The direction of prices in the year's first quarter also does a good job of forecasting April price rises. Since 1922, prices rose on the FTSE All Share Index or its pre-decessor index by +3.92% or more in the most recent three months in 31 different years. The stock market continued to rise in April in 29 of those years.

*Rose (29)*

*Fell (2)*

April record after a price rise of at least +3.92% in the past three months (FTSE All Share Index since 1922)

Prior three-
months signal
No.2

A similar trend (with slightly different figures) runs on the FT-Non-Financial Index, and its predecessor index since 1922.

*Rose (27)*

*Fell (2)*

April record after a price rise of at least +4.38% in the past three months (FT-Non-Financial Index since 1922)

Prior 10-months
signal

The April trend has been so strong for so many years that it is hard to find enough declining months to develop 'down indicators'. Here is one that has been running since 1924. During this period, there have been eight years with a weak trend in the last 10 months, a small loss of -1.89% to -6.79%, and a small loss in the last four months of -0.62% to -4.40%. April share prices fell in seven of those years.

*Rose (1)*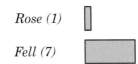

*Fell (7)*

April record after a price drop of -1.89% to -6.79%, in the past 10 months and a price drop in the past four months of -0.62% to -4.40%. (FTSE All Share Index since 1924)

## FIRST QUARTER OF APRIL – APRIL 1ST TO 8TH

For many years, the first quarter was one of the best quarters of the year. The chance of a price rise was good in bull and bear markets alike.

The trend weakened at the start of the 1980s as Spring Budgets were advanced to mid-March, and then improved in 1994–96 as soon as budgets were shifted to November. Clearly, the precise date of Budget Day has an effect upon first-quarter profitability.

Budget Day aside, first-quarter Thursdays rise 73% of the time, the best Thursday record of all 48 quarters.

Highly
profitable

The first quarter of April has been quite profitable over the long run (*see Table 4.3*). Prices rise 69% of the time, generating an average annual profit of +0.77%, one of the best quarterly performances for the entire year.

## PERCENTAGE PRICE CHANGE: APRIL 1936–96

|  | April 1–8 | April 9–15 | April 16–23 | April 24–30 |
|---|---|---|---|---|
| Annual average |  |  |  |  |
| 1935–39 | 1.59% | -0.34% | -0.26% | -1.01% |
| 1940–49 | 0.54% | 0.04% | 0.38% | 0.56% |
| 1950–59 | 1.96% | 1.20% | 0.88% | -0.45% |
| 1960–69 | 0.67% | 0.24% | 0.65% | 0.83% |
| 1970–79 | 0.58% | 0.48% | 2.89% | 0.47% |
| 1980–89 | 0.34% | 0.56% | 0.77% | 1.40% |
| 1990–96 | 0.29% | 1.96% | -0.44% | -0.35% |
| Average quarterly price change | 0.77% | 0.61% | 0.84% | 0.37% |
| Per cent of time prices rise | 69% | 64% | 62% | 64% |

*Source: Financial Times, Datastream/ICV*

Table 4.3: All four quarters of April have been quite profitable over the long run. However, the first, third and fourth quarters have been weaker than normal since 1985, coinciding with moves to ever-earlier March Budgets.

First five days

Shares increased in value in every single decade on record, with the best trading days of the quarter occurring up to April 5th, the end of the tax year *(see Figure 4.3)*. Prices rise much less often at the tail-end of the quarter.

Bear market profits

The odds of a price rise are especially high during bear market years when prices rise 74% of the time, the year's second-best quarter. The only quarter that does better during bear markets is the final quarter of December *(see Table 4.4)*.

Unfortunately, the trend weakened near the start of

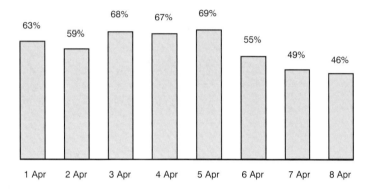

**PERCENTAGE OF TIME PRICES RISE EACH TRADING DAY IN APRIL'S FIRST QUARTER**

*Source: Financial Times, Datastream/ICV*

Figure 4.3: Over the long term, the first few trading days of the quarter (end of the tax year) are the most profitable. But profits are disappointing when April 2 lands on Monday or Friday.

**Budget Day effect**

the 1980s around the time that Spring Budgets were moved up to mid-March. Many of the losses were small so the decade still showed an average annual gain – of just +0.34%.

The 1990s record? More of the same with four up and three down. But three of those gains occurred in 1994–96, coinciding with the budget shift from mid-March to late-November. It is another good reason to watch for the date of each new Spring Budget with great interest.

**No help from PEPs**

The 1987 introduction of PEPs has not helped this final quarter of the tax year. The common assumption is that lots of PEP money pours into shares at the very last minute to beat the end-of-year tax deadline, driving up share prices. The theory is not supported by the facts. First-quarter prices have risen five times and fallen four times since PEPs were first introduced.

## APRIL FIRST-QUARTER PERFORMANCE IN BULL/BEAR MARKETS: 1936–1996

|  | Total | Bull Markets | Bear Markets |
|---|---|---|---|
| Average price change | 0.77% | 0.61% | 1.14% |
| Rank (of 48) | 7 | 20 | 2 |
| Per cent of time prices rise | 69% | 67% | 74% |
| Rank (of 48) | 3 | 15 | 2 |

Source: Financial Times, Datastream/ICV

Table 4.4: The odds of a first-quarter price rise are well above average during bear market years.

**Thursday**

One trend that has not changed is the pocket of extreme strength on first-quarter Thursdays. Although no one can explain why Thursday is such a strong performer, prices rise in three out of four years (73%), a trend that has been running for six decades *(see Figure 4.4)*. It is the best performing Thursday of all 48 quarters of the year.

**2 April**

Another trend worth noting is the high likelihood of a price rise when 2 April lands in mid-week. Since 1936, shares rose 19 out of the 26 times (73%) that 2 April landed on a Tuesday, Wednesday or Thursday versus just five rises in 15 attempts when the day landed on a Monday or Friday *(see Table 4.5)*.

**5 April**

Still another interesting deviation from the norm occurs on 5 April. No one can explain why but the odds of a price rise are lower when 5 April lands on Monday or Tuesday. Since 1936, shares rose 9 out of 18 times (50%) that 5 April landed on a Monday or Tuesday versus 20 out of 24 rises (83%) when this day landed later in the week *(see Table 4.6)*.

133

## PERCENTAGE OF TIME PRICES RISE EACH DAY OF WEEK IN APRIL'S FIRST QUARTER

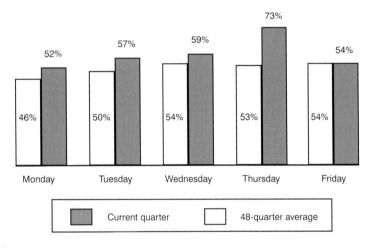

*Source: Financial Times, Datastream/ICV*

Figure 4.4: First-quarter Thursdays rise in three out of four years, the best Thursday performance of all 48 quarters.

### INCREASE YOUR PROFIT ODDS

March second-half signal No.1

Since 1969, the FTSE All Share Index drifted in the preceding two quarters within a range of -2.21% to +0.28% in 11 different years. First-quarter prices fell nine times. During the remaining 16 years of this period, the first-quarter record was 13 increases and three declines.

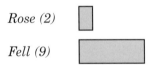

*Rose (2)*

*Fell (9)*

First-quarter record after a price shift in the preceding two quarters between -2.21% to +0.28% (FTSE All Share Index since 1969)

## PERCENTAGE OF TIME PRICES RISE ON 2 APRIL: 1936–1996

|  | Prices rise |
|---|---|
| Total | 59% |
| | |
| Monday or Friday | 33% |
| Tuesday, Wednesday or Thursday | 73% |

Source: Financial Times, Datastream/ICV

Table 4.5. Prices often rise when 2 April lands in mid-week. But the Monday and Friday record is quite poor.

## PERCENTAGE OF TIME PRICES RISE ON 5 APRIL: 1936–1996

|  | Prices rise |
|---|---|
| Total | 69% |
| | |
| Monday or Tuesday | 50% |
| Wednesday, Thursday or Friday | 83% |

Source: Financial Times, Datastream/ICV

Table 4.6. The chance of profit on 5 April is much better once the first two days of the week are out of the way.

March second-half signal No.2

On the up-side, an earlier edition of the *Schwartz Stock Market Handbook* observed that there have been 22 occasions since 1936 when the FT Ordinary Share Index rose

135

in the third quarter of March by any amount, and drifted in the fourth quarter, within a range of -1.00% to +2.42%. Prices rose in the first quarter of April each time.

From the time that advice was first provided, the FT Ordinary Share Index shifted in the third and fourth quarters of March within the target range two further times, in 1995 and 1996. Prices rose in the first quarter of April right on cue in both years. The record is now 24 rises and zero declines.

UPDATE

Rose (24)

Fell (0)

First-quarter record after a March third quarter rise and fourth-quarter price shift between -1.00% to +2.42% (FT Ordinary Share Index since 1936)

What makes us particularly keen on this indicator is that it was in effect back when the first quarter preceded Budget Day, and more recently when it followed Budget Day by several weeks.

March fourth-quarter signal

Here is a related indicator. Although it overlaps the March Second-Half indicator in some years, it often flashes independently.

Since 1936, there have been 30 years when the FT Ordinary Share Index shifted by a small margin of -1.35% to +0.72% in March's fourth quarter. (For the purposes of this indicator, ignore the third quarter.) The stock market rose during the first quarter of April in 26 of those years (87%). Each exception occurred after the introduction of a mid-March budget. Even better, the indicator regained its old form since the 1993 shift to a November Budget (see Table 4.7). Given its past record, this indicator could be useful in years with no early or mid-March budget.

**APRIL FIRST-QUARTER TREND AFTER MARCH
FOURTH-QUARTER SHIFT OF -1.35% TO +0.72%**

|  | First quarter Up | First quarter Down | Typical date of budget |
|---|---|---|---|
| 1936–49 | 10 | - | late-April |
| 1950–69 | 8 | - | mid-April |
| 1970–79 | 4 | - | late March & early April |
| 1980–89 | 1 | 2 | mid-March |
| 1990–93 | 1 | 2 | mid-March |
| 1994–present | 2 | - | November |
| Total | 26 | 4 |  |

UPDATE

*Source: Financial Times, Datastream/ICV*

Table 4.7: Prices usually rise in the first quarter after a March fourth-quarter price shift of -1.35% to +0.72%. The only exceptions occurred when budgets landed in mid-March.

## SECOND QUARTER OF APRIL – APRIL 9TH TO 15TH

Here comes the first quarter of a new fiscal year and another above-average performer. Unlike the first quarter, there have been no signs of trend weakness in recent years. Prices have fallen in just one year since the 1987 Crash.

Good long-term record

Over the long run, the second quarter has been good to investors. Shares rose 64% of the time between 1936 and 1996. Prices increased by +0.61% in the typical year *(see Table 4.8)*. Both figures are well above average compared to other quarters of the year.

137

### APRIL SECOND-QUARTER PERFORMANCE IN
### BULL/BEAR MARKETS: 1936–1996

|  | Total | Bull Markets | Bear Markets |
|---|---|---|---|
| Average price change | 0.61% | 0.89% | -0.01% |
| Rank (of 48) | 9 | 12 | 11 |
| | | | |
| Per cent of time prices rise | 64% | 69% | 53% |
| Rank (of 48) | 8 | 11 | 13 |

*Source: Financial Times, Datastream/ICV*

Table 4.8: The trend is above average in bull and bear markets. Unlike other quarters of the month, there have been no signs of weakness in recent years. The start of the new tax year continues to provide a solid if short-term boost to shares.

No recent weakness

Unlike the first quarter, the recent trend remains strong. The average annual increase in the 1970s was +0.48% (seven out of 10 years increased). The average annual increase for the 1980s was +0.56% with price increases in seven out of 10 years. Since 1990, second-quarter prices have fallen just one time, one of the year's best records during this decade *(see Table 4.9)*.

We are intrigued by its recent strong performance, given the stock market's weakness in the adjacent first and third quarters. A possible explanation: the start of a new tax year releases a short-lived flood of new money, providing a brief boost to prices.

Monday

Analysis of trading conditions by day of week shows a strong pocket of strength on second-quarter Mondays. Prices rise 62% of the time the best Monday of all 48 quarters *(see Figure 4.5)*. Given the more typical pattern of relative weakness on Monday, seeing it as the week's best performer is a refreshing change of pace.

## PERCENTAGE PRICE CHANGE: APRIL 1985–96

|  | April 1–8 | April 9–15 | April 16–23 | April 24–30 |
|---|---|---|---|---|
| 1985 | -0.08% | 0.71% | -0.16% | 0.49% |
| 1986 | 0.97% | -1.12% | -0.69% | 1.59% |
| 1987 | -0.91% | -2.42% | 1.97% | 3.80% |
| 1988 | 1.83% | 0.22% | -0.06% | 1.49% |
| 1989 | -1.63% | 0.20% | 0.22% | 2.54% |
| 1990 | -1.06% | -0.17% | -2.46% | -2.88% |
| 1991 | 2.68% | 0.32% | -1.35% | -0.82% |
| 1992 | -2.29% | 10.62% | -0.41% | 1.71% |
| 1993 | -1.64% | 0.51% | 0.55% | -0.78% |
| 1994 | 0.81% | 1.56% | -0.97% | -0.20% |
| 1995 | 2.12% | 0.01% | -0.15% | 0.61% |
| 1996 | 1.42% | 0.84% | 1.68% | -0.12% |
| | | | | |
| Average quarterly price change | 0.18% | 0.94% | -0.15% | 0.62% |
| | | | | |
| Number of years in which prices | | | | |
| Rose | 6 | 9 | 4 | 7 |
| Fell | 6 | 3 | 8 | 5 |

*Source: Datastream/ICV*

Table 4.9: Second-quarter prices have fallen just once since the 1987 crash, by far the best record of the month. Apparently, the start of the new tax year provides a brief boost to the stock market.

12 April     The price trend is strong throughout the quarter on a day-by-day basis, building to a climax on 15 April which rises 68% of the time *(see Figure 4.6)*. The only day that rises less than half the time is 12 April which produces profits just 45% of the time. But this weakness is largely

139

## PERCENTAGE OF TIME PRICES RISE EACH DAY OF WEEK IN APRIL'S SECOND QUARTER

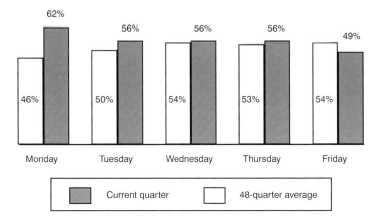

*Source: Financial Times, Datastream/ICV*

Figure 4.5: The Monday record is the best of all 48 quarters.

due to its record in the 1930s to '60s. In the last few decades, 12 April has performed as strongly as the other days of the period – profitable in most years. By way of example, since 1980, 12 April has risen eight times out of 10 opportunities.

### INCREASE YOUR PROFIT ODDS

Prior three-quarters signal

On balance, if you are thinking of selling shares around this point of the year, the odds favour holding on until the end of the quarter. You can improve upon these odds by watching the price trend over the preceding three quarters. Since 1969, there have been 12 occasions when the FTSE All Share Index fells by -1.59% or more in the prior three quarters. Second-quarter prices rose each time. In the remaining 16 years of this period, the second-quarter

**PERCENTAGE OF TIME PRICES RISE EACH TRADING DAY IN APRIL'S SECOND QUARTER**

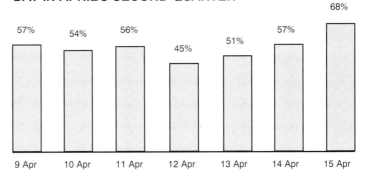

*Source: Financial Times, Datastream/ICV*

Figure 4.6: Most second-quarter trading days tend to be profitable. Even 12 April has had a strong record in recent years.

record was precisely 50:50, eight up and eight down.

*Rose (12)*

*Fell (0)*

Second-quarter record after a price decline in the preceding three quarters of -1.59% or more (FTSE All Share Index since 1969)

**First-quarter signal**

While the second quarter's profit odds are good, the preceding paragraph should make it clear that prices do not rise every year. Happily, a newly-developing trend may help to spot occasions when prices are due for a fall. Several years ago, we pointed out that since 1980, most second-quarter losses on the FT Ordinary Share Index have been tipped by a small price drop of -0.14% to

### CORRELATION BETWEEN APRIL'S FIRST AND SECOND QUARTERS: 1980–1996

| First-quarter shift | Second quarter | |
|---|---|---|
| | Up | Down |
| -0.13% or better | 7 | 1 |
| -0.14% to -1.44% | 2 | 3 |
| -1.45% or worse | 4 | – |

*Source: Datastream/ICV*

Table 4.10: Since 1980, small drops on the FT Ordinary Share Index in the first quarter of -0.14% to -1.44% are often associated with second-quarter declines. The record for all remaining years is quite good, 11 up versus one decline.

-1.44% in the first quarter. Since that warning was first issued, three years of new data have been obtained.

The more recent data continue to suggest that mild weakness in the last quarter of the tax year is often a stimulus for more of the same as the new year begins. But if bigger losses are incurred in the year's final quarter, perhaps triggered by tax-related considerations, the decks are cleared for a good start to the new year. On the up-side, investors who sense good trading conditions around the start of the new year tip their hand by bidding up shares in the last week of the old year.

This trend is based on a period of just 17 years. Treat it as a hypothesis, not a confirmed relationship. Likewise, our description of the underlying cause are guesses, not informed statements of fact *(see Table 4.10)*.

# THIRD QUARTER OF APRIL – APRIL 16TH TO 23RD

> The third quarter profit trend used to be very good but has weakened in recent years.
>
> The odds of a price rise are best near the beginning of the quarter and slip as the quarter progresses. The low point is reached on 22 April which rises 40% of the time, the worst day of the month.

**Good long-term record**

Like April's first quarter, the third quarter was traditionally quite good to investors, producing an average yearly profit in every complete decade since 1940. Between 1936 and 1996, third-quarter prices rose 62% of the time. The average annual profit was +0.84%.

This segment of the month has been good to investors in bear markets as well as bull markets. Over the long run, the stock market rose 58% of the time in bear markets, the eighth-best quarterly bear market record of the year (see Table 4.11).

**Recent trend change**

Also like the first quarter, things recently changed for the worse. Prices rose in the first three years of the 1980s and produced all of that decade's profits. A trend change then occurred. Even though a strong bull market dominated the decade, and the full month consistently generated high profits, prices rose in only two of the decade's remaining seven years. Note that the March budget was presented at least four weeks earlier during this period, reducing the odds that short-term budget effects were exerting pressure on third-quarter prices.

In the 1990s, third-quarter prices have risen in just two out of seven attempts, continuing the poor record of the 1980s. Unfortunately, the fourth quarter has also shown a weak trading pattern in recent years. On balance, history suggests little incentive to commit new money to the stock market at this point in the year.

Analysis of daily price records finds that trading

143

## APRIL THIRD-QUARTER PERFORMANCE IN BULL/BEAR MARKETS: 1936–1996

|  | Total | Bull Markets | Bear Markets |
|---|---|---|---|
| Average price change | 0.84% | 1.14% | 0.16% |
| Rank (of 48) | 4 | 5 | 7 |
| Per cent of time prices rise | 62% | 64% | 58% |
| Rank (of 48) | 12 | 18 | 8 |

*Source: Financial Times, Datastream/ICV*

Table 4.11: The long-term record has been good, especially in bear markets. But the trend has weakened in recent years. Prices rose just twice in the 1990s.

**Second half weak**

conditions are best in the first half of the quarter with the likelihood of a price rise peaking on April 19th when prices rise 67% of the time *(see Figure 4.7)*. From then on, the profit odds slip with the low point reached on 22 April which rises just 40% of the time, the worst performance of the month.

**22 April**

We see no sign of any recent improvement to trading conditions on 22 April. Since 1980, shares have risen in just five out of 13 attempts. The odds of a price rise are especially low when 22 April lands on a Monday or Tuesday. Since our records began, the stock market rose just twice out of 15 attempts on these two week days *(see Table 4.12)*.

**Wednesday**

The odds of a price rise on any single day of the week are close to average, with one notable exception. Over the long run, third-quarter Wednesdays rise in two out of three years (67%). It is a superb performance, the second-best Wednesday performance of the entire year. Even 22 April often rises when it lands on Wednesday *(see Figure 4.8)*.

## PERCENTAGE OF TIME PRICES RISE EACH TRADING DAY IN APRIL'S THIRD QUARTER

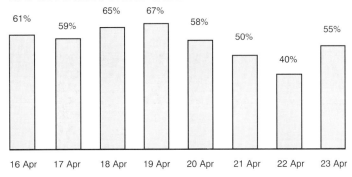

Source: Financial Times, Datastream/ICV

Figure 4.7: Trading conditions are quite good in the first half of the quarter, but weaken in the second half. 22 April is the weakest day of the month. The likelihood of a rise is especially poor on Monday and Tuesday.

### INCREASE YOUR PROFIT ODDS

Here are several historical trends that do a good job of forecasting third-quarter price shifts.

**Second-quarter signal No.1**   One involves second-quarter price fluctuations. If the FT Ordinary Share Index declines by -0.43% or more in the second quarter, it often rises in the third quarter. Since 1942, there have been 13 occasions when shares declined in the second quarter by a sufficient amount. The third quarter bounced back with an increase 11 times. During this period, Budget Day advanced from late April, through early April to mid-March, suggesting the trend is not Budget Day-related. The signal last flashed in 1987 when Budget Day was on March 17th. Nevertheless, April's second-quarter fall was followed by a third-quarter increase, right on cue.

145

## PERCENTAGE OF TIME PRICES RISE ON 22 APRIL: 1936–1996

|  | Prices rise |
|---|---|
| Total | 40% |
| | |
| Monday or Tuesday | 13% |
| Wednesday, Thursday or Friday | 56% |

*Source: Financial Times, Datastream/ICV*

Table 4.12: History shows that most of the pain dished out by the stock market on 22 April occurs on Monday and Tuesday. Prices rise at a more typical rate on the remaining three days of the week.

| IMPROVEMENT |
|---|

*Rose (11)*

*Fell (2)*

Third-quarter record after a second-quarter price decline of -0.43% or more (FT Ordinary Share Index since 1942)

**First-half signal**  A new signal has begun to rear its head. Since 1976, a rise of at least +1.32% in April's first half on the FT Ordinary Share Index has been associated with a decline in the third quarter in 11 out of 13 occurrences. As with other trends that appear during this part of the year, we are unsure of the effect of Budget Day and shall watch the situation carefully. Initial signs are good. The signal has flashed three times since Budget Day was shifted to November. Third-quarter prices fell in two of those years.

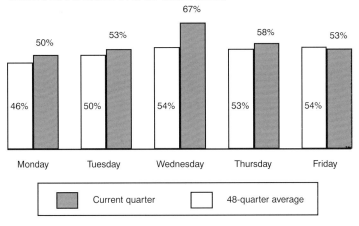

**PERCENTAGE OF TIME PRICES RISE EACH DAY OF WEEK IN APRIL'S THIRD QUARTER**

*Source: Financial Times, Datastream/ICV*

Figure 4.8: Third-quarter Wednesday provides the week's best return to investors. It is the second-best Wednesday of the year.

UPDATE

*Rose (2)*

*Fell (11)*

Third-quarter record after a first half price rise of at least +1.32% (FT Ordinary Share Index since 1976)

Second-quarter signal No.2

Here is a second newly-emerging trend that is worth monitoring. Since 1968, there have been six occasions when a bear market was running in the second quarter and the FTSE All Share Index either rose a small amount (up to +1.65%) or fell. Third-quarter prices fell each time.

147

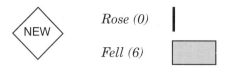

*Rose (0)*

*Fell (6)*

Third-quarter record in bear market years after a second-quarter price rise of up to +1.65% or a fall (FTSE All Share Index since 1968)

## FOURTH QUARTER OF APRIL – APRIL 24TH TO 30TH

Here comes a re-run of the third quarter story, another formerly strong performer whose trend has weakened in recent years.

A notable exception is 27 April which rises 70% of the time, the sixth-best day of the entire year.

Prices rise 64% of the time during the fourth quarter of April, the eighth-best quarter of the year. Between 1936 and 1996, the average annual increase in share prices was +0.37% (see Table 4.13).

**Recent weakness**

Like the first and third quarters of the month, signs of weakness have appeared in the fourth quarter in recent years. Since 1990, prices rose twice and fell five times, a worrying sign.

**25–27 April**

The profit odds for most days in the quarter are merely 50:50 over the long run. But three days do better than average – 25, 26 and 27 April. The performance of 27 April is especially noteworthy. Prices rise 70% of the time, the best day of the month and sixth-best of the entire year (see Figure 4.9). Tuesday, Wednesday and Friday rise more often than Monday and Thursday at this point in the month (see Figure 4.10).

## APRIL FOURTH-QUARTER PERFORMANCE IN BULL/BEAR MARKETS: 1936–1996

|  | Total | Bull Markets | Bear Markets |
| --- | --- | --- | --- |
| Average price change | 0.37% | 0.75% | -0.46% |
| Rank (of 48) | 17 | 18 | 20 |
| Per cent of time prices rise | 64% | 71% | 47% |
| Rank (of 48) | 8 | 9 | 18 |

*Source: Financial Times, Datastream/ICV*

Table 4.13: The long-term record looks good but there have been signs of weakness in recent years. Since 1990, prices have risen twice, versus five declines.

### INCREASE YOUR PROFIT ODDS

A new trend has recently developed which gives investors an edge during this final leg of the month.

**Third-quarter signal**

Since 1969, there have been 10 occasions when the FTSE All Share Index has shifted by a small amount during the third quarter of April, no more than -0.79% on the down-side and no higher than +0.22% on the up-side. Fourth-quarter prices rose each time. In the remaining years when third-quarter prices rose or fell by larger amounts, the fourth-quarter record was near 50:50.

This signal last flashed in 1995 and prices rose on cue, despite the absence of a Spring Budget.

*Rose (10)* ▭

*Fell (0)* |

Fourth-quarter record after a third-quarter shift of -0.79% to +0.22% (FTSE All Share Index since 1969)

149

### PERCENTAGE OF TIME PRICES RISE EACH TRADING DAY IN APRIL'S FOURTH QUARTER

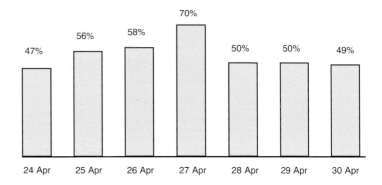

*Source: Financial Times, Datastream/ICV*

Figure 4.9: Over the long term, the odds of a profit on most days are around 50:50. A noticeable exception is 27 April, the best day of the month and sixth-best of the year.

**Prior three-quarters signal**

Here is another trend worth watching. If prices shift on the FT-Non-Financial Index by -1.90% to +1.37% in the first three quarters of April, the odds are high that the fourth quarter will rise as well. Since 1969, there have been 11 occasions with a price shift within the target range. Fourth-quarter prices rose in 10 of those years.

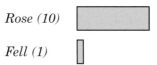

*Rose (10)*

*Fell (1)*

Fourth-quarter record after a shift in the three prior quarters of -1.90% to +1.37% (FT-Non-Financial Index since 1969)

## PERCENTAGE OF TIME PRICES RISE EACH DAY OF WEEK IN APRIL'S FOURTH QUARTER

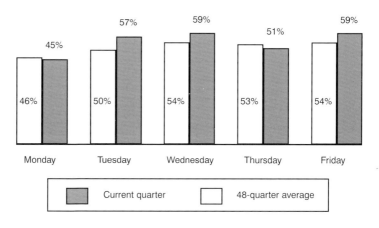

Source: Financial Times, Datastream/ICV

Figure 4.10: The profit odds are the best on fourth-quarter Tuesdays, Wednesdays and Fridays.

## LOOKING AHEAD

The next few months have a horrid reputation. One of the first things a novice investor learns is 'Sell in May and go away'. While the rule is a bit too simplistic for our taste, as subsequent chapters will demonstrate, there are times when shares do fall in value between May and September. Fortunately, the price trend for the year to date often tips how prices will shift during the next five months, to 30 September.

Falling prices by 30 September

Since 1929, there have been 16 years when the FTSE All Share Index or its predecessor index fell in the first four months of the year by -3.68% or more. Shares fell still further by 30 September in 15 of those years. The sole exception occurred in 1970 when they rose by just over 7% in the five months to 30 September.

151

IMPROVEMENT

*Rose (1)*

*Fell (15)*

Trend to 30 September after a January to April price drop of
-3.68% or more (FTSE All Share Index since 1929)

Rising prices by
31 October

On the up-side, there were 15 other years since 1925
with a mild price rise in the first four months of the year
within a range of +3.37% to +6.08%. Prices rose still
higher in the next six months to 31 October each time.

IMPROVEMENT

*Rose (15)*

*Fell (0)*

Trend to 31 October after a January to April price rise of +3.37%
to +6.08% (FTSE All Share Index since 1925)

When using either of these forecasting tools, keep in
mind that the lowest point may have been reached before
30 September and the highest point before 31 October.

Rising prices by
next 30 April

And finally, for a preview of the next 12 months, the
FT-Non-Financial Index and its predecessor index provide a useful perspective. Since 1921, there have been 21
occasions when prices rose +3.27% to +11.69% in the five
months from 1 December to 30 April. Shares continued to
rise in the next 12 months in 20 of those years.

NEW

*Rose (20)*

*Fell (1)*

Trend to 30 April (next year) after a December to April price rise
of +3.27% to +11.69% (FT-Non-Financial Index since 1921)

# CHAPTER 5 – MAY

At first glance, May is a poor month in which to hold shares, the eleventh-best of the year. Prices rise just half the time.

The chief problem in May are Big Hits – declines of at least 5% which occur every five or six years. They tend to occur more often in May (and June) than in other months and can easily wipe out months of accumulated profit.

Fortunately, the stock market often provides useful clues that tip off when a Big Hit is likely. The clues don't work flawlessly, but they reduce the odds of being caught by surprise.

Another fact not widely known is that the first quarter of the month is profitable in most years. When losses do occur, they most often occur in the second to fourth quarters.

It is fashionable to knock May's profit potential. According to conventional wisdom, May is a poor month in which to hold shares – and has been for three quarters of this century.

**Steady losses**

At first glance, the argument against a May investment in shares is quite persuasive. May investors have lost money in every single decade on record except for the 1950s. From 1919 to 1996, prices fell at a yearly average of -0.54%, equal to 22 points on a 4000 FTSE 100 *(see Table 5.1)*. Only June produces poorer results.

A May investor who started with £1,000 in 1919, shifting into cash for the other 11 months of the year, would now be worth just £540. To help to put this dismal performance into perspective, the same £1,000 invested in January and shifted into cash for the other 11 months would now stand at almost £6,000.

**Poor in bull and bear markets**

History shows that May's performance is poor in both bull and bear markets. During bull market months, prices rise just +1.12% in the average month, well below average. During bear markets, shares drop -3.33% on average each May, the worst bear market month of the year *(see Table 5.2)*. In other words, when things are good, they are good to a small degree. When things are bad, they are bad to a large degree.

**Big Hits**

The reason for May's poor bear market performance is linked with its propensity to suffer Big Hits, price declines of -5% or more. May has been hit by 14 Big Hits since our records began. Two more declines, in 1930 and 1981, clocked in at -4.9% and missed being called Big Hits by a hair.

A Big Hit seems to pop up every five or six years. On this dimension, May shares the dubious distinction of being ranked joint Number One, an honour shared with June. Further analysis reveals that 12 of the 14 Big Hits have occurred in bear markets.

If we massage the data a bit to look at it from another point of view, the danger of a May investment in bear

**MAY PRICE RISES AND DECLINES: 1919–1996**

|  | Average May price change | Up | Down/ No change |
|---|---|---|---|
| 1920–29 | -0.73% | 5 | 5 |
| 1930–39 | -1.45% | 3 | 7 |
| 1940–49 | -0.63% | 7 | 3 |
| 1950–59 | 0.52% | 6 | 4 |
| 1960–69 | -1.30% | 3 | 7 |
| 1970–79 | -1.74% | 5 | 5 |
| 1980–89 | -1.03% | 4 | 6 |
| 1990–96 | 1.54% | 4 | 3 |
| Average May change: 1919–96 | -0.54% | 49% | 51% |
| Rank (of 12) | 11 | 12 | |

*Source: BZW, Datastream/ICV*

Table 5.1: Even though May prices rise about half the time, the price of the average share fell in every decade but one since the 1920s. Big Hits of -5% or worse are the source of May's problems. If you can avoid Big Hits, a May investment can be quite profitable over the long run.

markets becomes even more apparent. Since 1919, there have been 29 bear market Mays. Prices fell in 22 of those years. More than half of those falls, 12 out of 22, were Big Hits.

Clearly, history signals high odds of dangerous market conditions during bear market Mays. You might profit in any single year of course but over the long-term, it pays to stand aside in May during bear market years.

Spotting bear markets

Given the potential problem with a May investment, it is quite useful to be able to gauge what is the likelihood

## MAY PERFORMANCE IN BULL/BEAR MARKETS: 1919–1996

|                                      | Bull Markets | Bear Markets |
|--------------------------------------|:------------:|:------------:|
| Average per cent price change        | 1.12%        | -3.33%       |
| Rank (of 12)                         | 9            | 12           |
|                                      |              |              |
| Per cent of time prices rise         | 63%          | 24%          |
| Rank (of 12)                         | 9            | 10           |
|                                      |              |              |
| Average per cent price change in:    |              |              |
| Rising years                         | 3.27%        | 3.43%        |
| Declining years                      | -2.59%       | -5.48%       |

*Source: BZW, Datastream/ICV*

Table 5.2: May's bear market record is very poor. Prices fall by more than 3% on average, the worst bear market month of the year.

of a bear market as May approaches. Fortunately, the April historical record provides a useful clue to help to answer this question *(see Figure 5.1)*. Over the long run, April price declines of -2.15% or more are associated with bear markets 89% of the time. There are exceptions to every rule of course but if April is hit by a loss of this magnitude, the odds strongly favour stormy stock market weather ahead.

Spotting bull markets

At the other end of the range, it is likely that a bull market is running at the beginning of May if the stock market rises by up to +3.51% during April. Remember that these figures say nothing about when either trend will end. It is conceivable that the following month will see the start of completely different stock market conditions. Nevertheless, the lessons from the past send a strong message – bull market prospects are generally

## ODDS OF BULL/BEAR MARKET TIPPED BY APRIL'S TREND

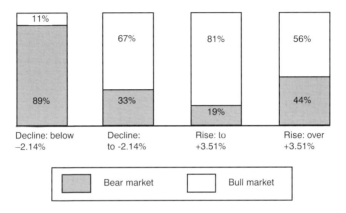

| | | | |
|---|---|---|---|
| 11% | 67% | 81% | 56% |
| 89% | 33% | 19% | 44% |
| Decline: below −2.14% | Decline: to -2.14% | Rise: to +3.51% | Rise: over +3.51% |

☐ Bear market    ☐ Bull market

*Source: BZW, Datastream/ICV*

Figure 5.1: April declines of -2.15% or more are usually associated with a bear market. A mild advance, no greater than +3.51%. is often a signal that good trading conditions lie ahead.

good following a strong April advance.

Going back to our main point, May's poor record has led many pundits to warn investors to 'Sell in May and go away. Don't come back 'til St Leger's Day'.

**Safer than you think**

In our opinion, conventional wisdom is wrong. May might not be as profitable as other months of the year but it is safer than many investors suspect. Before you back away from shares too far, consider these five important facts:

**OK in bull markets**

May's problem is primarily a bear market phenomenon. Prices rise most years during bull markets. You will not profit every year but will do well over the long run.

Most May losses occur in the second to the fourth

157

First quarter
profitable

segments of the month, especially the third quarter which rises just 41% of the time. The first quarter tends to be profitable. Prices rise 66% of the time, the fifth-best quarter of the year. The average annual profit is +0.42%. That's equal to 17 points on a 4000 FTSE 100 (see Figure 5.2). It's a perfectly safe time in which to own shares. Yes, you will lose money in some years but over the long run, the profits will outweigh the losses by a wide margin. So even if the May-bashers are right, in most years it does not pay to move out of shares on May 1st.

Global forces

We live in a global economy. Narrow national interests are increasingly undermined by international forces. This is especially true in the stock market. Organisations like the European Community and the World Trade Organisation have a large and rapidly growing effect on the profits of our local businesses. The actions or lack of by foreign governments play a huge role in our local economy and our stock market. Witness the wild gyration in share prices here when some distant international event takes place. Putting it another way, the effect of our local economic conditions on May price trends is growing ever smaller.

Foreign
investors

Foreign funds account for a constantly growing share of UK investment capital. Decisions by these foreign investors to buy or sell are often stimulated by conditions at the source of their funds – their local market, not ours.

'Smart money'

Multi-billion pound hedge funds, specifically set up to exploit short-term speculative opportunities, jump in and out of the world's stock markets at the flick of a computer button. Assuming May prices did drop with sufficient predictability to interest these investors, the weight of money would quickly change the underlying trend. For example: If 'smart money' knew May prices would drop, they would take action by selling at the end of April to avoid the damage. Prices would then fall steeply in late April because of this selling pressure, eliminating some of the downward pressure in May.

**QUARTERLY ODDS OF PRICE RISE IN MAY**

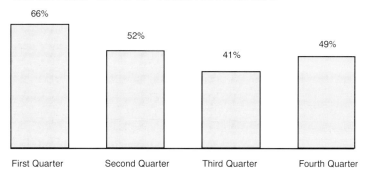

Source: *Financial Times, Datastream/ICV*

Figure 5.2:  First quarter prices rise in two out of three years, the fifth-best quarter of the year. Unfortunately, things soon take a turn for the worse. The low point is the third quarter which rises 41% of the rime, the third-worst quarter of the year.

| Big Hits are the problem | On balance, the key issue to address in this difficult investment month is not whether to sell in May and go away, but how to avoid occasional profit-wrecking Big Hits. If there were a way of avoiding Big Hit years, May investors would profit handsomely. They would still encounter some losing years but the winners would more than compensate for those 'normal'-sized losers. Is there such a way? In a word, yes. |

### INCREASE YOUR PROFIT ODDS[1]

| Avoid Big Hits: signal No.1 | A good way to avoid Big Hit years is to monitor the size of the April price change on the FT-Non-Financial Index. |

---

[1]We will provide closing prices on key indices for the last 12 months at no cost (see page 9).

If April prices shift by a small amount, declining by less than -1.66% or rising by no more than +2.81%, there is a low likelihood of a Big Hit in May. There have been 35 years in which April prices either rose or fell within this range. There was one Big Hit in all those years, the drop of 1994 which was triggered by an external event, an interest rate increase in the US.

Avoid Big Hits: signal No.2

Another way to avoid Big Hits is to watch the FT-Non-Financial Index price trend in the preceding 12 months. May prices never declined by 5% or more if prices moved within a range of -1.63% to +12.22% in the past 12 months. There have been 21 years in which prices either rose or fell within this range. There were no 5% plus May price declines in any of these years. Obviously, important fresh economic or political news could throw May prices into a tail-spin, regardless of what either historical trend suggests, but the odds of this happening are low unless the news catches the markets by surprise.

Eliminating duplication between these two trends finds 47 years when prices in the past month or past 12 months moved within the designated ranges. One Big Hit occurred in all of these years. In the remaining 31 years, a Big Hit occurred about half the time.

Aside from avoiding Big Hit years, you can also increase profits by identifying specific years when May prices are especially likely to rise. Short sellers or Put buyers can also profit by identifying years with a high likelihood of May price drops. Here are several trends which, historically, have done a good job of anticipating the direction of May price shifts.

Prior five-months signal No.1

During bull markets, a rise in the five-month run-up to May in the range of +7.05% to +18.42% is often associated with a May decline. Price shifts outside of this range are often followed by a May price rise. Here is the evidence.

Since 1963, there have been 23 years in which a bull market was running during the month of May. In 12 of those years, prices increased on the FTSE All Share Index within the range of +7.05% to +18.42% in the preceding December to April. The stock market fell during May in 10 of those years. One of the two exceptions was a small rise of +0.09% in 1989.

*Rose (2)*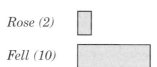

*Fell (10)*

May record after a December-to-April price rise of +7.05% to +18.42% (FTSE All Share Index since 1963)

**Prior five-month signal No.2**

In the remaining 11 bull market years that were enjoyed by UK investors since 1963, May prices rose 10 times.

*Rose (10)*

*Fell (1)*

May record after a December-to-April price rise or drop outside the range of +7.05% to -18.42% (FTSE All Share Index since 1963)

**March/April signal**

The next trend runs in bull and bear market alike. We first called attention to it in an earlier edition of the *Schwartz Stock Market Handbook*. At the time, we reported there have been 15 years in which the FT-Non-Financial Index or its predecessor index satisfied two conditions: (a) a rise in shares during March and April by at least +1.33% in total, and (b) a share price rise in April within a range of +0.70% to +2.81%. May prices rose each time.

These two conditions occurred once again in 1995 and May rose as expected. The record is now 16 increases and zero drops following this signal.

*Rose (16)*

*Fell (0)*

May record after a March/April price rise of over +1.32% and an April rise of +0.70% to +2.81% (FT-Non-Financial Index since 1922)

**April signal No.1**

On the other hand, if prices rise too high in April, May prices often suffer. There have been nine years when April increased between +5.59% to +8.31%. The May record in those years was zero rises and nine declines.

*Rose (0)*

*Fell (9)*

May record after an April price rise of +5.59% to +8.31% (FT-Non-Financial Index since 1922)

**April signal No.2**

A related trend runs on the FTSE All Share Index. Since 1958, there have been 14 occasions with an April price rise of +2.90% to +8.44%. May prices fell each time.

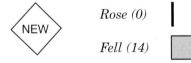

NEW

*Rose (0)*

*Fell (14)*

May record after an April price rise of +2.90% to +8.44% (FTSE All Share Index since 1958)

**Prior four-months signal**

Another way to flag occasions with a high probability of declining is to look for sharply falling prices in the first four months of the year. There have been 10 years on record with a decline of -5.28% to -12.66% in January to April. May shares fell nine times. Six were Big Hits. The single exception was in 1973 when shares rose about one tenth of a percent.

*Rose (1)*

*Fell (9)*

May record after a January to April price drop of -5.28% to -12.66% (FT-Non-Financial Index since 1920)

## FIRST QUARTER OF MAY – MAY 1ST TO 8TH

Prices rise 66% of the time, the best quarter of the month and fifth-best of the year. The trend is strong in bear markets as well as bull markets.

The chance of a price rise is best at the very beginning of the quarter. Unfortunately, first-quarter Tuesdays are an exception to the rule. Prices rise just 41% of the time.

Frequent profits

Although May can be a poor investment month, the first quarter is a consistent money-maker. Prices rise 66% of the time, the fifth-best quarter of the year. A first-quarter investment in each year since 1936 produced an average annual profit of +0.42%. Presumably the final phase of April's rally spills over to this segment of May. The recent record brought more of the same. Prices have risen in seven of the last 10 years.

In contrast, the rest of the month typically produces an average loss: second quarter, -0.14%; third quarter, -0.51%; fourth quarter, -0.43% *(see Table 5.3)*.

During bull market years, prices rise 68% of the time,

## PERCENTAGE PRICE CHANGE: MAY 1936–96

| | May 1–8 | May 9–15 | May 16–23 | May 24–31 |
|---|---|---|---|---|
| Annual average | | | | |
| 1935–39 | 1.10% | -1.08% | -1.12% | -0.24% |
| 1940–49 | 0.46% | 0.00% | -0.84% | -0.64% |
| 1950–59 | 0.75% | -0.23% | 0.14% | 0.61% |
| 1960–69 | -0.31% | 0.16% | -1.25% | -0.55% |
| 1970–79 | 0.91% | -0.63% | -0.15% | -1.87% |
| 1980–89 | -0.20% | -0.11% | -1.00% | 0.13% |
| 1990–96 | 0.70% | 0.38% | 0.48% | -0.07% |
| | | | | |
| Average quarterly price change | 0.42% | -0.14% | -0.51% | -0.43% |
| | | | | |
| Per cent of time prices rise | 66% | 52% | 41% | 49% |

Source: Financial Times, Datastream/ICV

Table 5.3: The first quarter rises in two out of three years. The remaining three quarters lose money in most decades. When they do produce a profit, the average annual return is usually quite low.

**Good bear market record**

somewhat above average compared with other quarters of the year. During bear markets, the quarter rises 62% of the time, the fifth-best bear market quarter of the entire year. This is quite impressive, given May's poor reputation *(see Table 5.4)*.

**Tuesday**

Analysis of first-quarter price trends by day of week reveals a curious fact. Shares rise at an above-average rate throughout the week, except Tuesday which rises just 43% of the time *(see Figure 5.3)*. Below-average Tuesdays are not limited to the first quarter alone. The odds of a price rise on Tuesday is below average for the

## MAY FIRST-QUARTER PERFORMANCE IN BULL/BEAR MARKETS: 1936–1996

|  | Total | Bull Markets | Bear Markets |
|---|---|---|---|
| Average price change | 0.42% | 0.50% | 0.28% |
| Rank (of 48) | 14 | 24 | 5 |
|  |  |  |  |
| Per cent of time prices rise | 66% | 68% | 62% |
| Rank (of 48) | 5 | 14 | 5 |

*Source: Financial Times, Datastream/ICV*

Table 5.4: Prices rise in two out of three years, the fifth-best quarterly record of the year. The trend is quite strong in bear market years as well.

rest of the month as well. Tuesday rises just 43% of the time in the second quarter, 40% in the third quarter and 45% in the fourth quarter. No one can explain why Tuesday is consistently weak in May.

The poor Tuesday record is solely a May issue, not part of a broader seasonal event. There are no signs of a poor Tuesday performance in either of the adjacent months.

**1–3 May**

Research also finds wide differences in profitability by day of month. Prices rise on 1–3 May about two-thirds of the time, the best three back-to-back trading days of the entire month. (Tuesday only rises about half the time on these three fine days.)

In recent years, 3 May has lost some of its sparkle with just five increases out of the last 10 opportunities. During this same period, prices have continued to follow the patterns of the past on 1–2 May with 15 rises out of 20 tries. On balance, if you are planning to sell shares at the very start of May, history suggests that waiting a few days will be a profitable decision in most years *(see*

165

## PERCENTAGE OF TIME PRICES RISE EACH DAY OF WEEK IN MAY'S FIRST QUARTER

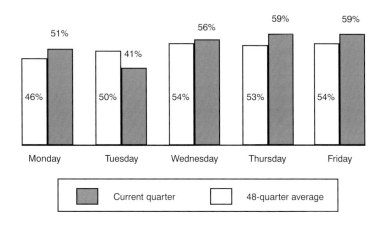

*Source: Financial Times, Datastream/ICV*

Figure 5.3:  It is difficult to make money on first-quarter Tuesdays. Prices rise just 41% of the time. The Tuesday problem is not limited to the first quarter. The likelihood of Tuesday profit is also low in the second to fourth quarters of May.

6 May

*Figure 5.4).*

The profit odds slip mid-way through the quarter. Prices rise less than half the time on three of the last four days of the quarter. The single exception, 6 May, rises 53% of the time, helped by a strong performance when it lands on Wednesday and Thursday *(see Table 5.5)*. But the likelihood of profit is much lower on 6 May when it lands on other days of the week.

Potential Big Hits

One important signal to watch out for is the possibility of a May Big Hit, using the two relationships discussed near the beginning of this chapter. If May turns out to be a potential Big Hit month, the odds are just 42%

## PERCENTAGE OF TIME PRICES RISE EACH TRADING DAY IN MAY'S FIRST QUARTER

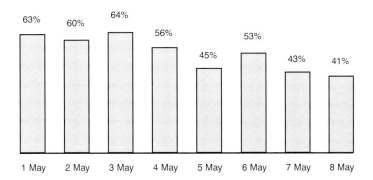

*Source: Financial Times, Datastream/ICV*

Figure 5.4: Over the long run, 1–3 May are the best three back-to-back trading days of the month, although 1 May has weakened in recent years. The other two days continue to be as profitable as ever.

that first quarter prices will rise, even if no Bit Hit strikes the month. But if no Big Hit is forecast, there is a 77% chance of profit in the first quarter.

### INCREASE YOUR PROFIT ODDS

April second-half signal No.1

Big Hits aside, the odds of a first-quarter profit can be improved by watching for a price rise on the FTSE All Share Index during the second half of April. Since 1965, there have been 20 occasions when stock market prices rose at least +1.22% in the previous two quarters. They continued to rise in the first quarter of May in 17 of those years.

In the remaining 12 years of this period when prices either rose by a smaller amount or fell, the first-quarter

**PERCENTAGE OF TIME PRICES RISE ON 6 MAY: 1936–1996**

|  | Prices rise |
| --- | --- |
| Total | 53% |
| | |
| Wednesday or Thursday | 72% |
| Rest of the week | 39% |

Source: Financial Times, Datastream/ICV

Table 5.5: The stock market rises three out of four times when 6 May lands on Wednesday or Thursday. Unfortunately, the likelihood of profit is much lower during the remainder of the week.

record was five up and seven down – in other words, profit odds of under 50:50.

Rose (17)

Fell (3)

First-quarter record after an April second-half price rise of +1.22% or more (FTSE All Share Index since 1965)

**April second-half signal No.2**

A related signal is provided by the FT Ordinary Share Index. If prices rise in the third quarter of April (by any amount) and the fourth quarter by up to +1.53%, the odds of a first quarter price rise are quite high. There have been 16 occasions when the April price trend followed this pattern. Prices rose in May's first quarter 14 times (88%). The average increase was +0.86%. This signal last failed to deliver in 1952.

Rose (14)

Fell (2)

First-quarter record after an April third-quarter price rise (any amount) and a fourth-quarter rise of up to +1.53% (FT Ordinary Share Index since 1939)

## SECOND QUARTER OF MAY – MAY 8TH TO 15TH

Prices rise three-quarters of the time in bull market years but the bear market record is grim. The chance of a price rise is just 18%, the worst bear market record of all 48 quarters.

Stock market weakness is observed once again on Tuesday, continuing a trend that began in the first quarter.

**Recent record unchanged**

Prices rise half the time in the second quarter of May. It is a long-running trend and nothing has changed in recent years. Prices rose just five times during the 1980s' Bull Market decade. The 1990s record is more of the same – four up and three down *(see Table 5.6)*.

**Potential Big Hits**

In years when May is classified as a potential Big Hit month (using the two indicators near the beginning of this chapter), there is a 46% likelihood of a second-quarter price rise. But if no Big Hit is forecast, there is a 63% chance of a price rise in the second quarter.

**Poor bear market record**

History reveals that there is a huge difference in performance in bull versus bear markets. Prices rise 72% of the time in bull markets but only 18% of the time in bear markets, the worst record of all quarters in bear market years *(see Table 5.7)*. Unbelievably, this dismal record has weakened in recent years. There have been 10 years

169

## PERCENTAGE PRICE CHANGE: MAY 1985–96

|  | May 1–8 | May 9–15 | May 16–23 | May 24–31 |
|---|---|---|---|---|
| 1985 | 1.25% | 2.08% | -0.40% | -0.97% |
| 1986 | -3.30% | -1.23% | 1.79% | -0.61% |
| 1987 | 3.58% | 3.02% | -0.71% | 1.18% |
| 1988 | 0.10% | -1.09% | -0.77% | 1.27% |
| 1989 | 0.17% | 1.26% | 0.09% | -1.42% |
| 1990 | 3.22% | 1.20% | 3.61% | 2.23% |
| 1991 | 1.25% | -2.22% | 0.66% | 0.26% |
| 1992 | 2.85% | -1.19% | 1.19% | -0.56% |
| 1993 | -0.68% | 1.68% | -0.71% | 0.77% |
| 1994 | -0.51% | -0.05% | -0.32% | -4.17% |
| 1995 | 1.08% | 1.85% | -0.46% | 0.92% |
| 1996 | -2.32% | 1.40% | -0.58% | 0.03% |
| Average quarterly price change | 0.56% | 0.56% | 0.28% | -0.09% |
| Number of years in which prices |  |  |  |  |
| Rose | 8 | 7 | 5 | 7 |
| Fell | 4 | 5 | 7 | 5 |

Source: Datastream/ICV

Table 5.6: The odds of a price rise in the recent past for each quarter is similar to its long-term average. The third quarter continues to rise less often than other quarters. Since 1985, prices fell in seven out of twelve years including the last four times in a row.

since 1969 when a bear market was running at this point of the month. The FTSE All Share Index fell in nine of those years.

## MAY SECOND-QUARTER PERFORMANCE IN BULL/ BEAR MARKETS: 1936–1996

|  | Total | Bull Markets | Bear Markets |
|---|---|---|---|
| Average price change | -0.14% | 0.60% | -1.44% |
| Rank (of 48) | 34 | 21 | 42 |
| Per cent of time prices rise | 52% | 72% | 18% |
| Rank (of 48) | 25 | 7 | 48 |

*Source: Financial Times, Datastream/ICV*

Table 5.7: During bear market years, prices rise just 18% of the time, the worst quarterly record of the year. It is quite a change from this quarter's fine bull market record.

9–13 May

The weak daily share price trend observed at the tail-end of the first quarter continues through most of the second quarter. Prices rise less than half the time from 9 May to 13 May. There has been no sign of improvement in the recent past. Since 1980, each of these days has risen half the time or less often *(see Figure 5.5)*.

14–15 May

Profit trends improve in the final two days of the quarter, with prices rising 55% on 14 May and 60% on 15 May, the best day of the quarter.

Tuesday

As noted in Figure 5.6, the pattern of Tuesday weakness continues into the second quarter. Prices rise just 43% of the time, well below average compared with other Tuesdays of the year. The problem is especially severe on 12 May which has risen on Tuesday just once out of nine attempts since daily records began in 1935.

### INCREASE YOUR PROFIT ODDS

If you plan to bet against the market, increase the

**PERCENTAGE OF TIME PRICES RISE EACH TRADING DAY IN MAY'S SECOND QUARTER**

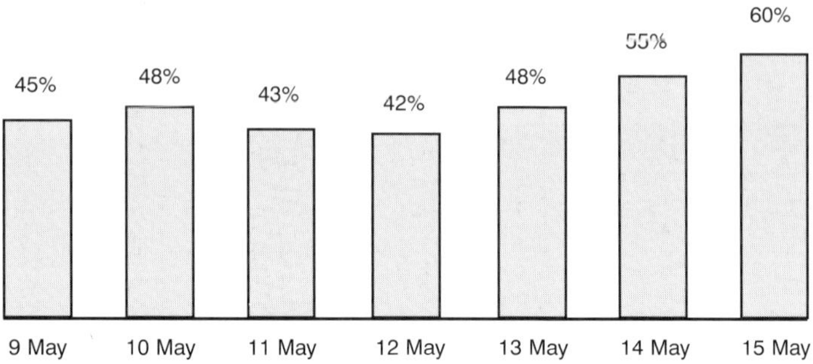


*Source: Financial Times, Datastream/ICV*

Figure 5.5: The first five days fall in most years. However, the chance of a price rise gradually increases as the quarter ends.

First-quarter signal No.1

chance of being right by watching the direction of first-quarter prices. Since 1969, there have been 10 occasions when the FTSE All Share Index either rose by a tiny amount or fell in the previous quarter. Second-quarter prices fell in nine of those years.

NEW

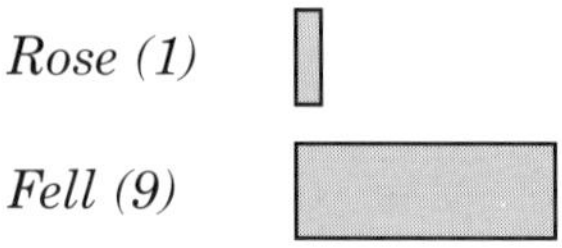


Second-quarter record after a first quarter drop or a rise no greater than +0.10% (FTSE All Share Index since 1969)

First-quarter signal No.2

Here is a second newly discovered trend which often tips the direction of second-quarter prices in bull market years. Since 1969, there have been 11 occasions when prices rose by +0.17% or more in the first quarter.

## PERCENTAGE OF TIME PRICES RISE EACH DAY OF WEEK IN MAY'S SECOND QUARTER

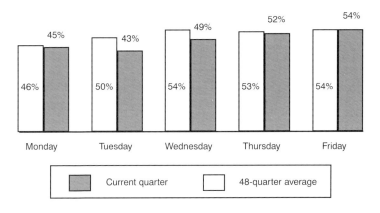

*Source: Financial Times, Datastream/ICV*

Figure 5.6: Tuesday weakness exists in the second quarter as well as the first quarter. Shares are especially weak on 12 May which has risen just once on Tuesday out of nine attempts since 1936.

Second-quarter prices rose in 10 of those years.

*Rose (10)*

*Fell (1)*

Second-quarter record during bull markets after a first-quarter rise of +0.17% or more (FTSE All Share Index since 1969)

April/May first-quarter signal

Another trend that tips second-quarter increases in bull and bear markets alike is a rise in April followed by a rise in the first quarter of May. There have been 21 years

173

when the FT-Non-Financial Index or its predecessor index rose in April by no more than +5.48%, followed by a first-quarter prices rise of +0.62% to +4.15%. Second-quarter prices continued to rise in 18 of those years (86%).

*Rose (18)*

*Fell (3)*

Second-quarter record after an April price rise of up to +5.48% and a rise in May's first quarter of +0.62% to +4.15% (FT-Non-Financial Index since 1941)

## THIRD QUARTER OF MAY – MAY 16TH TO 23RD

> You might profit this year but over the long run, a steady third-quarter investment is a money-losing proposition. Prices rise just 41% of the time, the third-worst quarter of the entire year.
> The chance of a price rise is especially poor during the first half of the week.

Money-losing
time

Investors often lose money during the third quarter.

Between 1936 and 1996, third-quarter prices rose just 41% of the time, the 46th-ranked quarter of the year, and generated an average loss of -0.51%, the 47th-ranked or second-worst quarter of the year. Even during the fabulous 1980s, prices fell seven times. The only way to profit over the long run is to bet on falling prices.

The likelihood of making money is poor in bull markets as well as bear markets. Prices rise less than half the time in either environment *(see Table 5.8)*.

Unlike other quarters of May, third-quarter profit odds

## MAY THIRD-QUARTER PERFORMANCE IN BULL/BEAR MARKETS: 1936–1996

|  | Total | Bull Markets | Bear Markets |
|---|---|---|---|
| Average price change | -0.51% | -0.11% | -1.16% |
| Rank (of 48) | 47 | 46 | 38 |
| Per cent of time prices rise | 41% | 45% | 35% |
| Rank (of 48) | 46 | 46 | 34 |

*Source: Financial Times, Datastream/ICV*

Table 5.8: The price trend is quite weak during bull market years. Prices rise 45% of the time, one of the worst quarterly records of the year.

are the same in potential Big Hit months and in so-called 'safe' months.

**Recent trend unchanged**

From 1989 to 1992, prices increased in four consecutive years, for the first time ever. The previous best was three ups in a row back in 1971–73. We wondered if this was a preliminary sign that the trend was improving. No such luck. The up-trend record decisively ended with four drops in a row from 1993–96.

On balance, the evidence is clear. If you want to invest during this segment of the year, use extreme caution. Although you might profit in any single year, the odds favour standing on the side-lines over the long-run or betting against the market.

**16 May**

There are few pockets of strength during the quarter. Prices rise just over half the time on 16 May, a continuation of good trading conditions at the tail-end of the second quarter. All other days in this quarter rise less often *(see Figure 5.7 )*.

Examining price trends by day of week shows

### PERCENTAGE OF TIME PRICES RISE EACH TRADING DAY IN MAY'S THIRD QUARTER

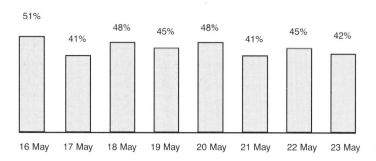

*Source: Financial Times, Datastream/ICV*

Figure 5.7: Another poor segment of the month. All but one day rise less than half the time.

**Thursday is best**

Thursday to be the only day that rises an average number of times, compared to the rest of the year. All of the other days are substandard, particularly Monday to Wednesday *(see Figure 5.8)*. Third-quarter Mondays rise 41% of the time. Tuesdays rise 40% of the time, 46th-ranked of all 48 quarters. Third-quarter Wednesdays rise 42% of the time, the worst Wednesday performance in all 48 quarters.

**18–19 May**

The Tuesday problem is especially apparent on 18–19 May. Since 1936, the stock market has risen just four times out of 18 attempts when either of these two days landed on Tuesday versus slightly over half the time when they landed on other days of the week *(see Table 5.9)*.

**16–17 May**

Happily, we can report upon one positive trend to help investors during this disappointing segment of the year. Share prices tend to rise on 16 or 17 May when either one lands on Thursday. Since 1936, prices have risen in

## PERCENTAGE OF TIME PRICES RISE EACH DAY OF WEEK IN MAY'S THIRD QUARTER

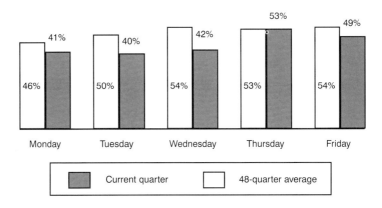

Source: *Financial Times, Datastream/ICV*

Figure 5.8: Monday is weak but Tuesday and Wednesday are much worse, relative to other quarters. Third-quarter Tuesday is 46th-ranked of all 48 quarters. Third-quarter Wednesday is the weakest of all 48 quarters.

12 out of 17 years (71%) on Thursday. During the other four days of the week, the 16th and 17th rise just 40% of the time *(see Table 5.10)*.

### INCREASE YOUR PROFIT ODDS

We find no trends that help to increase the odds of spotting a rise in this quarter. But if you plan to bet on the down-side, there are several ways to maximise your return.

Prior four-quarters signal

Here is a newly-discovered trend that has been running since 1969. During bull markets, a price swing on the FTSE All Share Index in the preceding four quarters

177

## PERCENTAGE OF TIME PRICES RISE ON
## 18–19 MAY: 1936–1996

|  | Prices rise |
|---|---|
| Total | 47% |
| Tuesday | 22% |
| Rest of the week | 53% |

*Source: Financial Times, Datastream/ICV*

Table 5.9: The odds of a price rise are stacked against investors when 18 or 19 May land on Tuesday.

of -3.12% to +12.94% is typically associated with a price decline in the third quarter. During the period surveyed, there were 13 price shifts within the target range. Third-quarter prices fell 12 times.

*Rose (1)*

*Fell (12)*

Third-quarter record during bull markets after a previous four-quarter swing of -3.12% to +12.94% (FTSE All Share Index since 1969)

Prior three-quarters signal

In all market conditions, bull and bear alike, history shows that steady rises in the preceding three quarters are often followed by a third-quarter decline. Since 1943, the FT Ordinary Share Index rose in each of the three preceding quarters 16 times. Third-quarter prices fell 13 times. Two of the three exceptions to the rule saw a third-quarter rise of less than two-tenths of a per cent. In other words, even when prices rose, the rise was a small one,

178

**PERCENTAGE OF TIME PRICES RISE ON
16–17 MAY: 1936–1996**

|  | Prices rise |
|---|---|
| Total | 46% |
| Thursday | 71% |
| Rest of the week | 40% |

*Source: Financial Times, Datastream/ICV*

Table 5.10: Prices often rise when 16 or 17 May land on a Thursday.

equivalent to less than eight points on an FTSE 100 in the area of 4000.

*Rose (3)*

*Fell (13)*

Third-quarter record after price rise in each of three preceding quarters (FT Ordinary Share Index since 1943)

**April signal**

Another indicator worth monitoring is the relationship between the month of April and the third quarter of May. Since 1944, April prices rose +1.72% to +5.80% on the FT Ordinary Share Index 25 times. Third-quarter prices fell in 22 of those years regardless of what happened in the first half of May.

This signal flashed most recently in 1996 and third-quarter prices fell on cue.

What we like about this trend, despite our inability to explain why the first and second quarters have no role in the relationship, is that it has been running steadily for six decades including the 1970s and '80s, through all of Budget Day's many schedule changes.

IMPROVEMENT

*Rose (3)*

*Fell (22)*

Third-quarter record after an April price rise of +1.72% to +5.80% (FT Ordinary Share Index since 1944)

April second-half signal

We also find that a price surge in the second half of April on the FT Ordinary Share Index is often associated with a decline in the second half of May. There have been 27 years with a price rise of +1.50% or more in the second half of April. Either the third quarter or the fourth quarter of May, or both, fell in 26 of those years. So be alert for a price drop at this point in the month following a strong second half of April. And if the decline doesn't occur by the end of this quarter, be doubly cautious in the fourth quarter.

*Rose (1)*

*Fell (26)*

Odds of a decline in the third or fourth quarter after a price rise of +1.50% or more in April's second half (FT Ordinary Share Index since 1944)

May first-half signal

A final way to maximise your gain by betting on the down-side is to monitor first- and second-quarter prices. Once again, this indicator is based upon the FT Ordinary Share Index. If prices fall in the first quarter or rise a little bit (no more than +0.94%), and fall in the second quarter, the odds of a third-quarter decline increase.

Since 1936, there have been 20 occasions with first- and second-quarter price trends within the designated limits. In 17 of those years, prices continued to decline in the third quarter.

*Rose (3)*

*Fell (17)*

Third-quarter record after a first-quarter price shift of +0.94% or less and a second-quarter fall (FT Ordinary Share Index since 1936)

## FOURTH QUARTER OF MAY – MAY 24TH TO 31ST

> Here comes another weak quarter, especially during bear markets when prices rise in just one out of four years. The profit odds are especially poor on Monday which rises 29% of the time, the worst Monday record of all 48 quarters.

Poor record

Between 1936 and 1996, prices rose in the fourth quarter of May 49% of the time and generated an average loss of -0.43%, the fourth-worst record of the year *(see Table 5.11)*. The trend is especially poor during bear market years when prices rise just one out of four times.

Trend change?

But things may be changing. Fourth-quarter prices have risen in seven of the last 10 years. We shall watch the future performance of this quarter with great interest.

One important signal to watch out for is the possibility of a May Big Hit, using the two relationships discussed near the beginning of this chapter. If May turns out to be a potential Big Hit month, the odds are just 38%

**MAY FOURTH-QUARTER PERFORMANCE IN
BULL/BEAR MARKETS: 1936–1996**

|                              | Total  | Bull Markets | Bear Markets |
|------------------------------|--------|--------------|--------------|
| Average price change         | -0.43% | 0.29%        | -1.70%       |
| Rank (of 48)                 | 45     | 33           | 46           |
|                              |        |              |              |
| Per cent of time prices rise | 49%    | 59%          | 27%          |
| Rank (of 48)                 | 31     | 23           | 44           |

*Source: Financial Times, Datastream/ICV*

Table 5.11: The odds of a price rise are about average in bull market years. Unfortunately, shares rise just once every four years in bear markets which is well below average compared with other quarters.

that fourth-quarter prices will rise, even if no Bit Hit strikes the month. But if no Big Hit is forecast, there is a 60% chance of profit in the fourth quarter.

**Monday and Friday**

Analysis of daily price trends over the last six decades shows a steady pattern of below-average performance each day of the week. Mondays and Fridays are especially disappointing. Fourth-quarter Mondays rise just 29% of the time, the worst Monday performance of all 48 quarters. Friday's record is, in a relative sense, not much better. Prices rise just 42% of the time, the 47th-ranked Friday of the year *(see Figure 5.9).*

**25 and 29 May**

Most days in the quarter rise less than half the time. There are two exceptions worth noting.

Prices rise 60% of the time on 29 May and 53% of the time on 25 May. *(see Figure 5.10).* The 25 May record is helped by its Thursday performance where prices have risen eight times in nine attempts. The record for the rest of the week is more typical for this part of May, producing

## PERCENTAGE OF TIME PRICES RISE EACH DAY OF WEEK IN MAY'S FOURTH QUARTER

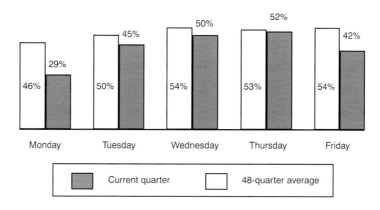

Source: *Financial Times, Datastream/ICV*

Figure 5.9: The profit odds are low on Mondays and Fridays. Monday rises 29% of the time, the worst Monday of all 48 quarters. Friday is ranked in 47th place on the Friday league rankings.

a 43% chance of profit *(see Table 5.12)*.

### INCREASE YOUR PROFIT ODDS

Third-quarter signal

History provides several clues to help investors increase the chance of profits on the up-side as well as the down-side.

One way to maximise gains is to monitor third-quarter price swings on the FT Ordinary Share Index. Our historical review found nine occasions when third-quarter prices fell by -3.10% to -4.73%. The fourth quarter continued to fall in eight of those years. The signal last failed in 1945. Since then, it has correctly flagged a fourth-

## PERCENTAGE OF TIME PRICES RISE EACH TRADING DAY IN MAY'S FOURTH QUARTER

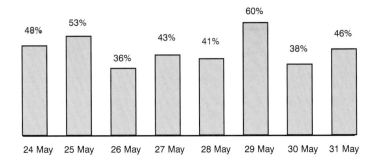

*Source: Financial Times, Datastream/ICV*

Figure 5.10: 29 May is the best day of the quarter. Second-best is 25 May which is helped by a very strong record when it lands on Thursday.

quarter decline six times in a row.

*Rose (1)*

*Fell (8)*

Fourth-quarter record after a third-quarter fall of -3.10% to -4.73% (FT Ordinary Share Index since 1936)

Second/third-quarter signal No.1

Another down-side indicator is the trend in the second and third quarters of May. If the price of an average share falls in both quarters on the FTSE All Share Index or its predecessor index by at least -0.86% per quarter, fourth-quarter prices will probably fall. Since 1938, there have been nine moves within this range and fourth-quarter prices fell eight times.

### PERCENTAGE OF TIME PRICES RISE ON
### 25 MAY: 1936–1996

|  | Prices rise |
|---|---|
| Total | 53% |
| Thursday | 89% |
| Rest of the week | 43% |

*Source: Financial Times, Datastream/ICV*

Table 5.12: Prices are very likely to rise when 25 May lands on a Thursday.

UPDATE

*Rose (1)*

*Fell (8)*

Fourth-quarter record after a second- and third-quarter fall of at least -0.86% each (FTSE All Share Index since 1938)

**Prior three-quarters signal**

It is also possible to profit on the up-side during this segment of May. Watch for a steady up-trend on the FT Ordinary Share Index in the first three quarters of the month. There have been 11 years since 1936 when prices rose in the first, second and third quarters of the month. Fourth-quarter prices rose in nine of those years.

*Rose (9)*

*Fell (2)*

Fourth-quarter record after a rise in the first, second, and third quarters (FT Ordinary Share Index since 1936)

The two exceptions to the rule are instructive. In 1989, prices rose in the third quarter by just +0.01%, thereby qualifying but by just a whisker. Clearly, a real third-quarter rise is needed to push share prices up in the fourth-quarter.

And, at the other extreme, in 1975, an April price rise of +16.23% was followed by +1.19%, +1.33% and +5.81% in the first three quarters of May. Prices finally fell in the fourth quarter. The stock market simply ran out of steam in the short run because of the enormous rally that had just taken place.

**Second/third-quarter signal No.2**

The following trend has been running during bear markets in the last six decades. Since 1938, there have been 18 bear market years when the FTSE All Share Index or its predecessor index fell in the preceding two quarters or rose by a very small amount, no more than +0.08% in total. Fourth-quarter prices fell in 16 of those years.

*Rose (2)*

*Fell (16)*

Fourth-quarter record during bear markets after a fall in the preceding two quarters or a rise of up to +0.08% (FTSE All Share Index since 1938)

Reminder: we mentioned in the preceding section that price surges in the second half of April of at least +1.50% on the FT Ordinary Share Index have occurred 27 times. In all but one of those years, prices fell in the third and/or fourth quarters of May. So if a strong April run-up is followed by rising prices in May's third quarter, consider it to be a strong warning that prices are due to fall in this quarter.

## LOOKING AHEAD

To help you to gauge the odds of a price rise or fall in the months ahead, history suggests that you should pay careful attention to the price trend over the last several months.

Rising prices by 31 August

If a bull market is running as May ends, the following trend is quite useful. Since 1922, the FTSE All Share Index or its predecessor index shifted in the 11 months that run from 1 July to 31 May by -13.35% to +16.15% in 26 different years. Prices rose in the next three months each time.

*Rose (26)*

*Fell (0)*

Trend to 31 August in bull markets after a July to May price shift of -13.35% to +16.15% (FTSE All Share Index since 1922)

Falling prices by 31 August

If a bear market is running as May ends, a price swing on the FTSE All Share Index or its predecessor index within a range of -11.46% to +26.61% in the last 12 months is a sign of trouble ahead. Since 1921, there have been 15 bear markets with a price swing within the last 12 months in the target range. Prices fell in the next three months in 14 of those years.

In all remaining bear market years with 12-month price swings outside this range, prices fell just 50% of the time.

*Rose (1)*

*Fell (14)*

Trend to 31 August in bear markets after a June to May price shift of -11.46% to +26.61% (FTSE All Share Index since 1921)

187

Rising prices by
28 February

The next trend can be used to monitor in all years, bull and bear alike. If prices have risen between 1 December and 31 May on the FT-Non-Financial Index or its predecessor index by +1.94% to +13.96%, it is a clear signal that shares will rise still further in the nine months to follow. Since 1925, there have been 31 years on record with a six-month price rise within this range. By 28 February of the following year, prices had risen still higher 28 times.

We called attention to this indicator in an earlier edition of the *Schwartz Stock Market Handbook*. Since that time, shares rose into the target range in 1995 and 1996 and prices continued to rise in the next nine months as expected, both times.

UPDATE

*Rose (28)*

*Fell (3)*

Trend to next 28 February after a December to May price rise of +1.94% to +13.96% (FT-Non-Financial Index since 1925)

A similar up-trend runs on the FTSE All Share Index if prices rise in December to May within a range of +2.18% to +13.26%.

Falling prices
by 31
December

On the down-side, a price decline on the FT-Non-Financial Index or its predecessor index in the five-month period from January to May within a range of -3.45% to -12.42% is a strong signal that prices will fall even lower by 31 December.

There have been 14 occasions since 1929 when prices fell within the defined range in the first five months of the year. By the end of the year, shares were even lower in 12 of those years. The two exceptions were +5.27% in 1962 and a minuscule +1.17% increase in 1994. The 1994 exception was particularly instructive. Prices had steadily fallen throughout the spring in response to fears of rising interest rates. In the final week of May, the FTSE 100 fell yet another 150 points in response to fears of a further rate rise, bringing prices down to near their 1994 bear market bottom. Despite this low price, the best shares could do was climb +1.17% by the end of the year.

*Rose (2)*

*Fell (12)*

Trend to December 31 after a January-to-May price decline of -3.45% to -12.42% (FT-Non-Financial Index since 1929)

# CHAPTER 6 – JUNE

June offers investors very poor profit potential. You may profit in some years but will lose money with a steady June investment over the long term.

The only good news worth looking forward to is the strong profit odds on 6 June, the best day of the entire year. Prices rise in three out of four years, a trend that has been running since the 1930s.

6 June aside, this month shares a number of problems with May including being slammed by a large number of Big Hits, price declines of 5% or more. They seem to pop up every six years or so. Fortunately, the historical record provides some useful clues that often tip off when a Big Hit is likely. The clues don't work flawlessly, but they reduce the odds of being caught by surprise.

Also like May, the first quarter of the month is profitable in most years. The remaining three quarters are money-losers over the long run with the third- and fourth-quarter record growing even weaker in recent years.

**Long-term weakness**

It has been said that the best way for investors to finish up with a small fortune in June is to start with a large one. It is the year's worst month. Prices rise half the time. From 1919 to 1996, the stock market fell at an average rate of -0.60% each June, equal to 24 points on a 4000 FTSE 100.

This poor record is not just a recent trend. Going back through history, it was 10th-ranked in the 1960s and 12th-ranked in the 1970s. The trend seemingly improved in the 1980s. Prices rose +2.26% per year with a record of eight up and two down. But the rise was more a function of broad trading conditions affecting all months, rather than an improvement in June's relative strength. Furthermore, June prices rose by +10.65% in 1980, accounting for a sizeable portion of the entire decade's gain *(see Table 6.1)*.

**Recent record poor**

The trend remained weak in recent years. Since 1990, the record is two up and five down. The average loss of -1.68% over the past seven years places June, once again, in 12th place on the monthly profit rankings for the current decade.

June shares a number of traits with May. It rises about half of the time. Also, like May, the first quarter of the month tends to be profitable with price rises in six out of ten years. The losses most often occur in the second to fourth segments of the month *(see Figure 6.1)*.

**Big Hits**

Another problem common with May is Big Hits, price declines of 5% or more. Since records began, June investors have suffered 14 Big Hits versus just five increases of that magnitude. A Big Hit seems to pop up every five or six years on average. June is tied with May for having the worst Big Hit record of the entire year.

**Bull market**

The price trend is weak in bull and bear markets alike. In bull market years, June prices rise +0.50% on average, the worst bull market performance of the year. This problem is caused by the small size of the typical price rise, not the frequency with which prices rise.

## JUNE PRICE RISES AND DECLINES: 1919–1996

| | Average June price change | Up | Down/ No change |
|---|---|---|---|
| 1920–29 | -1.39% | 4 | 6 |
| 1930–39 | 0.79% | 6 | 4 |
| 1940–49 | -2.93% | 5 | 5 |
| 1950–59 | 1.45% | 7 | 3 |
| 1960–69 | -0.93% | 4 | 6 |
| 1970–79 | -2.80% | 3 | 7 |
| 1980–89 | 2.26% | 8 | 2 |
| 1990–96 | -1.68% | 2 | 5 |
| | | | |
| Average June change: 1919–96 | -0.60% | 51% | 49% |
| | | | |
| Rank (of 12) | 12 | 9 | |

*Source: BZW, Datastream/ICV*

Table 6.1: June rises half the time but has lost money over the long term. The key problem at this point in the year is Big Hits, price declines of 5% or more which seem to strike every six years or so. The odds of a Big Hit are even higher in bear market years.

History shows that they rise 66% of the time which is about average for bull market months *(see Table 6.2)*.

Bear market

Bear market Junes are also poor performers. Over the long run, prices rise just 20% of the time, the 11th-best bear market month. Only February's 17% odds of a price rise is lower. Unfortunately, June's bear market record is getting worse. Prices fell in nine of the last 10 bear market Junes. In other words, the profit odds have fallen to 10%.

History also shows that if prices fall in a bear market, the odds of a Big Hit are very high. Prices have fallen 20

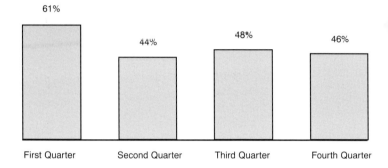

## QUARTERLY ODDS OF PRICE RISE IN JUNE

*Source: Financial Times, Datastream/ICV*

Figure 6.1: The first quarter rises in six out of 10 years and is the month's most profitable segment. The second quarter has a poor long-term record but has shown some signs of improvement in recent years. No such luck in the third and fourth quarters which continue to lose money in most years.

**Spotting bull markets**

times in bear markets since our records began. Ten were Big Hits.

Given the drastically different profit odds in bull versus bear markets for June, it is critically important for investors to know if we are in a bull or bear market. Figure 6.2 provides useful information to help to answer this question. History shows that May price rises in excess of +2.77% are usually associated with a bull market advance.

There are exceptions, of course. Prices rose by +6.22% in May 1939, right in the middle of a major bear market. And in 1990, prices rose by +10.65%, in a sharp but temporary rebound from poor conditions in the preceding months. Despite these exceptions, the lessons from the past send a strong message – that stock market prospects for the month of June generally look good

## JUNE PERFORMANCE IN BULL/BEAR MARKETS: 1919–1996

|  | Bull Markets | Bear Markets |
|---|---|---|
| Average per cent price change | 0.50% | 2.93% |
| Rank (of 12) | 12 | 10 |
|  |  |  |
| Per cent of time prices rise | 66% | 20% |
| Rank (of 12) | 6 | 11 |
|  |  |  |
| Average per cent price change in: |  |  |
| Rising years | 2.93% | 3.61% |
| Declining years | -4.21% | -4.56% |

*Source: BZW, Datastream/ICV*

Table 6.2: Prices rise an average number of times in bull market years but the size of the typical rise is substandard. The bear market record is poor and getting worse. Shares fell in nine of the last 10 bear market Junes.

following a strong May advance.

Keep in mind that these figures do not tell you when the bull market will end. It is conceivable that the following month will see the start of a reversal. Still, as a useful bull market signal, large May price advances are worth heeding.

Avoiding Big Hits

As far as Big Hits are concerned, if there were a way of avoiding them, long-term June investors would profit handsomely. They would still encounter losing years but the winners would more than compensate for those 'normal' sized losers. Our historical record shows that Big Hit years are well sign-posted. Big Hits have never appeared if any single one of the following conditions has occurred on the FT-Non-Financial Index or its predecessor index.

195

## ODDS OF BULL/BEAR MARKET TIPPED BY MAY'S TREND

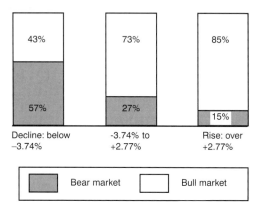

Source: BZW, Datastream/ICV

Figure 6.2: A large May advance is a good sign that a bull market is in progress.

| Time frame | Trend* | Number of years | Number of Big Hits |
|---|---|---|---|
| December–May | 0.00% to +11.57% | 29 | 0 |
| March–May | +1.11% to + 4.81% | 15 | 0 |
| April–May | +5.13% to +10.57% | 18 | 0 |
| May | +2.43% to + 6.01% | 16 | 0 |

*FT-Non-Financial Index

UPDATE

There is a good deal of overlap between these safety zones. In total, there have been 43 years touched by at least one of them. A Big Hit has not occurred in any of them. Prices have fallen in just 16 of those years or 37% of the time so you would have made money in most years.

196

The typical profit in these 43 'safe' years is +1.06%, equal to about 42 points on a FTSE 100 in the area of 4000.

**Poor odds in other years**

In the 35 years outside these safety ranges, the June record has been simply awful. A Big Hit has occurred 14 times or 40% of the time. Prices fell by less than 5% in nine other years and rose just 12 times (or 34% of the time).

A similar trend runs on the FTSE All Share Index (and its predecessor), with some minor changes.

| Time frame | Trend* | Number of years | Number of Big Hits |
|---|---|---|---|
| December–May | 0.00% to +11.69% | 31 | 0 |
| March–May | +1.70% to + 3.86% | 15 | 0 |
| April–May | +5.13% to +10.57% | 16 | 0 |
| May | +2.43% to + 3.98% | 15 | 0 |

*FTSE All Share Index

Could a Big Hit occur in the future on either index in a so-called 'safe' year? Of course. But it hasn't happened yet.

**Mild rises**

Notice the single common element that links each safe year. Up until now, Big Hits have not occurred when share prices were rising at a comfortable rate. The odds of one occurring increase when markets rise too strongly and become overheated, or are very weak in the run-up to June.

In using these signals, resist the temptation to round off to the nearest whole percent. Fractions of a percent count. Take the May rule for example. There were two years close to but just below the 'safety zone', a +2.04% May increase on the FT-Non-Financial Index in 1985 and a +2.00% increase on the same index in 1992. June prices fell by -6.72% and -7.45% in those two years. Imagine your pain if you modified the rule and purchased shares at the beginning of June in those two years because you considered any May increase in the area of 2% to be a safe signal.

Here are some other ways to tell if this is a Big Hit year.

Watch May

- If a Big Hit is experienced in May, it is less likely that one will also occur in June. Out of 14 May Big Hits, two were followed by a June Big Hit. One was in 1940, during the darkest days of the war when there was a real risk that Britain might lose. June prices fell -22.10%, one of the biggest monthly falls in history, after a May fall of -11.60%. The other exception was in the worst stretch of the 1973–74 bear market, the spring of 1974, when prices fell -20.74% in March, -8.39% in May and -10.37% in June. So, unless market conditions are catastrophically poor, the odds of back-to-back Big Hits in May and June are quite low.

June's first quarter

- Since 1936, when daily indices were first published in the United Kingdom, there have been 11 June Big Hit years. In nine of them, prices fell during the first quarter of June on the FT Ordinary Share Index . The two exceptions were in the tumultuous years of 1974 and 1975 when Big Hits occurred despite a first-quarter price rise. As a rough rule of thumb, if the first-quarter price trend is up, it is likely that June will not be subjected to a Big Hit. Prices might fall, but by less than 5%.

May's second half

- The third backup signal to watch is the direction of prices in the second half of May. Nine of the 11 post-1936 Big Hits occurred after a price decline on the FT-Ordinary Share Index. The two exceptions: 1992 when second-half prices rose by just +0.04%, the equivalent of one point on the FTSE 100 and in the atypical 1975. Implication: If prices rise in the second half of May, a Big Hit is not very likely, even if one of the price trends listed earlier has flashed a warning signal.

### INCREASE YOUR PROFIT ODDS

A number of long-running trends can help investors to improve the profit odds in this difficult investment month.

**May signal**

During bull markets, a decline of -0.38% to -7.09% on the FTSE All Share Index or its predecessor index in May is usually followed by a June price rise. Since 1936, the stock market has fallen within this range in 14 different bull market years. June prices rose in 13 of those years.

The single exception occurred in 1996 when a sudden Conservative leadership challenge in the final few days of the month temporarily caused shares to slip.

*Rose (13)*

*Fell (1)*

June record during bull markets after a fall in May of -0.38% to -7.09% (FTSE All Share Index since 1936)

During the remaining 29 bull market years since 1936, the June record was 16 up and 13 down.

**Prior eight-months signal**

Each of the remaining trends are effective in bull and bear markets alike. The first is based on the FT Ordinary Share Index, the UK's longest-running daily index. Since 1937, prices have shifted in the preceding eight months within a range of +2.60% to -9.09% on 14 occasions. The stock market fell in June in 12 of those years.

*Rose (2)*

*Fell (12)*

June record after a preceding eight-month shift of +2.60% to -9.09% (FT Ordinary Share Index since 1937)

**Prior 12-months signal**

Another price trend that does a very good job of tipping when June's prices will fall is the direction of prices in the preceding 12 months (June 1st to May 31st) on the FT-Non-Financial Index and its predecessor index. If prices have fallen in the preceding 12 months by any amount, and have fallen between -0.06% to -13.38% in the past six months, June prices will probably fall. Out of 11 years which followed this scenario, June prices fell in 10 of those years. Five of the 10 were Big Hits.

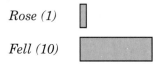

*Rose (1)*

*Fell (10)*

June record after a preceding 12-month fall and a six-month fall of -0.06% to -13.38% (FT-Non-Financial Index since 1924)

**Prior four-months signal No.1**

Shares are also likely to continue to fall if they have fallen during the February to May period within a range of -1.99% to -17.78%. Since 1948, prices on the FTSE All Share Index or its predecessor index has fallen within this range on 14 occasions. June prices fell 12 times.

NEW

*Rose (2)*

*Fell (12)*

June record after a preceding four-month fall of -1.99% to -17.78% (FTSE All Share Index since 1948)

**Prior four-months signal No.2**

A similar trend runs on the FT-Non-Financial Index. Since 1940, prices have fallen within a range of -2.67% to -15.90% on 12 occasions in the four month run-up to June. Shares fell in June in 11 of those years by an average of -5.03%. Six of the 11 falls were Big Hits.

*Rose (1)*

*Fell (11)*

June record after a four-month fall of -2.67% to -15.90% (FT-Non-Financial Index since 1940)

April-May signal No.1

If the FTSE All Share Index or its predecessor index shift within a range of -1.88% to +1.17% during April and May, the odds of a June price rise are low. There have been 18 swings within this target range since 1921 and June prices fell 15 times.

*Rose (3)*

*Fell (15)*

June record after a two-month swing of -1.88% to +1.17% (FTSE All Share Index since 1921)

April-May signal No.2

On the up-side, if shares rise on the FT-Non-Financial Index or its predecessor index in April by +3.75% to +13.03%, and shift in May by -1.61% to +3.96%, the odds favour a June price rise. Since 1935, there have been 14 years with price shifts of this magnitude in the run-up to June. Shares rose in 12 of these years. Be warned, though. The two exceptions to the rule were whoppers, -8.25% in 1961 and -7.45% in 1992.

*Rose (12)*

*Fell (2)*

June record after an April rise of +3.75% to +13.03%, and a May shift of -1.61% to +3.96% (FT-Non-Financial Index since 1935)

The message to long-term investors is quite clear. Despite June's poor reputation, it can be profitable to invest in this month if you pick your years carefully.

# FIRST QUARTER OF JUNE – JUNE 1ST TO 8TH

The first quarter is a consistent money-maker, especially during bull markets when it rises in three out of four years. The odds of a price rise are quite good on 6 June which rises 77% of the time, the most profitable day of the year.

Consistent profits

Although June is often painful for investors, the first quarter has been a consistent money-maker. Prices rise 61% of the time, which makes it the best quarter of the month *(see Table 6.3)*.

The trend is even better than it looks to be at first glance. The last bad stretch ran from 1961 to 1972 when first-quarter prices fell in 10 out of 12 years. Since then, the first-quarter trend has been incredibly good. From 1973 to the present, prices rose in 20 of 24 years at an average rate of +1.20% per year.

Bull market rises

Prices are especially likely to rise in bull market years. Since 1936, bull market first quarters were profitable 74% of the time, the fifth-best quarterly bull market record of the year *(see Table 6.4)*.

6 June

Although the first quarter is profitable in most years, the chance of a price rise on most trading days is just 50:50. A noteworthy exception is 6 June which rises 77% of the time, the best day of the entire year. It is quite surprising to encounter such a profitable day in so poor a month. Even more surprising, it is not a recent event. The trend has been running since our daily price records

## PERCENTAGE PRICE CHANGE: JUNE 1936–96

|  | June<br>1–8 | June<br>9–15 | June<br>16–23 | June<br>24–30 |
|---|---|---|---|---|
| Annual average |  |  |  |  |
| 1935–39 | -0.22% | -1.30% | 1.39% | -0.13% |
| 1940–49 | -0.49% | -0.09% | -1.71% | -0.18% |
| 1950–59 | 0.94% | 0.00% | 0.86% | -0.56% |
| 1960–69 | -0.76% | -0.56% | -0.81% | 0.91% |
| 1970–79 | 0.90% | -2.61% | -0.27% | -0.74% |
| 1980–89 | 1.51% | 0.23% | 0.48% | 0.14% |
| 1990–96 | 0.24% | 0.08% | -0.90% | -1.13% |
|  |  |  |  |  |
| Average quarterly |  |  |  |  |
| price change | 0.35% | -0.59% | -0.23% | -0.22% |
|  |  |  |  |  |
| Per cent of time |  |  |  |  |
| prices rise | 61% | 44% | 48% | 46% |

*Source: Financial Times, Datastream/ICV*

Table 6.3: The first quarter has been steadily profitable in the last few decades. The second quarter went through a stormy stretch in the 1960s and 1970s but has improved in recent years. The final two quarters have frequently disappointed investors in recent years.

began in 1936 and has shown no sign of weakening in the recent past. Since 1980, 6 June has risen in 10 out of 12 different years *(see Figure 6.3)*.

3 June

Another day to watch is 3 June. Prior to 1980, prices rose less than half of the time. But the recent trend has improved. Since 1980, 3 June has risen 10 out of 13 times.

Monday and
Tuesday
strength

Analysing price shifts by day of week shows a pattern of strength on Monday and Tuesday. Both rise much more often than the average Monday or Tuesday.

### JUNE FIRST-QUARTER PERFORMANCE IN
### BULL/BEAR MARKETS: 1936–1996

|  | Total | Bull Markets | Bear Markets |
|---|---|---|---|
| Average price change | 0.35% | 0.94% | -0.70% |
| Rank (of 48) | 18 | 10 | 28 |
| Per cent of time prices rise | 61% | 74% | 36% |
| Rank (of 48) | 15 | 5 | 31 |

*Source: Financial Times, Datastream/ICV*

Table 6.4: The long-term record is good. The short-term record is even better. Prices have risen in 20 of the last 24 years. Bull markets are associated with a price rise 74% of the time, the fifth-best bull market quarter of the year.

**Wednesday weakness**

Wednesday is the opposite, the weakest day of the first quarter and well below average compared with other Wednesdays of the year *(see Figure 6.4)*.

Wednesday is at its worst on 1–2 June. Prices rise 28% of the time when either day lands on a Wednesday versus 55% of the time on the other four days of the week.

### INCREASE YOUR PROFIT ODDS[1]

Here are several historical relationships that increase the odds of correctly forecasting which way prices will move.

**Prior three-quarters signal**

During the last three decades, there have been 12 occasions when prices rose on the FTSE All Share Index in the prior three quarters, or fell by no more than -0.08%. Prices rose in the first quarter in 11 of those years. The

---

[1]We will provide closing prices on key indices for the last 12 months at no cost (see page 9).

## PERCENTAGE OF TIME PRICES RISE EACH TRADING DAY IN JUNE'S FIRST QUARTER

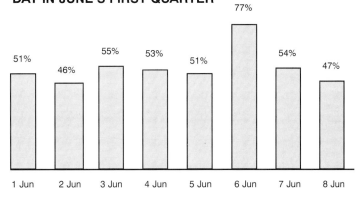

Source: Financial Times, Datastream/ICV

Figure 6.3: Prices rise around 50% of the time for most days. 6 June is a remarkable exception. Prices rise 77% of the time, the best day of the year. There has been no sign of weakness in recent years.

single exception was a tiny fall of -0.09%, equal to four points on an FTSE 100 in the area of 4000.

*Rose (11)*

*Fell (1)*

First-quarter record after a price rise in the prior three quarters, or a drop of -0.08% or less (FTSE All Share Index since 1969)

May signal

A related trend is the direction of prices on the FT-Non-Financial Index and its predecessor index during the month of May. If May prices rise moderately by +2.47% to +3.96%, first-quarter prices will probably rise

## PERCENTAGE OF TIME PRICES RISE EACH DAY OF WEEK IN JUNE'S FIRST QUARTER

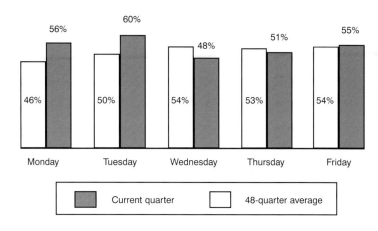

*Source: Financial Times, Datastream/ICV*

Figure 6.4: Tuesday is the most profitable day in the first quarter. Both Monday and Tuesday rise much more often than average.

too. We first called attention to this indicator in an earlier edition of the *Schwartz Stock Market Handbook*. Since then, shares rose within the target range in May 1995 and June's first quarter rose on cue.

In total, there have been 11 occasions since 1942 when May prices rose within the target range. June's first quarter rose in 10 of those years. The one exception was in 1971.

UPDATE

*Rose (10)*

*Fell (1)*

First-quarter record after a price rise of +2.47% to +3.96% in May (FT-Non-Financial Index since 1942)

May fourth-
quarter signal
No.1

Since 1969, there have been 11 occasions when the FT-Non-Financial Index fell in the final quarter of May by -1.15% to -5.98%. First-quarter prices rose in 10 of those years.

Rose (10)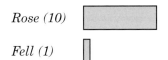

Fell (1)

First-quarter record after a price drop in May's fourth quarter of -1.15% to -5.98% (FT-Non-Financial Index since 1969)

Bull market
signal

During bull markets, the odds of a first-quarter rise are quite good. Since 1972, there have been 17 occasions when a bull market was running as the first quarter began. Prices rose on the FTSE All Shares Index in 15 of those years.

Rose (15)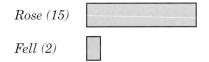

Fell (2)

First-quarter record during bull markets (FTSE All Share Index since 1972)

May fourth-
quarter signal
No.2

The following signal is for use in months with a low probability of a Big Hit (as defined by the Big Hit warning signals discussed earlier in this chapter). In such months, the odds of a first-quarter profit are especially high if FT Ordinary Share Index prices rose in May's fourth quarter by +0.27% to +1.51%. Since 1936, there have been 11 years when prices moved in the designated range. First-quarter prices rose each time.

This signal last flashed in 1995 and prices rose in the first quarter by +1.52%

*Rose (11)*

*Fell (0)*

First-quarter record after a price rise of +0.27 % to +1.51% in May's fourth quarter (FT Ordinary Share Index in 'safe' years since 1936)

May second-
half signal

On the down-side, it is possible to pin-point years when prices are especially likely to fall by watching the price trend during May's second half. The losses are often large enough to give speculators a short-term opportunity to profit by betting against the market. Since 1948, there have been 14 years with a decline in the second half of May of under -5.00% and a fourth-quarter decline of -0.20% to -2.98%. Prices fell in June's first quarter in 12 of those years (86%). The average loss during those 14 years was -1.30%.

*Rose (2)*

*Fell (12)*

First-quarter record after a price fall of up to -5.00% in May's second half and fourth-quarter price fall of -0.20% to -2.98% (FT Ordinary Share Index since 1948)

# SECOND QUARTER OF JUNE – JUNE 9TH TO 15TH

On some dimensions, the second quarter is the worst quarter of the year. The record is poor in bull and bear markets alike. Happily, the second-quarter trend has shown signs of improvement in recent years.

Unfortunately, the chance of a price rise continues to be poor on second-quarter Wednesdays and Thursdays. Be especially cautious on Thursday which rises in just one year out of three, the worst Thursday performance of the year.

**Year's worst record**

The average share price drops -0.59% each year in the second quarter of June, the worst quarterly performance of the year. Prices rise just 44% of the time during this quarter, well below average compared with other segments of the year.

This quarter's performance is weak in bull and bear markets alike *(see Table 6.5)*. Prices rise about half the time in bull market years and less than one-third of the time in bear market years. Both figures are below average compared with other quarters of the year.

But under the surface, some interesting trend changes have occurred in recent years. From 1936, when quarterly records first began, until 1968, the second quarter was an average performer. Prices rose about half the time. Suddenly, the trend changed for the worse. From 1969–77, second-quarter prices fell nine times in a row. No one can explain why the second-quarter trend turned so sour.

**Recent improvement**

The next nine years to 1986 saw a slight improvement with three rises and six declines. More recently, the trend has improved yet again. Prices have risen in six of the last 10 years, a return to traditional second-quarter patterns *(see Table 6.6)*.

Analysis of daily price swings reveals a pattern of consistent weakness. Prices rise less than half the time every single day of the quarter with the worst days at the

**JUNE SECOND-QUARTER PERFORMANCE IN
BULL/BEAR MARKETS: 1936–1996**

|  | Total | Bull Markets | Bear Markets |
|---|---|---|---|
| Average price change | -0.59% | -0.06% | -1.46% |
| Rank (of 48) | 48 | 43 | 43 |
| Per cent of time prices rise | 44% | 53% | 30% |
| Rank (of 48) | 42 | 37 | 38 |

*Source: Financial Times, Datastream/ICV*

Table 6.5: The odds of a price rise are below average in bull and
bear markets alike.

Wednesday
and Thursday

very beginning and very end *(see Figure 6.5)*.

The stock market's performance is particularly poor on
second-quarter Wednesday and Thursday. Wednesday
rises 43% of the time, the 47th-ranked Wednesday of all
48 quarters. Thursday's performance is even worse, rising just once every third year, the worst Thursday record
of all 48 quarters of the year *(see Figure 6.6)*. There are
no guarantees for any single year of course, but over the
long run, holding shares at this point of the week is a losing proposition.

### INCREASE YOUR PROFIT ODDS

Clearly, the only way to profit consistently in the second
quarter is to invest selectively when market conditions
are favourable. To help you improve the odds of a profitable investment, the market sends several useful signals. One of the best is the interaction between May's
fourth quarter and June's first quarter.

If a May fourth-quarter advance of +0.64% to +2.90%
is followed by a first-quarter price rise of at least +0.18%,

## PERCENTAGE PRICE CHANGE: JUNE 1985–96

|  | June 1–8 | June 9–15 | June 16–23 | June 24–30 |
|---|---|---|---|---|
| 1985 | 0.08% | -2.87% | -0.81% | -2.60% |
| 1986 | 0.68% | -1.57% | 2.52% | 1.77% |
| 1987 | 1.10% | 3.64% | -1.18% | 1.50% |
| 1988 | 2.32% | 2.19% | 0.52% | -0.80% |
| 1989 | 1.02% | -0.87% | 1.58% | -0.74% |
| 1990 | 1.02% | 1.06% | -0.55% | -0.06% |
| 1991 | 0.20% | 0.63% | -1.37% | -2.85% |
| 1992 | -2.17% | -2.26% | -1.41% | -1.62% |
| 1993 | 0.32% | 0.73% | 0.87% | 0.13% |
| 1994 | 1.79% | -0.09% | -3.29% | -0.88% |
| 1995 | 1.59% | -0.47% | 0.20% | -1.84% |
| 1996 | -1.04% | 0.99% | -0.73% | -0.77% |
| Average quarterly price change | 0.58% | 0.09% | -0.30% | -0.73% |
| Number of years in which prices | | | | |
| Rose | 10 | 6 | 5 | 3 |
| Fell | 2 | 6 | 7 | 9 |

*Source: Datastream/ICV*

Table 6.6: The first quarter has fallen just twice since 1985. The second quarter improved in recent years from its sorry performance in the 1970s, but is still much weaker than the first quarter. No signs of improvement are apparent for the two later quarters.

**Prior two-quarters signal No.1**

prices will probably continue to rise in the second quarter. The FT Ordinary Share Index rose in 11 out of 13 years with the two prior-quarter price trends in the appropriate range.

211

**PERCENTAGE OF TIME PRICES RISE EACH TRADING DAY IN JUNE'S SECOND QUARTER**

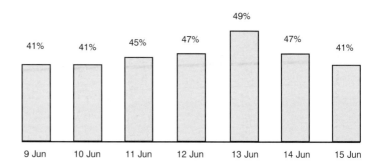

*Source: Financial Times, Datastream/ICV*

Figure 6.5:  Shares rise less than half of the time throughout the quarter. The chance of a price rise is weakest at the very beginning and the very end of the quarter.

*Rose (11)*

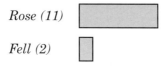

*Fell (2)*

Second-quarter record after a price rise in May's fourth quarter of +0.64% to +2.90% and a first-quarter price rise of at least +0.18% (FT Ordinary Share Index since 1936)

May fourth-quarter signal No.1

On the other hand, if FT Ordinary Share Index prices are weak in May's fourth quarter, second-quarter prices will probably fall regardless of what happens in the first quarter. Here is the evidence. Since 1971, there have been 16 years when the price of the average share fell in May's fourth quarter. Second-quarter prices declined in 14 of those years.

## PERCENTAGE OF TIME PRICES RISE EACH DAY OF WEEK IN JUNE'S SECOND QUARTER

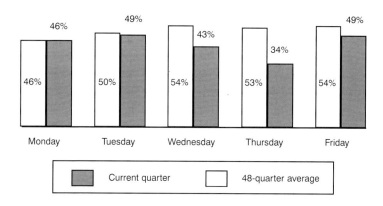

Source: Financial Times, Datastream/ICV

Figure 6.6: The odds of a mid-week price rise are well below average. Thursday is ranked in last place on the day-of-the-week performance league tables. Wednesday is 47th-ranked.

NEW

*Rose (2)*
*Fell (14)*

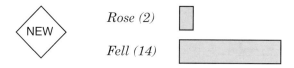

Second-quarter record after a price drop in May's fourth quarter (FT Ordinary Share Index since 1971)

May fourth-quarter signal No.2

A similar trend runs on the FTSE All Share Index. Since 1969, the fourth quarter of May has fallen by -0.04% or more in 15 different years. Second-quarter prices continued to decline in 14 of those years, regardless of how they moved in the first quarter of June.

*Rose (1)*

*Fell (14)*

Second-quarter record after a price drop of -0.04% or more in May's fourth quarter (FTSE All Share Index since 1971)

**Prior two-quarters signal No.2**

Also on the FTSE All Share Index, a decline in the prior two quarters is often associated with further declines during the second quarter. Since 1969, there have been 14 occasions when prices fell -0.06% or more during the prior two quarters. Second-quarter prices fell in 13 of those years. During the other years of this period, the second-quarter record was nine rises and five declines.

*Rose (1)*

*Fell (13)*

Second-quarter record after a price drop in the prior two quarters of -0.06% or more (FTSE All Share Index since 1969)

**Prior four-quarters signal**

A final indicator worth watching is the direction of prices on the FT-Non-Financial Index in the previous four quarters. Since 1970, a drop of -2.74% or worse was followed by a second-quarter decline in nine out of 10 years. The single exception was an advance of just +0.06% in 1994.

*Rose (1)*

*Fell (9)*

Second-quarter record after a price drop in the prior four quarters of -2.74% or more (FT-Non-Financial Index since 1970)

# THIRD QUARTER OF JUNE – JUNE 16TH TO 23RD

> Here comes another poor quarter. Unlike the previous quarter, there have been no signs of improvement in recent years.

**Poor record**

Investors typically lose money by investing during the third quarter. Between 1936 and 1996, third-quarter prices rose 48% of the time and generated an average loss of -0.23% per year. The profit picture may not be as grim as in the second quarter but it is not good.

**No sign of improvement**

The trend continued to show weakness in the last few decades. Shares fell in the average year during the 1960s and '70s. In the Bull Market 1980s, the record was five up and five down. The 1990s continues to be weak with just two rises out of seven attempts.

Over the long run, the third quarter has risen 59% of the time in bull market years, about average for bull markets, but has done quite poorly in bear markets, rising just 29% of the time *(see Table 6.7)*.

**Wednesday to Friday**

There is a general pattern of weakness on third-quarter Wednesdays, Thursdays and Fridays. The odds of a price rise are well below average when compared with the other 47 quarters of the year *(see Figure 6.7)*.

**16–17 June**

Analysis of price trends by calendar day reveals that the best trading day of the quarter is the opening day, 16 June. Prices rise 57% of the time *(see Figure 6.8)*. On both 16 and 17 June, the odds of a price rise are much higher on Monday compared with the rest of the week. Prices rise in three out of four years when either one lands on Monday versus just half the time when they land on other days of the week *(see Table 6.8)*.

**19 June**

Be especially cautious when 19 June, the worst trading day of the quarter, lands on Wednesday. Since 1936, 19 June prices rose on Wednesday just once in nine attempts *(see Table 6.9)*.

## JUNE THIRD-QUARTER PERFORMANCE IN
## BULL/BEAR MARKETS: 1936–1996

|  | Total | Bull Markets | Bear Markets |
|---|---|---|---|
| Average price change | -0.23% | 0.56% | -1.46% |
| Rank (of 48) | 39 | 23 | 43 |
| Per cent of time prices rise | 48% | 59% | 29% |
| Rank (of 48) | 37 | 22 | 41 |

Source: Financial Times, Datastream/ICV

Table 6.7: The bull market record is about average but the bear market record is substandard. Prices rise less than one-third of the time.

### INCREASE YOUR PROFIT ODDS

We find no trends which consistently forecast a price rise in the third quarter.

June second-quarter signal

If you are betting on the down-side, one way to increase your odds of success is to watch second-quarter prices on the FT Ordinary Share Index. If they fall by -1.23% or more, the odds of a third-quarter decline increase. Since 1973, second-quarter prices have fallen within this range 10 times. In nine of them, the fall was immediately followed by a decline in the third quarter. The average loss was -2.29%, equal to 92 points on a 4000 FTSE 100.

Rose (1)

Fell (9)

Third-quarter record after a price drop in June's second quarter of at least -1.23% (FT Ordinary Share Index since 1973)

## PERCENTAGE OF TIME PRICES RISE EACH DAY OF WEEK IN JUNE'S THIRD QUARTER

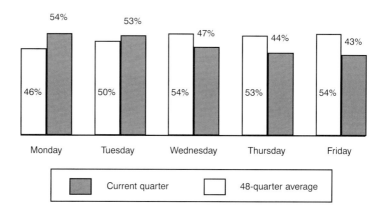

Source: Financial Times, Datastream/ICV

Figure 6.7: The odds of a price rise are well below average on third-quarter Wednesdays, Thursdays and Fridays.

**June first-half signal**

Another trend to watch on the FT Ordinary Share Index is the direction of prices in the first half of June. If they fall by -2.79% to -6.83%, the odds are high that prices will also decline in the third quarter.

Out of 13 years in which the stock market fell in the first half within the defined range, the third quarter declined 10 times. Two of the exceptions were associated with atypical events. The Conservatives won a mid-June election in 1970 and third-quarter prices rose +10.68%. One year later, prices rose sharply when the markets got wind of a July tax cut.

These exceptions confirm the point that news-making events can overwhelm even the strongest of trends. If you put these two atypical years aside for the moment, a first-half drop in share prices within a range of -2.79% to

217

## PERCENTAGE OF TIME PRICES RISE EACH TRADING DAY IN JUNE'S THIRD QUARTER

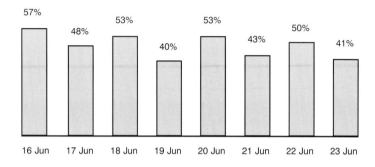

*Source: Financial Times, Datastream/ICV*

Figure 6.8: Prices often rise on 16 June, especially when it lands on Monday.

-6.83% is associated with a third-quarter drop in 10 out of the remaining 11 years.

*Rose (3)*

*Fell (10)*

Third-quarter record after a price drop in June's first half of -2.79% to -6.83% (FT Ordinary Share Index since 1936 – two exceptional years included)

Prior four-quarters signal No.1

The stock market also often declines after prices drop in the second half of May and first half of June. Since 1940, there have been 15 occasions when prices declined in both periods on the FT Ordinary Share Index, by at least -0.33% in May and -0.77% in June. The third quarter declined 13 times.

## PERCENTAGE OF TIME PRICES RISE ON
## 16–17 JUNE: 1936–1996

|  | Prices rise |
|---|---|
| Total | 52% |
| Monday | 76% |
| Rest of the week | 46% |

*Source: Financial Times, Datastream/ICV*

Table 6.8: The chance of a rise is best when 16–17 June land on Monday

Third-quarter record after a price drop in May's second half by at least -0.33% and June's first half by at least -0.77% (FT Ordinary Share Index since 1940)

Prior four-quarters signal No.2

Here is a related trend that has been running for three decades. Since 1969, there have been 10 occasions when the FTSE All Share Index fell during the prior four quarters by -1.34% to -5.76%. Third quarter prices fell in nine of those years.

Third-quarter record after a price drop in the prior four quarters of -1.34% to -5.76% (FTSE All Share Index since 1969)

**PERCENTAGE OF TIME PRICES RISE ON
19 JUNE: 1936–1996**

Prices rise

| | |
|---|---|
| Total | 40% |
| | |
| Wednesday | 11% |
| Rest of the week | 47% |

*Source: Financial Times, Datastream/ICV*

Table 6.9:  A price drop is likely when 19 June lands on a Wednesday.

Prior four-quarters signal No.3

Since 1976, there have been 10 occasions when the FT-Non-Financial Index fell during the prior four quarters by -0.26% to -5.67%. Third-quarter prices fell in each of those years.

*Rose (0)* ▌

*Fell (10)* ▭

Third-quarter record after a price drop in the prior four quarters of -0.26% to -5.67% (FT-Non-Financial Index since 1976)

# FOURTH QUARTER OF JUNE – JUNE 24TH TO 30TH

Here comes another quarter with low profit potential. There are no signs of any recent improvement. Prices have fallen in eight of the last 10 years in the fourth quarter, one of the year's worst records.

**Poor record**

The fourth quarter of June offers poor investment potential. In the long run, investors have lost money by consistently investing during the fourth quarter. Between 1936 and 1996, the fourth quarter rose 46% of the time and generated an average loss of -0.22%.

Nothing has changed recently. The record over the last 10 years is eight declines and two rises, one of the worst performances of the year.

**Bear markets weak**

The odds of a price rise are especially poor in bear market years. Prices rise just 25% of the time, the 46th-ranked bear market quarter of the year (*see Table 6.10*).

The beginning of the quarter tends to be weaker than its end. Prices rise less than half the time in three of the first four days of the quarter. The profit trend for the final three days is better with each rising more than half the time (*see Figure 6.9*).

Analysis of price trends by day of the week shows that each day performs very close to average (*see Figure 6.10*).

### INCREASE YOUR PROFIT ODDS

Despite the difficult stock market conditions that are often encountered during this quarter, we find several good price signals worth watching.

**Prior four-quarters signal**

On the FT-Non-Financial Index, a price rise over the last four quarters or a small decline no greater than -0.54% is usually followed by a fourth-quarter decline. Since 1970, there have been 14 occasions with a price shift within this range. Fourth-quarter prices dropped in

## JUNE FOURTH-QUARTER PERFORMANCE IN BULL/BEAR MARKETS: 1936–1996

|  | Total | Bull Markets | Bear Markets |
|---|---|---|---|
| Average price change | -0.22% | -0.02% | -0.64% |
| Rank (of 48) | 38 | 42 | 27 |
| Per cent of time prices rise | 46% | 56% | 25% |
| Rank (of 48) | 40 | 29 | 46 |

*Source: Financial Times, Datastream/ICV*

Table 6.10: The likelihood of a price rise is quite poor in bear market years. Prices rise just one out of four times on average, the third-worst bear market quarter of the year.

12 of those years. In the remaining 13 years, the fourth-quarter record was roughly 50:50 – seven up and six down.

⟨NEW⟩

*Rose (2)*

*Fell (12)*

Fourth-quarter record after a price rise in the prior four quarters, or a drop no greater than -0.54% (FT-Non-Financial Index since 1970)

Prior three-quarters signal No.1

Over to the FT Ordinary Share Index, if prices rise in the first half of June by no more than +2.92%, and shift in the third quarter within a range of -1.24% to +0.49%, fourth-quarter prices will probably rise. There have been 13 years with price shifts within this range. Fourth-quarter prices rose in 11 of those years.

## PERCENTAGE OF TIME PRICES RISE EACH TRADING DAY IN JUNE'S FOURTH QUARTER

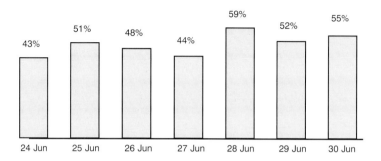

*Source: Financial Times, Datastream/ICV*

Figure 6.9: The fourth quarter starts off slowly but ends with a big finish. The three best days are the final three.

UPDATE

*Rose (11)*

*Fell (2)*

Fourth-quarter record after a price rise in June's first half by no more than +2.92% and a shift in the third quarter of -1.24% to +0.49% (FT Ordinary Share Index since 1936)

Prior three-quarters signal No.2

There is also a tendency for the FT Ordinary Share Index to fall in the fourth quarter if it rises in each of June's first, second, and third quarters. Here is the rule that seems to be developing. There have been eight years in which prices rose in the three preceding quarters, with a third-quarter rise of at least +0.50%. Fourth-quarter prices fell in each of those years. The average annual decline was -1.12%.

## PERCENTAGE OF TIME PRICES RISE EACH DAY OF WEEK IN JUNE'S FOURTH QUARTER

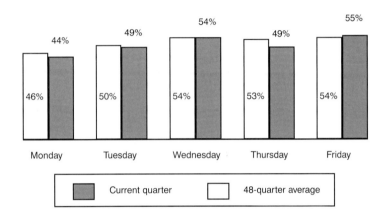

Source: Financial Times, Datastream/ICV

Figure 6.10: For each day of the week, the chance of a price rise is very close to average.

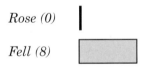

*Rose (0)*

*Fell (8)*

Fourth-quarter record after a price rise in three consecutive quarters, with a third-quarter rise of at least +0.50% (FT Ordinary Share Index since 1936)

## LOOKING AHEAD

Here is a long-running trend that gives good insights into the expected direction of shares in the three months ahead.

**Rising prices by 30 September**

Since 1941, a small shift on the FTSE All Share Index or its predecessor index in April to June is usually followed by higher share prices in the three months ahead. During this period, there were 20 occasions when prices shifted within a range of -4.89% to +3.49% in April–June. In 18 of those years, the stock market had risen by the end of September. One of the two exceptions was in the summer of 1973 in the midst of our worst-ever bear market.

*Rose (18)*

*Fell (2)*

Trend to 30 September after a April–June price shift of -4.89% to +3.49% (FTSE All Share Index since 1941)

**Rising prices by next 30 June**

Looking further ahead, there is a very pronounced tendency for the June price trend to tip off where prices are heading in the next 12 months, that is, to June 30 of the following year. Since World War 1, there have been 25 occasions when the FTSE All Share Index or its predecessor index shifted in June within a relatively narrow range of -3.38% to +0.63%. In 22 of those 25 occasions, share prices were sharply higher 12 months later. All but four were in double digits. There were just three exceptions to the rule: 1937, 1947 and 1973.

After the June 1937 signal flashed, prices remained flat during July and August. But fear of war and of higher taxes to pay for re-armament then hit the stock market hard. In the 10 months that followed, prices dropped by almost 18%.

The cold winter and spring floods of 1947 brought the

225

post-war economy almost to a stand-still. Things began
to look up in April and May. Sterling was made convert-
ible in June and the June signal flashed. Soon after, the
stock market's optimism turned sour. The government
was forced to suspend Sterling's convertibility in August.
Food rations were reduced to well below war-time levels.
US aid ran out amidst considerable uncertainty about
America's upcoming Marshall Plan aid package. Share
prices dropped by over 19% in the year that followed a
good June signal.

In 1973, the June signal was followed by a relatively
small price drop of around 6% by October. Suddenly, the
oil crisis smashed Britain. Crude oil prices rose by 66%.
The government was in turmoil. Interest rates rose to 13
percent. A three-day work week was introduced. A
December mini-Budget introduced massive spending
cuts, credit controls and tax increases. Labour won a surprise victory in February. By June 1974, prices were
down 44% from the previous June, despite a favourable
June signal.

Clearly, there are no certainties when it comes to the
stock market. Equally clear: throughout all of recorded
history, each exception to the June rule was associated
with truly extraordinary economic and political events.

| UPDATE |
| --- |

*Rose (22)*

*Fell (3)*

Trend to 30 June (next year) after a June price shift of -3.38% to
+0.63% (FTSE All Share Index since 1919)

# CHAPTER 7 – JULY

Over the long run, July rises exactly 50% of the time, below average compared to other months.

The amount of profit that would have been gained after seven decades of steady investing is not much different than what might have been obtained from a building society savings account.

The chance of a price rise is below average in bull and bear markets alike. The recent bear market trend has been especially weak with just one rise in the last 10 bear markets.

Shares tend to rise most often in the first two quarters of the month. The final two quarters lose money over the long run.

July is the third 50:50 month in a row, rising 50% of the time like May and June. Fortunately, it is buffeted by Big Hits less often than May and June. As a result, it is the most profitable of the three.

**Ranked seventh**

Over the long run, July is ranked seventh on monthly profitability and investors typically make a small profit. Between 1919 and 1996, prices rose at a yearly average of +0.43%, equal to about 17 points on a 4000 FTSE 100 *(see Table 7.1)*.

A profit of this size is no great shakes. To put the figure into perspective, a start-up investment of £1,000, placed in shares each July from 1919 to 1996, and in cash for the rest of each year, would have grown to £1,306 after eight decades of steady investing. If the same sum were deposited each July into a risk-free building society savings account earning an average of 4% per year, it would have grown to £1,296 by 1996, a small difference.

**Recent trend unchanged**

We repeated this experiment from 1975 to the present, the best two decades in stock market history. The results were similar. A July investment of £1,000 in shares grew to £1,102. A deposit of the same size in a saving account each July would now stand at £1,076, almost the same amount.

In the highly favourable stock market conditions of the 1980s, July posted its best performance since World War Two. Note though, that the average annual increase of +0.98% merely reached ninth place on the monthly profitability rankings for this profitable decade. And much of this profit was due to 1989 when prices rose by +6.50%.

**Quarterly differences**

Although it is not widely known, there are some interesting performance differences within various segments of this month worth watching. History shows that prices rise more often in the first half of the month than the second half. Be cautious during the third quarter. In recent years, the stock market has been quite disappointing during this stretch of time. Prices have fallen nine times

## JULY PRICE RISES AND DECLINES: 1919–1996

| | Average July price change | Up | Down/ No change |
|---|---|---|---|
| 1920–29 | -0.86% | 3 | 7 |
| 1930–39 | 1.51% | 6 | 4 |
| 1940–49 | 2.20% | 6 | 4 |
| 1950–59 | 0.73% | 6 | 4 |
| 1960–69 | -2.04% | 4 | 6 |
| 1970–79 | 0.08% | 4 | 6 |
| 1980–89 | 0.98% | 6 | 4 |
| 1990–96 | 1.17% | 4 | 3 |
| | | | |
| Average July change: 1919–96 | 0.43% | 50% | 50% |
| | | | |
| Rank (of 12) | 7 | 10 | |

*Source: BZW, Datastream/ICV*

Table 7.1: In some respects, July is a lacklustre month. It rises half of the time over the long term and produces a small profit. Its performance has been quite consistent for many decades, steadily rising around half the time in each 10 year cycle since the 1930s.

in the last 12 years in the third quarter *(see Figure 7.1)*.

**Poor in bull and bear markets**

The monthly price trend tends to be weak in bull and bear markets alike. During bull markets, July typically rises just under two-thirds of the time. In bear market years, it rises in one out of four years. Both figures are below average compared to other months.

An ominous bear market trend change has developed in recent years. Prior to 1960, there were 16 bear market years. Prices rose in six of them, a 40% success rate. After 1960, there were 10 further bear market years. Prices

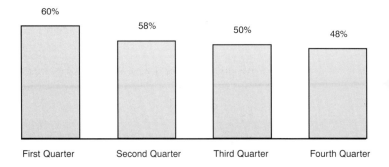

**QUARTERLY ODDS OF PRICE RISE IN JULY**

*Source: Financial Times, Datastream/ICV*

Figure 7.1: The long term profit odds are highest in the first two quarters. Be very cautious in the third quarter. Its 50:50 long term record is a product of past strength and recent weakness. By way of example, prices have risen just three times in the last 12 years.

Spotting bear markets

rose just once (10%), an abnormally low level even for bear markets *(see Table 7.2)*.

Given the danger of exposure to shares in July during bear markets, here is a useful signal that might help investors determine if a bear market is running or not.

Over the long run, two out of three large June price declines, -3.48% or more, were associated with bear markets. The data suggest that if June is hit by a large loss, invest in July with caution until the situation gets clarified.

Remember that these figures do not tell you when the bear market will end. It is conceivable that the following month will see the start of a new bull market. Also, it is possible for a bear market to be in progress without being flagged by this indicator. Still, as a bear market warning signal, a large July price drop should not be ignored.

## JULY PERFORMANCE IN BULL/BEAR MARKETS: 1919–1996

|  | Bull Markets | Bear Markets |
|---|---|---|
| Average per cent price change | 1.77% | -2.25% |
| Rank (of 12) | 5 | 7 |
|  |  |  |
| Per cent of time prices rise | 62% | 27% |
| Rank (of 12) | 11 | 9 |
|  |  |  |
| Average per cent price change in: |  |  |
| Rising years | 4.07% | 2.31% |
| Declining years | -1.92% | -3.93% |

*Source: BZW, Datastream/ICV*

Table 7.2: The odds of a price rise are substandard in bull and bear markets alike. Even worse, the bear market record is getting worse. Since 1960, July rose just once in 10 tries during bear markets.

**Spotting bull markets**

On the up-side, large June price rises are often associated with bull markets. There have been 13 large price rises exceeding +3.38% since 1931. A bull market was running after 12 of those rises.

The lessons from the past send a strong message – prospects for the months ahead are generally good following a strong June advance. You may not profit each and every time but you will do quite well over the long term *(see Figure 7.2)*.

### INCREASE YOUR PROFIT ODDS

Despite July's unexceptional record, investors can profit if they invest selectively and nimbly. Several historical price trends provide good insight into the expected direction of

## ODDS OF BULL/BEAR MARKET TIPPED BY JUNE'S TREND

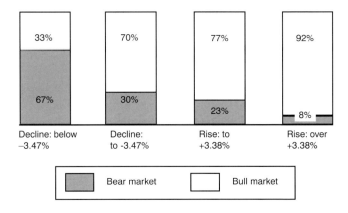

| | | | |
|---|---|---|---|
| 33% | 70% | 77% | 92% |
| 67% | 30% | 23% | 8% |
| Decline: below −3.47% | Decline: to -3.47% | Rise: to +3.38% | Rise: over +3.38% |

Bear market    Bull market

*Source: BZW, Datastream/ICV*

Figure 7.2: A sharp June price rise that exceeds +3.38% is usually associated with a bull market.

prices.

**January and April signal**

Since 1942, an interesting seasonal pattern has developed involving January and April, the opening months of the year's first and second quarter. Moderate rises in both of these months on the FT Ordinary Share Index[1] seems to tip rising prices in July, the start of the third quarter. Here is the evidence.

There have been 12 occasions with a January price rise of + 0.68% to +4.60% and an April rise of +0.70% to +4.54%. July rose in ten of those years.

---

[1]We will provide closing price trends on key indices for the last 12 months at no cost (see page 9).

*Rose (10)*

*Fell (2)*

July's record after a January price rise of + 0.68% to +4.60% and an April rise of +0.70% to +4.54% ( FT Ordinary Share Index since 1942)

**Prior six-months signal**

Here is an up-date of a signal first described in an earlier edition of the *Schwartz Stock Market Handbook* involving the FT-Non-Financial Index and its predecessor index. The signal relies on small or moderate price shifts, in either direction, from 1 January to 30 June. Since 1921, if prices fluctuate in the first half of the year by -2.22% to +9.85%, and in the preceding two months within a range of -1.98% to +4.25%, July prices will probably rise.

This pattern most recently occurred in 1995 and prices rose in July by +4.62%. Since our records began, July has risen in 16 out of the 17 years that were preceded by this pattern.

UPDATE

*Rose (16)*

*Fell (1)*

July's record after a previous six-month price shift of -2.22% to +9.85% and a previous two-month shift of -1.98% to +4.25% (FT-Non-Financial Index since 1921)

**May/June signal No.1**

Another trend is based solely on a moderate price rise in May and June. Since 1927, there have been 13 years when the FTSE All Share Index and its predecessor index rose in May/June by +1.07% to +4.25%. July prices rose in 12 of those years.

*Rose (12)*

*Fell (1)*

July's record after a May/June price rise of +1.07% to +4.25% (FTSE All Share Index since 1927)

**May/June signal No.2**

Since 1961, a price decline of at least -5.10% during May and June often signalled that July prices will also fall. Out of 13 years with a drop of this magnitude, July prices fell 11 times.

*Rose (2)*

*Fell (11)*

July's record after a drop of -5.10% or more during May and June (FT-Non-Financial Index since 1961)

**Prior five-months signal**

Be warned that both exceptions to the rule were big ones, rises of almost 6% in 1972 and 1994.

During bull markets, a rise on the FTSE All Share Index or its predecessor index in February to June in the range of +3.30% to +7.81% is usually followed by a July rise. Since 1923, there have been 10 bull market occasions with a price rise in the five month run-up to July within the target range. The stock market rose in July each time.

*Rose (10)*

*Fell (0)*

July's record after a February to June rise of +3.30% to +7.81% (FTSE All Share Index since 1923)

## FIRST QUARTER OF JULY – JULY 1ST TO 8TH

---

Here comes the most profitable quarter of the month. Prices rise 60% of the time.

There was a weak stretch in the 1960s and 1970s but the profit trend now seems to be back on track. By way of example, prices rose in seven of the last 10 years.

---

The first quarter is the month's most profitable time period. Prices have risen 60% of the time since 1935 and produced an average profit of +0.64% per year, the eighth-best quarter of the year *(see Table 7.3)*.

Good record    During bull markets, the first-quarter record is even better with prices rising 69% of the time, also well above-average *(see Table 7.4)*.

Weak in 1960s    There was an atypical weak stretch in the 1960s and
and 1970s    1970s. In the 1960s, prices rose just three times. The profits of the 1970s were entirely due to an +8.82% increase in the abnormal year of 1975, the largest-ever price rise during this quarter. On July 1st of that year, Denis Healey electrified the markets by warning unions he would introduce wage controls unless they voluntarily reduced their wage demands. Share prices exploded upwards. The record for the rest of the decade was four up and five down, and an average annual loss of -0.28%.

The recent trend contains evidence of a return to profitable trading conditions. Prices have risen in seven of the last 10 years.

1 July    Analysis of daily price trends shows that shares rise 65% of the time on 1 July, the second-best trading day of the entire month. This continues the run of profitable trading conditions encountered on the final three trading days of June. Shares are especially likely to rise when 1 July lands on Monday. Since 1935, the Monday record is seven up versus one down *(see Figure 7.3)*.

## PERCENTAGE PRICE CHANGE: JULY 1935–96

|  | July 1–8 | July 9–15 | July 16–23 | July 24–31 |
|---|---|---|---|---|
| Annual average |  |  |  |  |
| 1935–39 | 0.65% | -0.46% | 0.66% | 0.80% |
| 1940–49 | 1.77% | 0.34% | 0.21% | -1.13% |
| 1950–59 | 1.07% | 0.08% | 0.06% | -0.50% |
| 1960–69 | -0.36% | -0.96% | -0.49% | -1.26% |
| 1970–79 | 0.63% | 1.30% | -0.62% | -1.15% |
| 1980–89 | 0.30% | 0.23% | 0.07% | 0.41% |
| 1990–96 | 0.35% | 0.71% | -0.19% | 0.26% |
|  |  |  |  |  |
| Average quarterly price change | 0.64% | 0.20% | -0.09% | -0.49% |
|  |  |  |  |  |
| Per cent of time prices rise | 60% | 58% | 50% | 48% |

*Source: Financial Times, Datastream/ICV*

Table 7.3: The superior first-quarter trend owes much to its performance in 1940–59 when it was much more profitable than the rest of the month. After a patch of stormy weather in the 1960s and 1970s, its record seems to have got back on track. The third quarter also went through a period of weakness in the 1960s and 1970s. Unfortunately, there are no recent signs of improvement as there are in the first quarter.

4 July

Another above-average performer is 4 July which rises 60% of the time over the long run. One possible reason for this good record is that Wall Street is closed for its annual Independence Day holiday and without US leadership, the UK stock market can follow its normal inclination which is to rise nearly two-thirds of the time.

When 4 July lands on Saturday, the American stock market observes its Independence Day holiday on Friday,

## JULY FIRST-QUARTER PERFORMANCE IN
## BULL/BEAR MARKETS: 1935–1996

|  | Total | Bull Markets | Bear Markets |
|---|---|---|---|
| Average price change | 0.64% | 1.06% | -0.23% |
| Rank (of 48) | 8 | 6 | 14 |
| Per cent of time prices rise | 60% | 69% | 40% |
| Rank (of 48) | 16 | 11 | 25 |

*Source: Financial Times, Datastream/ICV*

Table 7.4: Over the long term, the first quarter rose an above-average number of times in bull market years.

3 July. Here too, UK shares perform as expected when not under the influence of Wall Street. Although 3 July generally rises 47% of the time, prices have risen on six of the last nine Fridays.

**8 July**  The quarter ends on 8 July which has a 50:50 chance of profit, over the long run. But the trend changed recently so be cautious on this day. Since 1980, prices have risen just three times out of 12 attempts.

Analysis of price trends by day of week shows that prices rise at a near average rate on Monday, Wednesday and Thursday, and a bit above-average on first-quarter Tuesdays and Fridays *(see Figure 7.4)*.

### INCREASE YOUR PROFIT ODDS

Here are several ways to improve the odds of a profitable first quarter investment. The first two involve an upturn in June's second half.

**June second-half signal No.1**  Since 1936, there have been 14 years when June's second half rose by +0.94% to +3.01% on the FT Ordinary

**PERCENTAGE OF TIME PRICES RISE EACH TRADING DAY IN JULY'S FIRST QUARTER**

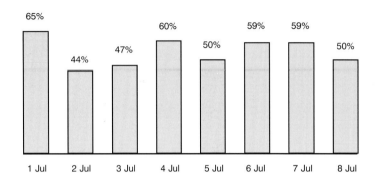

*Source: Financial Times, Datastream/ICV*

Figure 7.3: The strength of 1 July is a continuation of good trading conditions on the final three days of June. Although 3 July is a weak trading day, prices often rise when it lands on a Friday.

Share Index. First quarter prices rose in 12 of those years.

*Rose (12)*

*Fell (2)*

First-quarter record after a rise of +0.94% to +3.01% in June's second half (FT Ordinary Share Index since 1936)

| June second-half signal No.2 | A variation on the second-half theme is based on the direction of prices in June's third and fourth quarters. There is some duplication with the previous signal but it sometimes flashes independently of the Second-Half signal. |

## PERCENTAGE OF TIME PRICES RISE EACH DAY OF WEEK IN JULY'S FIRST QUARTER

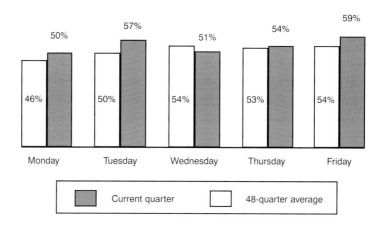

Source: *Financial Times, Datastream/ICV*

Figure 7.4: The week's best days, Tuesday and Friday, rise at an above-average rate compared to other quarters.

Since 1936, price increases in both quarters have frequently been associated with a further increase during July's first quarter. Out of 11 years in which prices rose by at least +0.09% in the third quarter and at least +0.27% in the fourth quarter, first-quarter prices rose 10 times (91%).

*Rose (10)*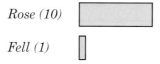

*Fell (1)*  ▯

First-quarter record after a rise of at least +0.09% in June's third quarter and at least +0.27% in June's fourth quarter (FT Ordinary Share Index since 1936)

June fourth-
quarter signal
No.1

Here is a newly-discovered trend based upon the FTSE
All Share Index. Since 1969, there have been nine occasions when prices fell by -0.80% or more during June's
fourth quarter. Prices rose in eight of those years.

*Rose (8)*

*Fell (1)*

First-quarter record after a decline of at least -0.80% in June's
fourth quarter (FTSE All Share Index since 1969)

June fourth-
quarter signal
No.2

A comparable trend runs on the FT-Non-Financial Index.
Since 1975, shares have fallen by -0.27% or more in 12
different years during the fourth quarter of June. The
first quarter rose in 11 of those years.

*Rose (11)*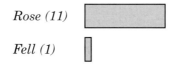

*Fell (1)*

First-quarter record after a decline of at least -0.27% in June's
fourth quarter (FT-Non-Financial Index since 1975)

240

## SECOND QUARTER OF JULY – JULY 8TH TO 15TH

---

Shares rise in most second quarters, with the odds of an increase well above-average in bear market years.

Thursdays are the best day of the week, bull or bear market. Prices rise 61% of the time, the fifth-best Thursday record of all 48 quarters.

---

**Mostly profitable**

Over the long run, the second quarter rises 58% of the time and typically produces a small annual profit, about average compared to other quarters.

The recent record remains unchanged. Since 1985, prices have risen six out of 12 times. Most losses were quite small. As a result, the quarter produced an average annual profit of +0.77% *(see Table 7.5)*.

**Bull and bear markets**

Prices rise 56% of the time in bull market years, also about average compared to other quarters. Oddly, prices rise even more often in bear market years. Since our records began in 1935, the second quarter has risen 62% of the time in bear market years, the fifth-best quarter of the year. Bear market strength continues right up to the present. Prices rose during this quarter in six of the last seven bear market years *(see Table 7.6)*.

**13 and 15 July**

The odds of a profit on any individual day are typically higher than 50:50 throughout the quarter. The likelihood of a rise is best at the end of the quarter, reaching its high point on 13 July which rises 64% of the time and 15 July which rises 66% of the time, the month's best day. Both are long-running trends that show no sign of weakening. Since 1980, prices have risen on each day nine times versus just three falls *(see Figure 7.5)*.

**14 July**

Sandwiched between these two profitable days is 14 July which rises just 45% of the time. The poor profit trend on this day is most apparent on Mondays which has risen just once out of eight tries since 1935 *(see Table 7.7)*.

**12 July**

A second poor day is 12 July which also rises 45% of

## PERCENTAGE PRICE CHANGE: JULY 1985–96

|  | July 1–8 | July 9–15 | July 16–23 | July 24–31 |
|---|---|---|---|---|
| 1985 | 1.72% | -1.10% | -0.66% | 1.90% |
| 1986 | -2.53% | -0.53% | -1.39% | -1.03% |
| 1987 | 3.30% | 3.05% | -3.20% | 1.18% |
| 1988 | 1.08% | -0.50% | -0.68% | 0.33% |
| 1989 | 1.88% | 3.34% | 0.57% | 0.58% |
| 1990 | -1.47% | 1.28% | -0.81% | -1.07% |
| 1991 | 1.73% | 2.13% | 2.30% | 0.15% |
| 1992 | -2.24% | 0.17% | -3.63% | -0.43% |
| 1993 | -1.46% | -0.38% | -0.26% | 3.31% |
| 1994 | 1.29% | 3.39% | 1.50% | -0.63% |
| 1995 | 4.13% | -0.45% | -0.25% | 1.44% |
| 1996 | 0.46% | -1.18% | -0.18% | -0.94% |
| Average quarterly price change | 0.66% | 0.77% | -0.56% | 0.40% |
| Number of years in which prices |  |  |  |  |
| Rose | 8 | 6 | 3 | 7 |
| Fell | 4 | 6 | 9 | 5 |

*Source: Datastream/ICV*

Table 7.5: Most quarters (including the second quarter) have risen at least half the time in recent years. The third quarter continues to be a notable exception. Prices have risen just three times in the last 12 years.

the time. There are no signs of improvement in recent years. Since 1984, trading conditions on the 12th have been poor – two up and seven down. We don't suggest that prices will decline each and every July 12 but the

## JULY SECOND-QUARTER PERFORMANCE IN BULL/BEAR MARKETS: 1935–1996

|  | Total | Bull Markets | Bear Markets |
|---|---|---|---|
| Average price change | 0.20% | 0.39% | -0.16% |
| Rank (of 48) | 20 | 28 | 12 |
| Per cent of time prices rise | 58% | 56% | 62% |
| Rank (of 48) | 18 | 29 | 5 |

*Source: Financial Times, Datastream/ICV*

Table 7.6: The second quarter is a strong performer in bear market years. Its long-term strength continues right up to the present with price rises in six of the last seven bear markets. The bull market record is about average.

**Good Thursday record**

recent weakness is an important point to consider for anyone buying or selling around this time in the month.

Analysis of price trends by day of week reveals that the best odds of a price rise occur late in the week. Thursday's record is especially strong, rising 61% of the time, the year's fifth-best Thursday of all 48 quarters *(see Figure 7.6)*. Monday and Tuesday are less profitable. A good example of this tendency toward late-week strength is seen in the price trend for 9 July which rises just over half the time. As shown in Table 7.8, the odds of a price rise on Monday or Tuesday are just 18%.

### INCREASE YOUR PROFIT ODDS

**Prior three-quarters signal No.1**

The stock market sends some useful signals to help second-quarter investors improve their profit record. A good starting point is to monitor the price trend on the FT Ordinary Share Index in the last half of June and the

**PERCENTAGE OF TIME PRICES RISE EACH TRADING DAY IN JULY'S SECOND QUARTER**

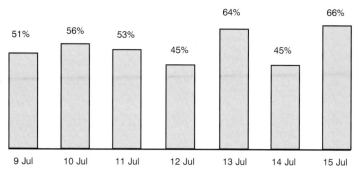

*Source: Financial Times, Datastream/ICV*

Figure 7.5: The chance of a price rise is best on 15 July, the most profitable day of the entire month.

first quarter of July.

There have been eight occasions since 1965 when the price of the average share fell in June's second half (by any amount) and July's first quarter (by at least -0.52%). Second-quarter prices rose each time.

*Rose (8)*

*Fell (0)*

Second-quarter record after a fall in June's second half and in July's first quarter by at least -0.52% (FT Ordinary Share Index since 1965)

Prior three-quarters signal No.2

There have been 11 other occasions when the FT Ordinary Share Index rose in June's second half by +1.38% to +5.35%, and shifted in July's first quarter

**PERCENTAGE OF TIME PRICES RISE ON 14 JULY:
1935–1996**

|  |  | Prices rise |
|---|---|---|
| Total |  | 45% |
|  |  |  |
| Monday |  | 13% |
| Rest of week |  | 53% |

*Source: Financial Times, Datastream/ICV*

Table 7.7: It is hard to make money when 14 July lands on a Monday. Prices have risen just once in eight attempts since our records began in 1935.

within a range of -2.76% to +5.55%. Second-quarter prices rose in 10 of those years. The average increase during this period was +1.80%.

*Rose (10)*

*Fell (1)*

Second-quarter record after a rise in June's second half by +1.38% to +5.35%, and a shift in July's first quarter of -2.76% to +5.55% (FT Ordinary Share Index since 1935)

**Prior three-quarters signal No.3**

Here is a newly-discovered trend derived from the FTSE All Share Index. History shows that a decline in the prior three quarters by -2.05% or more is often associated with a price rise in the second quarter. Since 1969, there have been 10 declines of sufficient size. The second quarter rose in nine of those years. In the remaining 17 years of this period, prices rose seven times and fell 10 times, a 41% success rate.

## PERCENTAGE OF TIME PRICES RISE EACH DAY OF WEEK IN JULY'S SECOND QUARTER

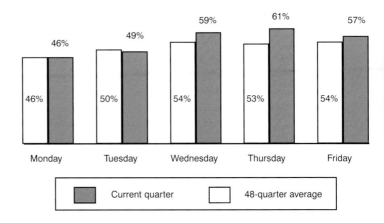

*Source: Financial Times, Datastream/ICV*

Figure 7.6: Shares tend to rise more often late in the week, especially on Thursday, the fifth-best of all 48 quarters.

Second-quarter record after a decline in the prior three quarters of at least -2.05% (FTSE All Share Index since 1969)

**PERCENTAGE OF TIME PRICES RISE ON 9 JULY:**
**1935–1996**

|  | Prices rise |
|---|---|
| Total | 51% |
| Monday and Tuesday | 18% |
| Rest of week | 73% |

*Source: Financial Times, Datastream/ICV*

Table 7.8: The chance of profiting on 9 July is quite poor on Monday and Tuesday.

## THIRD QUARTER OF JULY - JULY 16TH TO 23RD

Third-quarter profitability has been weak in recent decades. The poor trend continues right to the present. Prices fell in five or the last seven years.

Be cautious on 18 July. Its poor long-term record has continued to deteriorate in recent years.

**Recent trend poor**

Over the long run, prices rise exactly half the time in the third quarter. Unfortunately, this statistic hides the fact that third-quarter profitability has been poor in recent years. Prices fell in the typical year in the 1960s and 1970s. Even during the 1980s bull market decade, prices rose just four times and produced the weakest profit record of all four July quarters. So far in the 1990s, prices rose in two out of seven tries.

**Bull and bear markets**

Prices rise in bear markets 43% of the time, about average compared to other quarters. The likelihood of a

247

**JULY THIRD-QUARTER PERFORMANCE IN
BULL/BEAR MARKETS: 1935–1996**

|  | Total | Bull Markets | Bear Markets |
|---|---|---|---|
| Average price change | -0.09% | 0.10% | -0.42% |
| Rank (of 48) | 32 | 39 | 19 |
| Per cent of time prices rise | 50% | 54% | 43% |
| Rank (of 48) | 29 | 34 | 21 |

*Source: Financial Times, Datastream/ICV*

Table 7.9: Prices rise just over half the time in bull markets, a little below average compared to other quarters.

price rise is unimpressive in bull market years. Prices rise 54% of the time, a little below average compared with other quarters of the year *(see Table 7.9)*.

**Monday weakness**

The tendency toward Monday weakness that is often observed throughout the year intensifies in the third quarter. Monday prices rise just 41% of the time. The Monday trend weakens even further in the fourth quarter, providing investors with a relatively lengthy stretch of substandard Monday trading conditions *(see Figure 7.7)*.

**15–17 July**

A notable exception to Monday's weakness occurs on 15–17 July. Over the years, these three days have landed on Monday 26 times. Prices have risen 21 times, an 81% success rate. No one can explain why this is so.

**19 July**

Another day worthy of note is 19 July which rises 45% of the time. Most of its strength occurs on Tuesday and Wednesday which rise 67% of the time. The odds of a price rise on other days of the week are much lower *(see Table 7.10)*.

**18 July**

The weakest day of the quarter is 18 July which rises

## PERCENTAGE OF TIME PRICES RISE EACH DAY OF WEEK IN JULY'S THIRD QUARTER

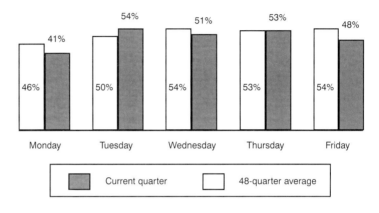

Source: Financial Times, Datastream/ICV

Figure 7.7: Once again, the weakest weekday in the quarter is Monday. Prices rise in four out of 10 years. The trend strikes from 18 July onwards. No one knows why but 15–17 July are not affected by the Monday trend as often as the rest of the quarter.

just 42% of the time, the 29th-ranked day of the quarter. The recent trend has worsened. Since 1986, prices have fallen in six out of seven years *(see Figure 7.8)*.

### INCREASE YOUR PROFIT ODDS

Second-quarter signal No.1

Despite the generally weak conditions, history provides several clues to help investors to spot short-term trading opportunities.

We start with the FTSE All Share Index which does a good job of spotting third-quarter declines. History shows that second-quarter declines of -0.38% or more are usually

249

**PERCENTAGE OF TIME PRICES RISE ON 19 JULY:
1935–1996**

|  | Prices rise |
|---|---|
| Total | 45% |
| Tuesday and Wednesday | 67% |
| Rest of week | 31% |

*Source: Financial Times, Datastream/ICV*

Table 7.10:  Prices rise two out of three times when 19 July
lands on Tuesday or Wednesday but only one out of three times
in the rest of the week.

associated with third-quarter declines. Out of 10 occasions with a decline of sufficient size, prices fell in nine of
those years.

NEW

*Rose (1)*

*Fell (9)*

Third-quarter record after a second quarter drop of -0.38% or
more (FTSE All Share Index since 1969)

First-half signal
No.1

The price trend in the prior two quarters also does a good
job of tipping third-quarter declines. There is some duplication with the previous trend but this one also spots up-
coming declines on its own. Since 1969, there have been
14 occasions when the FTSE All Share Index shifted
within a range of +0.59% to -4.36% during the prior two
quarters. Third-quarter shares fell in 13 of those years.
In the remaining 14 years untouched by this trend, the
third-quarter record was 10 up versus just four down.

## PERCENTAGE OF TIME PRICES RISE EACH TRADING DAY IN JULY'S THIRD QUARTER

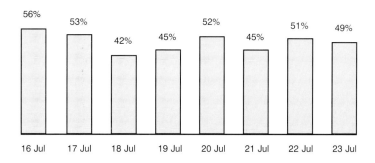

*Source: Financial Times, Datastream/ICV*

Figure 7.8: The stock market rises around half the time on most trading days of the third quarter. 18 July is an exception. It is the worst day in the quarter. Although the long-term trend is poor, the recent record even worse – one rise in the last seven attempts.

NEW

*Rose (1)*

*Fell (13)*

Third-quarter record after a price shift in the prior two quarters of +0.59% to -4.36% (FTSE All Share Index since 1969)

First-half signal No.2

On the up-side, third-quarter price increases on the FT Ordinary Share Index are often tipped off by a moderate price rise in the first half of July. Since 1935, prices rose in the first half of the month by +1.07% to +3.06% on 13 different occasions. Third-quarter prices rose in 11 of those years.

251

IMPROVEMENT

*Rose (11)*

*Fell (2)*

Third-quarter record after a rise in the two prior quarters of +1.07% to +3.06% (FT Ordinary Share Index since 1935)

Second-quarter signal No.2

Here is a second trend involving the FT Ordinary Share Index. History shows that, if second-quarter prices shift slightly, within a range of -0.45% to +0.44%, it is a good sign that shares will rise in the third quarter. Out of 12 years with a second-quarter shift within this range, third-quarter prices rose 10 times.

*Rose (10)*

*Fell (2)*

Third-quarter record after a shift in the second quarter of -0.45% to +0.44% (FT Ordinary Share Index since 1935)

Prior three-quarters signal

Another FT Ordinary Share Index signal to look for is the trend over the previous three quarters – the last quarter in June and the first two in July. If shares steadily move in the same direction in all three periods, they are likely to move in the opposite direction in the third quarter.

● Shares fell in three consecutive quarters on seven occasions since 1936. Third-quarter prices rose all seven times. The last time this signal flashed was in 1993. After a drop of over 2% in the three preceding quarters, prices rose in the third quarter.

● On six other occasions, prices rose in each of the three

preceding periods, with a second-quarter rise of at least +0.94%. Third-quarter prices fell each time.

What of the remaining years not preceded by three consecutive rises or declines? Here again, the market sends a pretty clear signal.

Since 1969, in years not touched by the three-prior-up/three-prior-down rule, first-half prices fell ten times. Each of the ten falls was immediately followed by a decline in the third quarter. The average loss was well over 2%. This signal last flashed in 1996 and third-quarter prices fell right on cue.

*Rose (0)*

UPDATE

*Fell (10)*

Third-quarter record after a drop in the first half in years unaffected by the three-prior-up/three-prior-down rule (FT Ordinary Share Index since 1969)

# FOURTH QUARTER OF JULY – JULY 24TH TO 31ST

---

Here comes another disappointing quarter. The record is especially poor in bear markets when prices rise less than one year in four.

Be cautious on fourth-quarter Mondays which rise just one-third of the time, one of the worst Monday records of the year.

---

**Poor recent trend**

The fourth quarter of July offers little profit potential. In the long run, investors have consistently lost money with a fourth-quarter investment. The only full decade on record in which profits were made was during the bull market 1980s. The trend for the 1990s has reverted to form with four out of seven declines.

Between 1935 and 1996, the fourth quarter of July rose 48% of the time and generated an average loss of -0.49%, the third-worst quarterly performance of the entire year.

**Bull and bear markets**

History shows that the stock market rises 63% of the time during bull markets, about average compared to other quarters. But the bear market record is poor. Prices rise less than one out of four times, the second-worst bear market quarter of the year *(see Table 7.11)*.

**Monday weakness**

Analysis of price trends by day of week shows, once again, a pattern of weakness on Monday. Fourth-quarter Mondays rise just 34% of the time, the 46th-ranked Monday of all 48 quarters. The only weekday of this quarter that does well is Wednesday which rises 59% of the time, above average compared with the Wednesday record in the other 47 quarters. *(see Figure 7.9)*.

**25, 27 and 29 July**

The two worst trading days of the fourth quarter are the 25th which rises just 40% of the time, the second-worst day of the month, and the 27th which rises 36% of the time, the worst day of the month. For both days, the recent trend has brought more of the same with price drops in most years since 1980. On the bright side,

## JULY FOURTH-QUARTER PERFORMANCE IN BULL/BEAR MARKETS: 1935–1996

|  | Total | Bull Markets | Bear Markets |
|---|---|---|---|
| Average price change | -0.49% | 0.25% | -1.83% |
| Rank (of 48) | 46 | 35 | 48 |
| Per cent of time prices rise | 48% | 63% | 23% |
| Rank (of 48) | 34 | 21 | 47 |

*Source: Financial Times, Datastream/ICV*

Table 7.11: The chance of a price rise in bull markets is near average. But prices rise less than one quarter of the time in bear markets, the second-worst quarter of the year.

another formerly mediocre performer, 29 July, has been especially good to investors since 1984 with a record of seven up and one down *(see Figure 7.10).*

### INCREASE YOUR PROFIT ODDS

Third-quarter signal No.1

During bull markets, a small shift in the prior quarter, no more than -0.68% on the down-side and +2.30% on the up-side, is often associated with fourth-quarter rises. Since 1969, the FTSE All Share Index has shifted within this range 12 times. Shares rose in the fourth quarter in 10 of those years.

*Rose (10)*

*Fell (2)*

Fourth-quarter record during bull markets after a shift in the prior quarter of -0.68% to +2.30% (FTSE All Share Index since 1969)

**PERCENTAGE OF TIME PRICES RISE EACH DAY OF WEEK IN JULY'S FOURTH QUARTER**

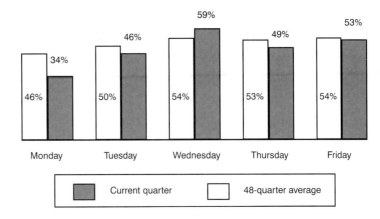

Source: Financial Times, Datastream/ICV

Figure 7.9: Prices often fall on fourth-quarter Mondays. It offers investors one of the worst Monday records of the year.

Third-quarter signal No.2

As noted earlier, the fourth-quarter bear market record is quite poor. Here is a useful trend that has run since 1949 on the FT-Non-Financial Index and its predecessor index. During this period, there have been 14 bear market years when prices rose in the previous quarter or fell no more than -3.52%. Fourth-quarter prices fell each time.

Fourth-quarter record during bear markets after a rise in the prior quarter or a decline of no more than -3.52% (FT-Non-Financial Index since 1949)

**PERCENTAGE OF TIME PRICES RISE EACH TRADING DAY IN JULY'S FOURTH QUARTER**

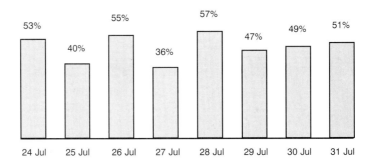

*Source: Financial Times, Datastream/ICV*

Figure 7.10: 25 and 27 July are the two worst days of the month. On the good side, 29 July has been quite strong since 1984, with a record of seven up and one down.

**Prior three-quarters signal**

In bull and bear markets alike, here is a relationship that has been in effect since 1938 on the FT Ordinary Share Index. If shares shift slightly in the first three quarters of July, no more than +0.28% on the up-side and no more than -1.49% on the down-side, they are likely to fall in the last quarter of July. Out of 14 years with this pattern, fourth-quarter prices fell 12 times.

We last saw this trend in operation in 1996 when a small decline in the first three quarters of July was followed by a further decline in the fourth quarter.

UPDATE

*Rose (2)*

*Fell (12)*

Fourth-quarter record after a shift in the first three quarters of -1.49% to +0.28% (FT Ordinary Share Index since 1938)

257

## LOOKING AHEAD

Falling prices
by 31
December

Since 1921, there have been 13 occasions when the stock market slipped in June and July by -1.12% to -4.64% on the FTSE All Share Index or its predecessor index. Shares continued to fall in the next five months in 11 of those years.

*Rose (2)*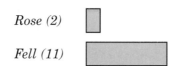

*Fell (11)*

Trend to 31 December after a June/July price drop of -1.12% to -4.64% (FTSE All Share Index since 1921)

Rising prices by
next 31 January

On the FT-Non-Financial Index and its predecessor index, a small shift during July, no more than -1.49% on the down-side and no more than +1.06% on the up-side, is a good sign that prices will rise six months ahead.

Since 1924, there have been 14 years with a small July price shift within the defined range. By the end of January of the following year, prices rose each time.

*Rose (14)*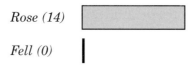

*Fell (0)* |

Trend to 31 January (next year) after a July price shift of -1.49% to +1.06% (FT-Non-Financial Index since 1924)

If the July signal does flash, don't be too quick to sell before the end of next January. In 13 of the 14 years when the signal flashed, prices reached their high point in January. The sole exception, back in 1925, saw a December price peak.

Buried in this statistic is another interesting price

258

signal to help you to maximise next year's January profits. In a round-about way, the data are telling us that January prices rose 13 out of 14 times following a July shift of -1.49% to +1.06%.

**Rising prices by 30 September**

On the FT Ordinary Share Index, a new trend has developed in recent years. The data suggest that a small rally in May to July is often followed by further rises by September.

Since 1980, there have been 15 occasions with a May to July price rise of +0.79% to +6.60%. The stock market continued to rise by 30 September in 13 of those years. Both exceptions were losses of around 1%.

*Rose (13)*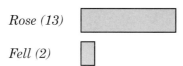

*Fell (2)*

Trend to 30 September after a May–July price rise of +0.79% to +6.60% (FT Ordinary Share Index since 1980)

# CHAPTER 8 – AUGUST

Investors long conditioned to 'Sell in May and go away. Don't come back to St. Ledger's Day' will be surprised to learn that August is a fine month in which to hold shares.

It is the third-best month of the year. Prices rise in two out of three years. In bull markets, August rises 86% of the time, the year's best bull market month.

The only problem with an August investment is that when things go wrong, they go wrong in a very big way. Since 1973, there have been seven occasions when the stock market fell in August. The smallest decline was over 3%. Most were much bigger.

As profitable as ever

When we first called attention to good trading conditions in August, many investors were surprised. Nothing has changed in recent years. The last four years are a good example. The stock market rose each time. Three of the rises were in excess of 5%. The ditty 'Shares will climb during August holiday time' says it all. Summer slumps often dramatically end with the arrival of August, just as many investors are departing to sunnier climes.

Third-best

Between 1919 and 1996, August rose 68% of the time. The average price rise was +1.24%, equal to 50 points on an FTSE 100 in the area of 4000. Historically, August is the third-best month in which to invest in shares. A hypothetical investor who invested in August only, from 1919 to 1996, would have run up his £1,000 to £2,344.

The last losing decade for the August investor was the 1940s when prices dropped at an average annual rate of -0.32%. But under the surface, things looked pretty good even then. Prices rose in seven of the decade's 10 years. A -17.04% drop in 1947, in response to the sudden suspension of sterling's convertibility, caused all of that decade's losses. It was the worst-ever month for August investors and the fourth-worst in history.

Each quarter is profitable

Since then, the month has been consistently profitable. In the 1980s, prices rose in eight out of 10 years, with an average price rise of +2.35% per month, the decade's third-best performer *(see Table 8.1)*. History shows that each quarter of the month rises in most years, especially the first quarter which has a superb long-term record. First-quarter prices have risen 68% of the time, the year's fourth-best quarter, at an average rate of +0.99%, the year's second-best record on this dimension *(see Figure 8.1)*.

There is only one problem with an August investment. When things go wrong, they go wrong in a big way. Since 1973, shares have fallen just seven times. The smallest decline of the group was -3.46% which is equivalent to 138 points on an FTSE 100 in the area of 4000. Most

## AUGUST PRICE RISES AND DECLINES: 1919–1996

|  | Average August price change | Up | Down/ No change |
|---|---|---|---|
| 1920–29 | 1.59% | 6 | 4 |
| 1930–39 | -1.07% | 4 | 6 |
| 1940–49 | -0.32% | 7 | 3 |
| 1950–59 | 3.12% | 8 | 2 |
| 1960–69 | 1.86% | 8 | 2 |
| 1970–79 | 1.32% | 6 | 4 |
| 1980–89 | 2.35% | 8 | 2 |
| 1990–96 | 1.10% | 5 | 2 |
| Average August change: 1919–96 | 1.24% | 68% | 32% |
| Rank (of 12) | 3 | 3 | |

*Source: BZW, Datastream/ICV*

Table 8.1: August is the year's third-best month. The last losing decade for the August investor was back in the 1940s. Since then, it has been a very profitable time period for investors.

Bull and bear markets

were much bigger.

History teaches that August's strength is primarily a bull market phenomenon. During bull markets, the stock market rises 86% of the time, tied with January as the best bull market month of the year. But during bear markets, August often disappoints investors. Prices fall by -3.05% on average, quite surprising for such a good month. The bear market problem is two-fold. Prices rise less than average in up years, and fall more than average in down years *(see Table 8.2)*.

Given the drastically different profit odds in bull versus bear markets, it is important to know if we are in a bull or

263

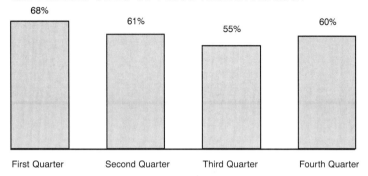

## QUARTERLY ODDS OF PRICE RISE IN AUGUST

68%    61%    55%    60%

First Quarter    Second Quarter    Third Quarter    Fourth Quarter

*Source: Financial Times, Datastream/ICV*

Figure 8.1: The likelihood of a price rise is high in each quarter of the month. The best segment is the first one which rises 68% of the time, one of the best quarterly records of the entire year. But even the weakest quarter of the month, the third quarter, rises more than half of the time.

bear market. Unfortunately, it is not always clear in the run-up to August. But occasionally, July's price trend provides a useful clue to help to answer this question.

**Spotting bear markets**

Over the long run, history reveals that large July price declines, -4.19% or more, are usually associated with bear markets. There are exceptions to every rule of course but the past record suggests that if July is hit by a large loss, there is a 90% likelihood that a bear market is running as August begins.

Keep in mind that these figures do not tell you when the bear market will end. The following month could see the start of a new bull market. Still, as a bear market warning signal, a large July price drop should not be ignored.

**Spotting bull markets**

On the up-side, price rises in excess of +1.89% are virtually always associated with a bull market advance.

## AUGUST PERFORMANCE IN BULL/BEAR MARKETS: 1919–1996

|  | Bull Markets | Bear Markets |
|---|---|---|
| Average per cent price change | 3.50% | -3.05% |
| Rank (of 12) | 2 | 11 |
|  |  |  |
| Per cent of time prices rise | 86% | 33% |
| Rank (of 12) | 1 | 8 |
|  |  |  |
| Average per cent price change in: |  |  |
| Rising years | 4.28% | 2.72% |
| Declining years | -1.37% | -5.93% |

*Source: BZW, Datastream/ICV*

Table 8.2: Prices rise 86% of the time in bull market years, quite an impressive record. In contrast, August's bear market record is substandard.

There have been 25 price rises of that magnitude since our records began. A bull market was running at the start of August in 22 of those years. A good example of this signal in action occurred in 1994. After an 18% drop in February to June, the stock market rose by more than 5% in July. It proved to be the first month of a new multi-year bull run.

The lessons from the past send a strong message – the likelihood of a bull market in the month ahead is generally good if July prices have risen strongly *(see Figure 8.2)*.

Small window     Unfortunately, the window of opportunity that August provides is small. Even in bull markets, the month that follows, September, is a relatively weak month in which to own shares. So if you are planning to sell, be prepared to act soon.

265

## ODDS OF BULL/BEAR MARKET TIPPED BY JULY'S TREND

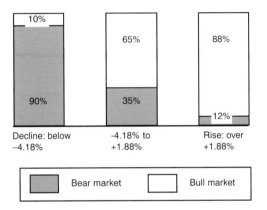

Source: *BZW, Datastream/ICV*

Figure 8.2: History shows that a July price decline of -4.19% or lower is usually associated with a bear market at the start of August. A July rise of +1.89% or more is typically associated with bull markets.

### INCREASE YOUR PROFIT ODDS[1]

Despite the good overall record, investors can improve their performance if they invest selectively. Here are several historic price trends that provide good insight into the expected direction of August's prices.

We start with one that is sure to intrigue *Schwartz Stock Market Handbook* readers, the relationship between Wall Street and the UK stock market.

---

[1]We will provide closing price trends on key indices for the last 12 months at no cost (see page 9).

**Wall Street signal**

History shows that if US prices have shifted during June and July within a range of +0.07% to -6.36%, the odds are especially good that UK prices will rise during August. Since 1928, there have been 23 occasions when Wall Street's Standard & Poors 500 Index shifted within the defined range. In 21 of those years, prices rose on the FTSE All Share Index or its predecessor index in August. This signal last flashed in 1994 when a Wall Street drop of -5.06% in June and July was followed by a UK rise of +5.15% in August.

Be warned however that the two exceptions were whoppers. In 1966, the UK stock market was wrong-footed by a set of July Measures which included increases in interest rates and taxes, the imposition of a £50 overseas travel allowance and a wage/price freeze. August prices fell -9.20%.

In 1990, prices fell -8.37% in the aftermath of Iraq's invasion of Kuwait due to a combination of higher oil prices and the threat of even higher oil prices in the months ahead.

Clearly, it has taken a surprise of major proportions to change the pattern during the last six decades.

| IMPROVEMENT |

*Rose (21)*

*Fell (2)*

August's record after a US June/July price swing of +0.07% to -6.36% (FTSE All Share Index since 1928)

**Prior 12-months signal No.1**

As far as UK-only indicators are concerned, one of the best predictors of the August price trend is the direction of prices in the preceding 12 months.

There have been 15 years in which the FTSE All Share Index or its predecessor index rose between +5.78% to +11.86% from 1 August to 30 July. August rose 13 times.

*Rose (13)*

| UPDATE |

*Fell (1)*

*Unchanged (1)*

August's record after a previous 12-month price rise of +5.78% to +11.86% (FTSE All Share Index since 1928)

This indicator recently flashed three times in a row in 1994, 1995 and 1996 and the stock market rose in August all three times.

Prior 12-months signal No.2

Also look for price increases on the FTSE All Share Index or its predecessor index between +15.10% to +49.91% in the preceding 12 months. There have been 24 years with a price rise of this magnitude. August rose in 22 of those years.

*Rose (22)*

| IMPROVEMENT |

*Fell (2)*

August's record after a previous 12-month price rise of +15.10% to +49.91% (FTSE All Share Index since 1920)

Combining the last two indicators provides an interesting insight. Since 1920, there have been 39 occasions when the FTSE All Share Index or its predecessor index climbed +5.78% to +11.86% or +15.10% to +49.91% in the last 12 months. The stock market fell in August in just three of those years, an 8% 'failure' rate. In the remaining 38 years of this period, August rose just 17 times, less than half the time.

January/March signal

The next indicator is based upon the FT-Non-Financial Index and its predecessor index. History shows that prices usually rise in August following a January price rise by any amount, and a March price rise by +2.92% or more. We cannot explain why August price increases correlate so closely with January and March but here are the facts. There have been 21 occasions since 1920 when stock market prices have shifted within the appropriate range in January and March. August prices rose in 19 of those years. The two exceptions occurred in 1930 and 1961. In both of those years, prices steadily fell in May, June and July as well as August.

UPDATE

*Rose (19)*

*Fell (2)*

August's record after a January price rise (any amount) and March price rise of +2.92% or more (FT-Non-Financial Index since 1920)

**Prior 12-months signal No.3**

Here is a new indicator that is based upon the FT Ordinary Share Index. Since 1936, there have been 14 occasions in which the FT Ordinary Share Index prices rose by +11.15% to +26.51% in the last 12 months. August continued to rise each time.

NEW

*Rose (14)*

*Fell (0)*

August's record after a previous 12-month price rise of +11.15% to +26.51% (FT Ordinary Share Index since 1936)

**June/July signal**

Also since 1936, there have been 19 occasions when the FT Ordinary Share Index rose between +0.38% to +5.95% in the last two months. August continued to rise in 17 of those years.

*Rose (17)*

*Fell (2)*

August's record after a previous two-month price rise of +0.38%
to +5.95% (FT Ordinary Share Index since 1936)

There have been 34 years since 1936 that were
untouched by either of the two preceding signals. The
stock market rose in August in 18 of those years and fell
16 times.

Stock markets don't always rise, even in historically
good months. Here are two useful down-side indicators
for August. Both are based on the FT-Non-Financial
Index and its predecessor index.

Prior five-
months signal

Since 1930, price drops of -3.86% to -8.79% in the five-
month run-up to August have usually been followed by
an August price decline. During this period, there were
10 occasions with price drops within the target range.
August prices fell eight times.

*Rose (2)*

*Fell (8)*

August's record after a previous five-month price drop of -3.86%
to -8.79% (FT-Non-Financial Index since 1930)

Prior 12-months
signal No.4

Since 1919, there have been seven occasions when prices
fell in the preceding twelve months by -18.21% or more.
August prices fell in six of those years. The single exception was in 1940, a time period heavily influenced by
war-related events.

*Rose (1)*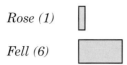

*Fell (6)*

August's record after previous 12-month price drop of -18.21% or more (FT-Non-Financial Index since 1919)

## FIRST QUARTER OF AUGUST – AUGUST 1ST TO 8TH

Here comes the best quarter of the month and fourth-best of the year. Prices rise in seven out of ten years. The record is strong in bull and bear markets alike.

The profit odds are high on virtually every day of the quarter. Unfortunately, 6 August has weakened in recent years. Prices have fallen in seven of the last nine years.

Although August is a good month in which to invest, there are wide differences in profitability during different segments of the month.

Month's best quarter

The best segment is the first quarter. It has risen 68% of the time (fourth-best of the entire year) and produced an average annual profit in every single decade on record. Between 1935 and 1996, the average first-quarter profit was +0.99% per year, the year's second-best *(see Table 8.3)*.

In the last 12 years, first-quarter profitability lagged behind the second quarter. Some analysts wondered if this was the start of a trend change. We think not. Much of the recent damage is due to 1987 when first-quarter prices fell -6.05% and 1990 with a decline of -4.26%. The first quarter out-performed the second quarter in seven of the other 10 years.

### PERCENTAGE PRICE CHANGE: AUGUST 1935–96

| | Aug<br>1–8 | Aug<br>9–15 | Aug<br>16–23 | Aug<br>24–31 |
|---|---|---|---|---|
| Annual average | | | | |
| 1935–39 | 0.62% | 0.28% | -2.55% | 0.37% |
| 1940–49 | 0.99% | 0.05% | -0.11% | 0.29% |
| 1950–59 | 0.74% | 1.02% | 0.14% | 0.57% |
| 1960–69 | 2.13% | 0.84% | 0.22% | 0.00% |
| 1970–79 | 1.29% | -0.11% | 0.21% | -0.15% |
| 1980–89 | 0.43% | 1.35% | 0.55% | 0.03% |
| 1990–96 | 0.34% | 0.26% | -0.11% | 0.59% |
| | | | | |
| Average quarterly<br>price change | 0.99% | 0.56% | -0.06% | 0.22% |
| | | | | |
| Per cent of time<br>prices rise | 68% | 61% | 55% | 60% |

*Source: Financial Times, Datastream/ICV*

Table 8.3: The first quarter rises 68% of the time, the fourth-best quarter of the year. But the other three quarters also rise more than 50% of the time.

**Bull and bear markets**

Our historical review finds that the first quarter usually does well in bull and bear markets alike, rising in three out of four years during bull markets and 50% of the time in bear markets. Both figures are above average *(see Table 8.4)*.

There is one distressing pattern worth noting that affects all August quarters including this one. When prices do fall, the drop is often a large one. Since 1980, there were 25 quarterly drops in August (out of 68 quarters in total). Eleven were in excess of 2%. Unfortunately, we find no forecasting tool which systematically anticipates all or even most of these Big Hits.

Analysis of daily price records over the long run finds

## AUGUST FIRST-QUARTER PERFORMANCE IN BULL/BEAR MARKETS: 1935–1996

|  | Total | Bull Markets | Bear Markets |
|---|---|---|---|
| Average price change | 0.99% | 1.50% | 0.06% |
| Rank (of 48) | 2 | 2 | 10 |
| Per cent of time prices rise | 68% | 78% | 50% |
| Rank (of 48) | 4 | 3 | 17 |

*Source: Financial Times, Datastream/ICV*

Table 8.4: The first quarter is ranked fourth but, during bull markets, the record is even better. Prices rise 78% of the time, the year's third-best bull market record.

**Good daily record**

very profitable trading conditions throughout the quarter. The four best trading days of the entire month land in this quarter. Even the so-called 'weaker days' are disappointing only in a relative sense, rising more than half the time *(see Figure 8.3)*.

**3 August**

An interesting trend runs on 3 August, the second-best day of the month. The odds of a price rise on this day are heavily affected by day of week. Since 1935, prices have risen when 3 August landed on Tuesday or Wednesday in 16 out of 18 years versus a little over half the time when the day lands on other weekdays *(see Table 8.5)*.

**6 August**

The record for 6 August is changing for the worse. Over the long run, it has been a profitable performer, but since 1982, the record has been two rises and seven declines.

Analysis of price trends for the first quarter by day of week shows a familiar pattern (3 August excepted). There is solid strength on most days of the week with Monday lagging behind the other four *(see Figure 8.4)*.

## PERCENTAGE OF TIME PRICES RISE EACH TRADING DAY IN AUGUST'S FIRST QUARTER

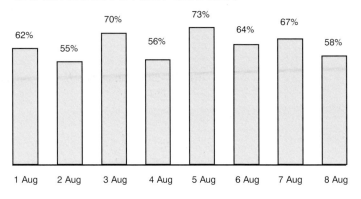

*Source: Financial Times, Datastream/ICV*

Figure 8.3: Prices often rise throughout this quarter. The four best days of the month land in this segment.

### INCREASE YOUR PROFIT ODDS

July second-half signal No.1

Happily, it is possible to pinpoint years with above-average profit prospects. Here is an update on a trend that has been running since 1941. During this period, there have been 29 years when the FT Ordinary Share Index shifted in the second half of July by -0.61% to +5.42%. Prices rose in August's first quarter in 26 of those years.

We find no sign of wear out in the recent past. The signal flashed in 1994 and 1995 and prices rose on cue.

UPDATE

*Rose (26)*

*Fell (3)*

First-quarter record after a price shift of -0.61% to +5.42% in July's second half (FT Ordinary Share Index since 1941)

274

## PERCENTAGE OF TIME PRICES RISE ON 3 AUGUST: 1935–1996

|  | Prices rise |
|---|---|
| Total | 70% |
| Tuesday and Wednesday | 89% |
| Rest of the week | 55% |

Source: Financial Times, Datastream/ICV

Table 8.5: Prices are very likely to rise when 3 August lands on Tuesday or Wednesday.

July fourth-quarter signal No.1

Another trend worth tracking on the FT Ordinary Share Index is the direction of prices in July's fourth quarter. We first called attention to this in an earlier edition of the *Schwartz Stock Market Handbook*. Since our records began in 1935, there have been 28 years when fourth-quarter prices shifted -0.18% to +2.64%. Prices rose in August's first quarter in 25 of those years. In the recent past, this signal correctly anticipated a first-quarter price rise in 1995 and 1996.

UPDATE

*Rose (25)*

*Fell (3)*

First-quarter record after a price shift of -0.18% to +2.64% in July's fourth quarter (FT Ordinary Share Index since 1935)

Obviously, there is some overlap between these two signals. But each tips some first-quarter rises that are overlooked by the other. Both signals have their counterparts

## PERCENTAGE OF TIME PRICES RISE EACH DAY OF WEEK IN AUGUST'S FIRST QUARTER

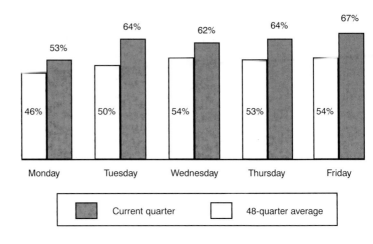

| | Monday | Tuesday | Wednesday | Thursday | Friday |
|---|---|---|---|---|---|
| Current quarter | 53% | 64% | 62% | 64% | 67% |
| 48-quarter average | 46% | 50% | 54% | 53% | 54% |

*Source: Financial Times, Datastream/ICV*

Figure 8.4: Once again, Monday lags behind the rest of the week in profitability. But the chance of a first-quarter price rise during the rest of the week is quite good, especially on a Friday.

**July second-half signal No.2**

on the FTSE All Share Index.

Since 1969, the FTSE All Share Index has risen within a range of +0.43% to +3.08% in the second half of July in 13 different years. Prices rose in the first quarter of August in 11 of those years.

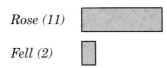

*Rose (11)*

*Fell (2)*

First-quarter record after a price rise of +0.43% to +3.08% in July's second half (FTSE All Share Index since 1969)

**July fourth-quarter signal No.2**

Also since 1969, the FTSE All Share Index has risen within a range of +0.33% to +3.31% in the final quarter of July in 10 different years. Prices rose in the first quarter of August in nine of those years. In the 17 years untouched by this signal, the first-quarter record is just seven rises and 10 declines.

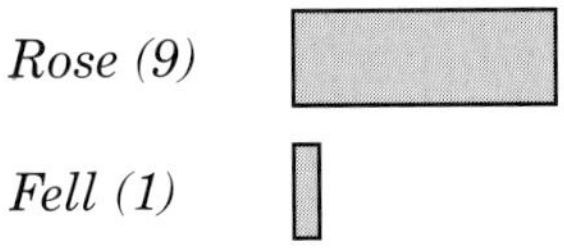
Rose (9)
Fell (1)

First-quarter record after a price rise of +0.33% to +3.31% in July's fourth quarter (FTSE All Share Index since 1969)

**July fourth-quarter signal No.3**

A good down-side indicator is a small decline on the FT Ordinary Share Index in July's fourth quarter. Prices fell by -0.24% to -1.23% on 10 occasions since 1938. First-quarter prices fell still further in nine of those years.

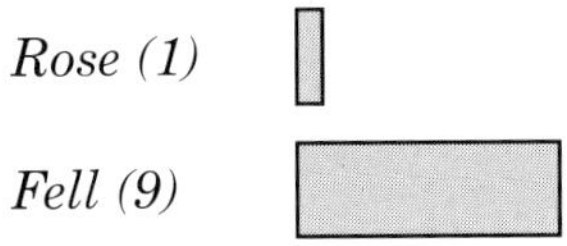
Rose (1)
Fell (9)

First-quarter record after a price fall of -0.24% to -1.23% in July's fourth quarter (FT Ordinary Share Index since 1938)

# SECOND QUARTER OF AUGUST – AUGUST 9TH TO 15TH

Although the historical trend is not quite as strong as in the first quarter, the second quarter has produced a respectable record over the long run, especially in bull market years.

Prices rise at least half the time on every trading day in this quarter. The record on 14 August has strengthened in recent years, rising 10 of the last 12 times.

Second-quarter prices rose 61% of the time between 1935 and 1996, slightly less often than the first quarter. Prices rose +0.56% in the average year, also less than in the first quarter but still highly respectable.

**Strong bull market record**

The second-quarter trend is especially strong in bull market years when it rises 70% of the time and produces an average profit of +1.15%, the year's fourth-best bull market quarter. But in bear markets, this quarter rises slightly less than half of the time, about average compared to other quarters of the year *(see Table 8.6)*.

In most decades, the second quarter has been the second- or third-best quarter of the month. The 1980s were an exception. It became the most profitable quarter of the month by far. A consistent second-quarter investor received an average annual quarterly profit of +1.35% during that decade. But the trend in the 1990s has reverted to form – a solid profit-maker but never the best performer of the month *(see Table 8.7)*.

**Good daily record**

Analysis of day-by-day trends reveals good profit odds throughout the quarter. While the frequency of profit is weaker than in the first quarter, shares rise at least half the time on every trading day of the second quarter *(see Figure 8.5)*.

**14 August**

Once again, the chance of profit is lowest on Monday when prices rise less than 50% of the time *(see Figure 8.6)*. An extreme example of the Monday 'problem' is

## AUGUST SECOND-QUARTER PERFORMANCE IN BULL/BEAR MARKETS: 1935–1996

|  | Total | Bull Markets | Bear Markets |
|---|---|---|---|
| Average price change | 0.56% | 1.15% | -0.52% |
| Rank (of 48) | 13 | 4 | 22 |
| Per cent of time prices rise | 61% | 70% | 45% |
| Rank (of 48) | 13 | 10 | 19 |

*Source: Financial Times, Datastream/ICV*

Table 8.6:  The second quarter is quite profitable in bull market years when it rises 70% of the time, well above average compared to other quarters of the year.

illustrated by the price trend on 14 August which rose 51% of the time over the long-term but just once out of nine attempts on Monday *(see Table 8.8)*.

The recent record for 14 August has improved. Since 1979, prices rose 10 times and fell just twice. In case you are wondering, both recent falls took place when 14 August landed on Monday.

### INCREASE YOUR PROFIT ODDS

Although the overall trend is quite good, the market sends several useful signals that can help second-quarter investors obtain even better returns.

Prior two-quarters signal No.1

Here is a newly emerging signal based on the FTSE All Share Index. History shows that if prices shifted in the last two quarters within a range of -2.90% to +0.94% the odds of a second-quarter price rise are good. Since 1972, prices shifted within this range on nine occasions. The second quarter rose in eight of those years.

## PERCENTAGE PRICE CHANGE: AUGUST 1985–96

|  | August 1–8 | August 9–15 | August 16–23 | August 24–31 |
|---|---|---|---|---|
| 1985 | 2.25% | 1.36% | 1.04% | 1.77% |
| 1986 | -1.89% | 4.37% | 0.49% | 2.87% |
| 1987 | -6.05% | 3.23% | -3.48% | 1.89% |
| 1988 | 1.39% | -2.98% | -0.06% | -3.97% |
| 1989 | 1.82% | -0.93% | 1.89% | 0.14% |
| 1990 | -4.26% | -0.12% | -7.62% | 3.73% |
| 1991 | 0.46% | 0.89% | 0.97% | 0.31% |
| 1992 | -2.09% | 0.05% | 0.31% | -2.34% |
| 1993 | 1.74% | 1.52% | 0.98% | 1.74% |
| 1994 | 2.72% | -0.68% | 0.98% | 2.15% |
| 1995 | 0.37% | -0.51% | 1.84% | -0.72% |
| 1996 | 3.42% | 0.71% | 1.74% | -0.76% |
| | | | | |
| Average quarterly price change | -0.01% | 0.58% | -0.08% | 0.57% |
| | | | | |
| Number of years in which prices | | | | |
| Rose | 8 | 7 | 9 | 8 |
| Fell | 4 | 5 | 3 | 4 |

*Source: Datastream/ICV*

Table 8.7: The recent record for each of August's four quarters is strong. Since 1985, apparent losses in the first and third quarters were both due to a large drop in a single quarter – a fall of just over 6% in the first quarter of 1987 and well over 7% in the third quarter of 1990. Although the overall picture is rosy, there is one distressing aspect to August's fine record. When prices fall, the drop is often a large one. Out of 48 recent quarters, prices fell 16 times. Eight of the declines were larger than 2%.

## PERCENTAGE OF TIME PRICES RISE EACH TRADING DAY IN AUGUST'S SECOND QUARTER

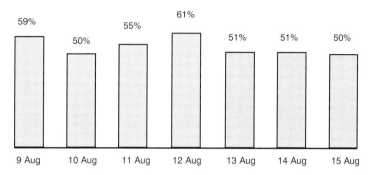

*Source: Financial Times, Datastream/ICV*

Figure 8.5: First-quarter strength often continues into the second quarter. Shares rise at least half of the time on every trading day in this quarter.

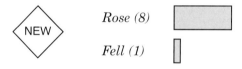

NEW

*Rose (8)*

*Fell (1)*

Second-quarter record after a price shift in two prior quarters of -2.90% to +0.94% (FTSE All Share Index since 1972)

Prior two-quarters signal No.2

Turning to the FT Ordinary Share Index, if July's fourth quarter is weak and August's first quarter strong, second-quarter prices will probably rise. Here is the evidence.

There have been 16 years when the fourth quarter shifted within a range of -7.45% to +0.17% and the first quarter rose by up to +4.29%. Prices rose in the second quarter in 14 of those years. The two losses were near misses. The most recent failure occurred in 1994 when

## PERCENTAGE OF TIME PRICES RISE ON 14 AUGUST: 1935–1996

|  | Prices rise |
|---|---|
| Total | 51% |
|  |  |
| Monday | 11% |
| Rest of week | 62% |

*Source: Financial Times, Datastream/ICV*

Table 8.8: 14 August is frequently a money-loser when it lands on Monday. Since 1979, prices have risen 10 times and fallen just twice on 14 August. Both declines took place on a Monday.

prices declined by just -0.09%.

*Rose (14)*

*Fell (2)*

Second-quarter record after a price shift in July's fourth quarter of -7.45% to +0.17% and rise in August's first quarter of up to +4.29% (FT Ordinary Share Index since 1935)

**Prior three-quarters signal No.1**

Another useful signal is provided by the FT Ordinary Share Index during July's second half and August's first quarter. If shares steadily shift in the same direction through both periods, the second quarter will probably rise.

Since 1949, there have been 13 years when FT Ordinary Share Index prices rose in July's second half and August's first quarter. The price rise continued through August's second quarter in 10 of those years. One of the three exceptions occurred in 1993 when

## PERCENTAGE OF TIME PRICES RISE EACH DAY OF WEEK IN AUGUST'S SECOND QUARTER

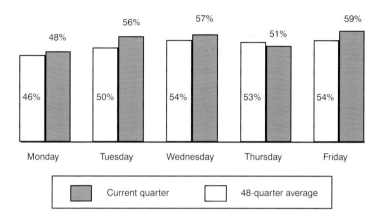

*Source: Financial Times, Datastream/ICV*

Figure 8.6: The profit odds are at their worst on second-quarter Mondays.

second-quarter prices fell by a minuscule -0.01% after a steady price rise in the two preceding periods. Another occurred in 1995 when second-quarter prices fell by -0.02% In other words, even when the signal fails, the odds of getting seriously hurt are quite low.

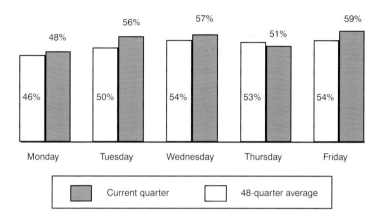

Rose (10)

Fell (3)

UPDATE

Second-quarter record after a price rise in July's second half and August's first quarter (FT Ordinary Share Index since 1949)

There have been 11 additional years since 1957 when

Prior three-quarters signal No.2

prices fell in July's second half and August's first quarter. Prices bounced back with an increase in August's second quarter in nine of those years. And one of the two exceptions to the rule, in 1990, saw a second-quarter drop of just -0.02%.

*Rose (9)*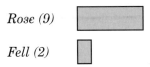

*Fell (2)*

Second-quarter record after a price fall in July's second half and August's first quarter (FT Ordinary Share Index since 1957)

Also since 1957, there have been 17 years when prices did not steadily rise or steadily fall in the second half of July and the first quarter of August. The second-quarter record was seven up and 10 down.

# THIRD QUARTER OF AUGUST – AUGUST 16TH TO 23RD

---

The third quarter is a bull market beauty and a bear market beast. Prices rise three-quarters of the time in bull markets but just one-quarter of the time in bear markets.

Most days rise around half the time over the long run. A pleasing exception is 21 August which rises 60% of the time.

---

If you slavishly accept the message portrayed by the averages, you would conclude that a steady investment every third quarter is a money-losing proposition. Since 1935 when our quarterly data trends first began, the third quarter averaged a -0.06% loss each year.

**Hidden under the surface**

But a closer look at the raw data tells a different story. There were big losses in the last half of the 1930s when share prices fell five years in a row, and in 1990 when the average share dropped -7.62%. In the intervening period, the results weren't all that bad – price rises in most years and average annual profits during the 1950s, '60s, '70s and '80s. Since the 1990 drop, prices rose six times in a row.

**Poor bear market record**

Be warned, however, that the third quarter is strictly a bull market investment opportunity. During bear markets, prices rise just 26% of the time, the fourth-worst bear market quarter of the year *(see Table 8.9)*.

**19 and 21 August**

Analysis of daily price swings shows a tendency for prices to rise about 50% of the time for most days of the quarter with two notable exceptions. The worst day of the month is 19 August when the odds of a price rise are just 41%. At the other extreme, the best performance of the quarter is two days later, on 21 August which rises 60% of the time *(see Figure 8.7)*.

The likelihood of a price rise on each day of the week is lower in the third quarter than the first and second quarter. The best two days of the week are Wednesday

### AUGUST THIRD-QUARTER PERFORMANCE IN BULL/BEAR MARKETS: 1935–1996

|  | Total | Bull Markets | Bear Markets |
|---|---|---|---|
| Average price change | -0.06% | 0.83% | -1.55% |
| Rank (ot 48) | 31 | 13 | 45 |
| Per cent of time prices rise | 55% | 72% | 26% |
| Rank (of 48) | 23 | 7 | 45 |

*Source: Financial Times, Datastream/ICV*

Table 8.9: The third quarter is quite profitable in bull market years. But its bear market record is poor. Prices rise just one out of four times, one of the year's worst quarterly records.

and Friday. But even on these two days, the odds of an increase are below average compared with the other 47 quarters of the year *(see Figure 8.8)*.

**17 and 18 August**

Throughout this book, we have frequently drawn attention to Monday weakness. Here is an interesting change of pace. The odds of a price rise on 17–18 August are about 50:50 over the long run but both days do especially well when they land on Monday. Since 1935, Mondays have risen in 12 out of 17 years on these two days, much better than the 17th and 18th record on the other four days of the week *(see Table 8.10)*.

17 August has a second claim to fame. Since 1980 prices have risen in 10 out of 12 occasions on this date.

### INCREASE YOUR PROFIT ODDS

**Second-quarter signal No.1**

A potentially profit-making statistical relationship emerged in 1967. Since then, there have been 12 years when prices dropped in August's second quarter on the

## PERCENTAGE OF TIME PRICES RISE EACH TRADING DAY IN AUGUST'S THIRD QUARTER

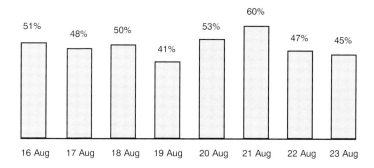

*Source: Financial Times, Datastream/ICV*

Figure 8.7: Prices rise about half the time on most days, with two exceptions. Prices rise 41% of the time on 19 August, the worst day of the month and 60% of the time on 21 August, two days later.

FT Ordinary Share Index. They bounced back with a third-quarter increase in 11 of these years. The average annual increase was +0.73%. And this average was pulled down quite substantially by the sole exception to the rule, the -8.24% decline of 1990 (on the FT Ordinary Share Index).

In the recent past, the Second-Quarter Signal flashed in 1993, 1994 and 1995 and prices rose each time, right on cue.

*Rose (11)*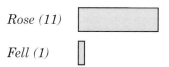

*Fell (1)* |

Third-quarter record after a price drop in August's second quarter (FT Ordinary Share Index since 1967)

**PERCENTAGE OF TIME PRICES RISE EACH DAY OF
WEEK IN AUGUST'S THIRD QUARTER**

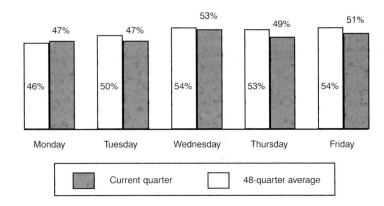

*Source: Financial Times, Datastream/ICV*

Figure 8.8: Prices rise about half the time each week day but the odds of a price rise on each day are considerably lower than in the first and second quarters.

Second-quarter signal No.2

Here is a newly discovered trend based upon the FTSE All Share Index, During bull markets, a small swing in the preceding quarter, no lower than -1.89% and no higher than +1.52%, is often associated with a third-quarter price rise. Since 1969, there have been 13 occasions that fit this profile. Third-quarter prices rose in 12 of those years.

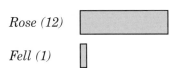

*Rose (12)*

*Fell (1)*

Third-quarter record after a price swing in August's second quarter of -1.89% to +1.52% (FTSE All Share Index since 1969)

## PERCENTAGE OF TIME PRICES RISE ON 17–18 AUGUST: 1935–1996

|  | Prices rise |
| --- | --- |
| Total | 49% |
| Monday | 71% |
| Rest of the week | 44% |

*Source: Financial Times, Datastream/ICV*

Table 8.10: For a change, the Monday record is better than the record for the other four days.

Prior four-quarters signal

On the FT-Non-Financial Index, a price shift in the last four quarters within a range of -1.79% to +5.38% is another good sign for the third quarter. Since 1969, prices have shifted within the target range in 15 different years. Shares rose in the third quarter in 13 of those years.

*Rose (13)*

*Fell (2)*

Third-quarter record after a price shift of -1.79% to +5.38% in the preceding four quarters (FT-Non-Financial Index since 1969)

# FOURTH QUARTER OF AUGUST – AUGUST 24TH TO 31ST

---

The stock market rises in the fourth quarter of August in most years. The record is especially strong in bear markets. Prices rise two-thirds of the time, the third-best bear market quarter of the year.

There is one fly in the ointment. Although no one can explain why, shares often fall on fourth-quarter Tuesdays.

---

**Recent trend is strong**

Prices rise 60% of the time during the fourth quarter of August. The average annual gain is +0.22%. The recent trend remains strong. Between 1985 and 1996, the fourth-quarter record is eight up and four down.

**Bull and bear markets**

During bull markets, the fourth quarter typically turns in an average performance compared to other quarters of the year. But the bear market trend is superb. Prices rise 64% of the time, the third-best quarter of the year in bear markets, and return a small profit in the typical year *(see Table 8.11)*.

**Daily trend looks good**

Analysis of daily price shifts shows a generally strong pattern of profitable days. Even 26 August, one of just two days that rises less than 50% of the time, has experienced a recent trend change. Since 1981, prices have risen eight times out of nine attempts on this day *(see Figure 8.9)*.

**27 August**

27 August remains a notable exception to the positive fourth-quarter trend. Prices rise 41% of the time, tied with one other as the worst day of the month. In an earlier edition of the *Schwartz Stock Market Handbook*, we warned of especially poor trading conditions when 27 August landed on a Tuesday (zero rises out of nine attempts). 27 August landed on Tuesday in 1996 and prices fell on cue. The Tuesday record is now zero rises and 10 declines

**Tuesday**

Incidentally, Tuesday problems in the fourth quarter are not unique to 27 August. The odds of a Tuesday price

## AUGUST FOURTH-QUARTER PERFORMANCE IN BULL/BEAR MARKETS: 1935–1996

|  | Total | Bull Markets | Bear Markets |
|---|---|---|---|
| Average price change | 0.22% | 0.28% | 0.10% |
| Rank (of 48) | 19 | 34 | 8 |
|  |  |  |  |
| Per cent of time prices rise | 60% | 58% | 64% |
| Rank (of 48) | 16 | 25 | 3 |

*Source: Financial Times, Datastream/ICV*

Table 8.11: The bull market record is average but the bear market record is quite strong. Prices rise two-thirds of the time, the year's third-best bear market quarter.

rise during this quarter are just 36%, the worst Tuesday performance of all 48 quarters *(see Figure 8.10)*. In contrast, fourth-quarter Wednesdays rise 63% of the time, the third-best record of all 48 quarters.

**September warning**

If you are contemplating a purchase to take advantage of a good trading environment, be careful about making any long-term investments. The impending arrival of risky September trading conditions means that, in some years, you should be thinking about closing out positions, not opening new ones.

### INCREASE YOUR PROFIT ODDS

If you do decide to make a purchase in the fourth quarter, the best time to do so is if prices have risen steadily or fallen steadily in the preceding periods.

**Prior three-quarters signal No.1**

There have been 12 occasions since 1942 when FT Ordinary Share Index prices rose in the first half of August by up to +3.56% and the third quarter by up to

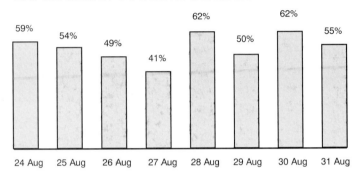

## PERCENTAGE OF TIME PRICES RISE EACH TRADING DAY IN AUGUST'S FOURTH QUARTER

*Source: Financial Times, Datastream/ICV*

Figure 8.9: Prices rise more than half of the time on most days. A notable exception is 27 August which turns in a poor record, especially on Tuesday.

+1.51%. Fourth-quarter prices rose in 10 of them.

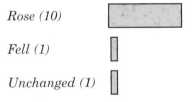

IMPROVEMENT

*Rose (10)*

*Fell (1)*

*Unchanged (1)*

Fourth-quarter record after a price rise in August's first half by up to +3.56% and a rise in the third quarter by up to +1.51% (FT Ordinary Share Index since 1942)

This signal last flashed in 1994 with a first-half rise of +3.55%, just within the range. Fourth-quarter prices followed with a rise of +1.82%.

Likewise, if the FT Ordinary Share Index falls in the

## PERCENTAGE OF TIME PRICES RISE EACH DAY OF WEEK IN AUGUST'S FOURTH QUARTER

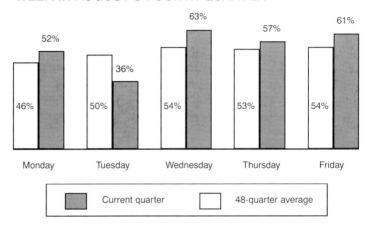

*Source: Financial Times, Datastream/ICV*

Figure 8.10: Tuesday's record is horrid, the worst Tuesday profit trend of all 48 quarters. But shares often bounce back on Wednesday.

**Prior three-quarters signal No.2**

first half and the third quarter, the odds favour a fourth-quarter rise. There have been 10 occasions on record since 1939 where a decline occurred in the first half and third quarter. Fourth-quarter prices rose nine times.

Since 1952, there have been 34 years untouched by either of the two previous indicators. The fourth-quarter record was disappointing: 11 up and 16 down.

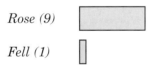

*Rose (9)*

*Fell (1)*

Fourth-quarter record after a price decline in August's first half and third quarter (FT Ordinary Share Index since 1939)

293

## LOOKING AHEAD

Here are three price signals that do a good job of fore-casting where prices are headed in the months ahead.

**Rising prices by 31 December**

If the stock market has risen in the first seven months of the year (to 31 July), and rises still further in August by +4.30% or more, there is a very good chance they will continue to rise by year-end.

There have been 15 years on record with price increases within these parameters. Shares rose still higher 14 times on the FT Non-Financial Index. The sole exception was in 1981 when prices suddenly fell by -16.94% in September in response to a sudden drop on Wall Street. But even here, the loss on 31 December was under 5%, a recovery of 12% during the last three months of the year.

*Rose (14)*

*Fell (1)*

Trend to 31 December after a January-to-July price rise and an August price rise of +4.30% or more (FT-Non-Financial Index since 1932)

**Rising prices by next 31 January**

An August price rise of +3.57% to +10.44% is a clear signal that prices will rise even higher in the next five months, that is, to the end of January.

Out of 26 times with a price shift within this range on the FT Non-Financial Index, shares rose in the next five months 24 times.

UPDATE

*Rose (24)*

*Fell (2)*

Trend to 31 January (next year) after an August price rise of +3.57% to +10.44% (FT-Non-Financial Index since 1925)

294

Rising prices by
30 November

Also on the FT-Non-Financial Index, a moderate decline in April to August is usually associated with further declines in the next three months. Since 1921, there have been 11 occasions with a price drop of -4.46% to -12.49% from 1 April to 31 August. Prices fell in the next three months nine times.

*Rose (2)*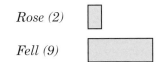

*Fell (9)*

Trend to 30 November after a price decline in the last five months of -4.46% to -12.49% (FT-Non-Financial Index since 1921)

# CHAPTER 9 – SEPTEMBER

The stock market rises about half of the time in September. Unfortunately, periodic Big Hits, price declines of 5% or more, drop the long-term September average into the red. A £1,000 investment in 1919, placed in shares every September and in cash for the rest of each year, would now have shrunk to just over £800.

Sad to say, no crystal ball is needed to forecast that September's record will probably worsen in future years. The source of the problem is Wall Street. September is the worst month of the year on Wall Street and the US stock market is exerting an increasingly larger influence on UK shares with each passing year.

But not all the news is bleak. The stock market frequently rises in the first quarter of September. When troubles do occur, they often cluster in the second to fourth segments of the month.

Tenth-ranked

Investors have not done well by holding shares during September in the long run. Although prices rise just over half of the time, occasional Big Hits, price drops of 5% or more, periodically wipe out years' worth of profits. As a result, September is ranked a lowly tenth on the monthly profit league tables. Only May and June are worse. Between 1919 and 1996, September prices fell at a yearly average of -0.13%, equal to five points on a 4000 FTSE 100 (see Table 9.1).

Bull markets

History cautions investors to expect a relatively weak performance in bull markets as well as bear markets. During bull markets, prices rise 62% of the time, eleventh-ranked of all 12 months on this dimension. The average price rise is +1.06% which is tenth-ranked. Even during rising months that occur within bull markets, the average price rise is +3.09% which is eleventh-ranked compared with other bull market up months. Put it all together and a pattern of relative weakness is quite apparent (see Table 9.2).

The bull market record is getting worse. Prior to 1978, there were 35 bull market Septembers. Prices rose 24 times (69%). Since then, September has risen 43% of the time in bull markets (six up and eight down) in a predominantly rising era when most other months out-performed their long-term average, not under-performed it.

Bear markets

During bear markets, September rises in four out of 10 years, about average compared to other months. However, when prices do decline, the typical drop is -6.14%. In other words, when things go wrong in bear market Septembers, they go wrong in a big way. Here too, the problem seems to be getting worse. Since 1972, there have been five bear market Septembers in which shares fell. Every one of those drops was over 6%.

Spotting bear markets

With stock market conditions like these, it obviously pays to stand aside during bear markets. As always, this is easier said than done. However, there is one historical trend that provides some help in this respect because of

298

## SEPTEMBER PRICE RISES AND DECLINES:1919–1996

| | Average September price change | Up | Down/ No change |
|---|---|---|---|
| 1920–29 | -1.01% | 3 | 7 |
| 1930–39 | -0.37% | 6 | 4 |
| 1940–49 | 1.26% | 8 | 2 |
| 1950–59 | -0.08% | 5 | 5 |
| 1960–69 | 1.08% | 5 | 5 |
| 1970–79 | -0.60% | 6 | 4 |
| 1980–89 | -0.97% | 5 | 5 |
| 1990–96 | -0.78% | 3 | 4 |
| Average September change: 1919–96 | -0.13% | 54% | 46% |
| Rank (of 12) | 10 | 8 | |

*Source: BZW, Datastream/ICV*

Table 9.1: Prices rise about half of the time over the long term. Unfortunately, September investors periodically get slammed by a Big Hit which wipes out months' worth of profits. A further problem is due to Wall Street where September is a very poor performer.

its past association with bear markets. As Figure 9.1 reveals, August price declines of -1.60% or more, are usually associated with bear markets. If August is hit by a large loss, the odds strongly suggest investing with extreme caution in September.

**Spotting bull markets**

On the up-side, an August price rise in excess of +4.42% is virtually always associated with a September bull market. Since our records began, there have been 21 occasions with a large August price rise. History shows that a bull market was running in September in 19 of

299

## SEPTEMBER PERFORMANCE IN BULL/BEAR MARKETS: 1919–1996

|  | Bull Markets | Bear Markets |
| --- | --- | --- |
| Average per cent price change | 1.06% | -2.26% |
| Rank (of 12) | 10 | 8 |
| | | |
| Per cent of time prices rise | 62% | 39% |
| Rank (of 12) | 11 | 5 |
| | | |
| Average per cent price change in: | | |
| Rising years | 3.09% | 3.75% |
| Declining years | -2.24% | -6.14% |

*Source: BZW, Datastream/ICV*

Table 9.2: On most dimensions, September provides below-average returns in bull market years. The bear market record is about average compared to other months.

those years. Clearly, prospects for September generally look good following a strong August advance.

**Future prospects poor**

As far as the future is concerned, we suspect that the September record will continue to deteriorate in bull and bear markets alike. The source of the problem is Wall Street where September has become the worst month of the year. Since 1974, Wall Street has had four Big Hits in September. UK prices fell by over 5% each time. Since 1985, Wall Street has fallen eight times in September. UK prices fell in seven of those years.

**First-quarter exception**

In other words, you may profit in any single September but over the long run, a September investment will probably be a money-loser. Note, however, that conditions are not uniform throughout the month. The first quarter has been quite profitable in most years. The problems, when they occur, tend to cluster in the second,

## ODDS OF BULL/BEAR MARKET TIPPED BY AUGUST'S TREND

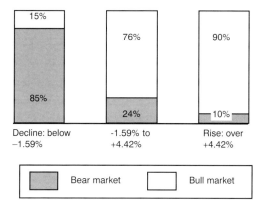

Source: *BZW, Datastream/ICV*

Figure 9.1: August price drops of -1.60% or greater are usually associated with bear markets. An August advance of +4.43% or higher is a strong bull market signal.

third, and fourth quarters *(see Figure 9.2)*.

### INCREASE YOUR PROFIT ODDS[1]

Despite the poor long-term record, there is money to be made in September if you can figure out how to avoid the bad years. Fortunately, history provides a number of clues.

April–August signal No.1

We start with a newly discovered trend that has done a good job of tipping off losing Septembers. Since 1952,

---

[1]We will provide closing price trends on key indices for the last 12 months at no cost (see page 9)

## QUARTERLY ODDS OF PRICE RISE IN SEPTEMBER

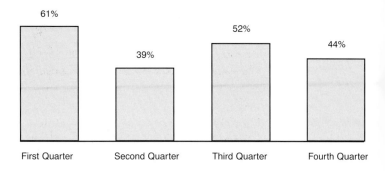

*Source: Financial Times, Datastream/ICV*

Figure 9.2: The first quarter is frequently profitable. When things go wrong in September, most of the damage occurs in the rest of the month, especially the second quarter which rises 39% of the time.

there have been 13 occasions when the FTSE All Share Index or its predecessor index rose in the preceding five months within a range of +4.08% to +9.33%. September prices fell in 11 of those years.

*Rose (2)*

*Fell (11)*

September's record after an April to August price rise of +4.08% to +9.33% (FTSE All Share Index since 1952)

**April–August signal No.2**

A similar trend runs on the FT-Non-Financial Index. Since 1952, there have been 15 occasions when it or its predecessor index rose in the preceding five months within a range of +3.69% to +9.28%. September prices fell in 13 of those years.

NEW

*Rose (2)*

*Fell (13)*

September's record after an April to August price rise of +3.69% to +9.28% (FT-Non-Financial Index since 1952)

May–August signal

Staying with the FT-Non-Financial Index, there have been nine occasions since 1952 when prices shifted within a range of -0.86% to +2.89% in the previous four months. September prices fell each time. The signal last flashed in 1994 and September prices fell by -7.38%.

*Rose (0)*

*Fell (9)*

September's record after a May to August price shift of -0.86% to +2.89% (FT-Non-Financial Index since 1952)

January signal

Another winning strategy: hold no shares (or move into Puts) in years when January share prices drop. We have refined the strategy a bit since our last edition. Here is an up-to-date version of it. Since 1937, there have been 15 years when January prices on the FTSE All Share Index or its predecessor index either rose by a tiny margin, no more than +0.04%, or dropped by up to -7.57%. In 13 of those years, September prices also dropped (87%).

*Rose (2)*

IMPROVEMENT

*Fell (13)*

September's record after a January shift of +0.04% to -7.57% (FTSE All Share Index since 1937)

**Prior 11-months signal**

Here is a final down-side indicator, this one based on the FT Ordinary Share Index. Since 1954, there have been 10 occasions when prices rose sharply in the preceding 11 months by +22.37% to +35.40%. September prices fell each time.

*Rose (0)*

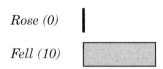

*Fell (10)*

September's record after a previous 11-month price rise of +22.37% to +35.40% (FT Ordinary Share Index since 1954)

Historical trend analysis also provides us with two trends that have done a good job of anticipating September price rises.

**Prior 12-months signal**

If the FTSE All Share Index or its predecessor index has fallen between -11.79% to -32.01% in the past twelve months, and the preceding three-month trend (June to August) is also negative, September prices will probably rise. Out of 11 years which followed this scenario since 1930, September prices fell just once.

*Rose (10)*

*Fell (1)*

September's record after a previous 12-month fall of -11.79% to -32.01% and a three-month fall of any size (FTSE All Share Index since 1930)

**March–August signal**

If the preceding six-month trend has risen on the FT-Non-Financial Index or its predecessor index within a range of +15.01% to +24.67%, September prices will probably rise. Out of 12 years with a price rise of this

304

magnitude in the run-up to September, September prices rose 11 times.

*Rose (11)*

*Fell (1)*

September's record after a previous six month rise of +15.01% to +24.67% (FT-Non-Financial Index since 1919)

# FIRST QUARTER OF SEPTEMBER – SEPTEMBER 1ST TO 8TH

Prices rise in most first quarters, bull and bear markets alike. In a rare change of pace, Monday is the most profitable weekday of the quarter.
   Despite the positive trends for the quarter as a whole, be cautious on 1 September which rises just 40% of the time.

Profitable

Although the month of September can be painful to investors, its first quarter is a consistent money-maker. Prices have risen in each of the five full decades on record. The average rate of increase is +0.42% per year. Prices rise in 61% of all September first quarters *(see Table 9.3)*. There has been no sign of a trend change in recent years. Prices have risen in six of the last 10 years.

   The first-quarter trend is strong in bull and bear markets alike. Shares rise more often than they do in the average quarter in both types of stock market conditions *(see Table 9.4)*.

Monday good news

   In most quarters of the year, Monday is a relatively poor day, frequently the worst or second-worst day of the week. This quarter is a welcome exception to the rule

305

## PERCENTAGE PRICE CHANGE: SEPTEMBER 1935–96

| | Sep 1–8 | Sep 9–15 | Sep 16–23 | Sep 24–30 |
|---|---|---|---|---|
| Annual average | | | | |
| 1935–39 | -0.16% | -2.63% | -1.54% | 0.67% |
| 1940 49 | 0.11% | 0.48% | 0.12% | -0.08% |
| 1950–59 | 0.06% | 0.15% | -0.58% | -0.09% |
| 1960–69 | 1.02% | -0.53% | 0.63% | -0.70% |
| 1970–79 | 0.88% | -0.30% | -0.56% | -0.65% |
| 1980–89 | 0.70% | -0.76% | -0.13% | -0.91% |
| 1990–96 | -0.15% | -0.46% | -0.19% | -0.05% |
| | | | | |
| Average quarterly price change | 0.42% | -0.42% | -0.23% | -0.34% |
| | | | | |
| Per cent of time prices rise | 61% | 39% | 52% | 44% |

*Source: Financial Times, Datastream/ICV*

Table 9.3: First-quarter prices have risen in every decade since the 1940s. The reverse pattern is apparent for the rest of the month – average annual losses in most decades.

with Monday turning in the best performance of the week and one of the best of all 48 quarters *(see Figure 9.3)*. In contrast, both Tuesday and Wednesday each rise less than half the time during this point of the month.

**1 September**     Analysis of daily price trends reveals a profitable outlook on most days of the quarter. 1 September is a notable exception. Over the long run, prices rise just 40% of the time. At the opposite end of the range, the odds of a price rise are highest on 7 September, rising 61% of the time, the best performer of the month. Close behind is 2 September which rises 60% of the time *(see Figure 9.4)*.

**5 September**     An interesting trend change has recently occurred on

### SEPTEMBER FIRST QUARTER PERFORMANCE IN BULL/BEAR MARKETS: 1935–1996

|  | Total | Bull Markets | Bear Markets |
| --- | --- | --- | --- |
| Average price change | 0.42% | 0.76% | -0.20% |
| Rank (of 48) | 14 | 17 | 13 |
|  |  |  |  |
| Per cent of time prices rise | 61% | 65% | 55% |
| Rank (of 48) | 13 | 17 | 10 |

*Source: Financial Times, Datastream/ICV*

Table 9.4: The chance of a price rise is above average in bull and bear markets alike.

5 September. For many years, the odds of a price rise were less than 50:50. But since 1977, prices have risen in 12 out of 14 different years. Both drops were less than one-third of a percent.

**8 September**

Another trend change recently occurred on 8 September, this one for the worse. Since 1971 prices have risen just four times out of 17 attempts, one of the worst records of the entire year during this period. Don't be too quick to dismiss this as a one-day fluke. The record for 9 September, to be discussed in the next section, is even worse.

### INCREASE YOUR PROFIT ODDS

**August signal No.1**

The direction that shares move in the first quarter is frequently tipped off by the August price trend. Since 1957, there have been 19 occasions in which prices on the FTSE All Share Index or its predecessor index rose by up to +5.15% during August. The first quarter rose 17 times. If prices shift outside of this range during August, the

307

## PERCENTAGE OF TIME PRICES RISE EACH DAY OF WEEK IN SEPTEMBER'S FIRST QUARTER

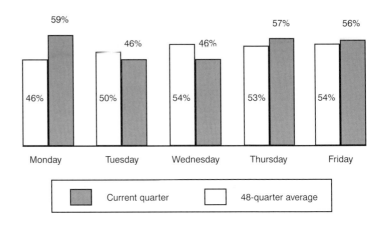

Monday | Tuesday | Wednesday | Thursday | Friday

Current quarter | 48-quarter average

*Source: Financial Times, Datastream/ICV*

Figure 9.3: Monday is the first quarter's best day and is the second-best Monday of all 48 quarters.

odds of a first-quarter price rise are just 50:50.

*Rose (17)*

*Fell (2)*

First-quarter record after a price rise of up to +5.15% in August (FTSE All Share Index since 1957)

August signal No.2

A similar trend runs on the FT Ordinary Share Index. Since 1942, a shift of -1.13% to +2.91% in August is often followed by a price increase in September's first quarter. Out of 17 years with an August shift within this range,

## PERCENTAGE OF TIME PRICES RISE EACH TRADING DAY IN SEPTEMBER'S FIRST QUARTER

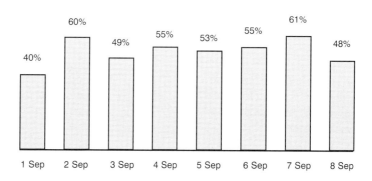

*Source: Financial Times, Datastream/ICV*

Figure 9.4: Prices rise more than half of the time on most days in the first quarter. 1 September is a notable exception.

September's first quarter rose 16 times.

IMPROVEMENT

*Rose (16)*

*Fell (1)*

First-quarter record after an August shift of -1.13% to +2.91% (FT Ordinary Share Index since 1942)

Above +2.91% in August and the prospects for September's first quarter are decidedly weaker, with the odds of a loss higher than 50:50.

Prior quarter signal No.1

Also on the FT Ordinary Share Index, if prices shift in the fourth quarter of August within a range of -0.66% to +1.19%, they usually rise in value during September's first quarter. Since 1960, there have been 14 years with

309

a shift in the previous quarter within the defined range.
First-quarter prices rose 12 times.

*Rose (12)*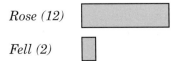

*Fell (2)*

First-quarter record after an August fourth-quarter shift of -0.66%
to +1.19% (FT Ordinary Share Index since 1960)

Prior quarter
signal No.2

During bull markets, a swing on the FTSE All Share
Index in the previous quarter within the range of -3.84%
to +0.43% has been associated with a first-quarter price
rise nine times in a row.

*Rose (9)*

*Fell (0)*

First-quarter record in bull markets after an August fourth-quarter
shift of -3.84% to +0.43% (FTSE All Share Index since 1969)

310

## SECOND QUARTER OF SEPTEMBER – SEPTEMBER 9TH TO 15TH

Prices rise just 39% of the time, the worst record of all 48 quarters. There is no relief in sight with the recent record bringing more of the same.

The odds of a price rise are especially poor near the beginning of the week. Monday and Tuesday each rise about one-third of the time over the long run.

Poor prospects

As a general rule, think twice before buying shares in the second quarter of September. Not only are the odds of making a profit loaded against you, but the third and fourth quarters of the month are also lacklustre. If you are thinking of selling shares you already own, the odds favour doing so at the beginning of the quarter.

On average, shares drop -0.42% each year during this quarter. Prices have risen in just 24 of the last 62 years (39%). Even during the 1980s' bull market decade the record was three up, seven down and an average decrease of -0.76%. Thus far into the 1990s, prices have fallen in four out of seven years *(see Table 9.5).*

Bull and bear markets

The second-quarter trend is weak in bull and bear markets alike. In fact, during bull market years, prices rise just 40% of the time, the worst bull market quarter of the year *(see Table 9.6).*

Monday weak

Analysis by day of week shows a huge reversal to Monday's fortunes, compared with its sterling first-quarter performance. While prices rise an impressive 59% of the time in the first quarter, second-quarter Mondays rise just 36% of the time, one of the year's weaker performances. Tuesdays are also quite weak in the second quarter *(see Figure 9.5).*

Daily price trends are generally weak throughout the quarter. Prices rise less than half the time on most days of the quarter *(see Figure 9.6).*

311

## PERCENTAGE PRICE CHANGE: SEPTEMBER 1985–96

|  | Sep 1–8 | Sep 9–15 | Sep 16–23 | Sep 24–30 |
|---|---|---|---|---|
| 1985 | -0.24% | -1.59% | -0.96% | -0.33% |
| 1986 | 0.72% | -2.30% | -1.21% | -3.22% |
| 1987 | 1.30% | -0.29% | 3.49% | 0.86% |
| 1988 | -0.83% | 1.44% | 1.20% | 2.01% |
| 1989 | 1.52% | -2.08% | 0.16% | -2.72% |
| 1990 | -1.90% | -1.27% | -3.96% | -1.58% |
| 1991 | 1.22% | -1.16% | -1.46% | 1.23% |
| 1992 | 0.86% | 1.11% | 8.78% | -0.88% |
| 1993 | -1.81% | -1.37% | 0.29% | 0.91% |
| 1994 | -1.88% | -2.26% | -2.59% | -0.57% |
| 1995 | 2.03% | 0.08% | -1.22% | -0.03% |
| 1996 | 0.44% | 1.68% | -1.16% | 0.57% |
| Average quarterly price change | 0.12% | -0.67% | 0.11% | -0.31% |
| Number of years in which prices | | | | |
| Rose | 7 | 4 | 5 | 5 |
| Fell | 5 | 8 | 7 | 7 |

*Source: Datastream/ICV*

Table 9.5: Recent quarterly trends follow past patterns. Prices continue to rise more often in the first quarter than in the rest of the month.

9 September

Be especially cautious on 9 September which has had an atrocious record in recent years, a continuation of the weakness observed on 8 September. Since 1971 prices have risen just three times out of 17 attempts, one of the worst records of the entire year during this time period.

## SEPTEMBER SECOND QUARTER PERFORMANCE IN BULL/BEAR MARKETS: 1935–1996

|  | Total | Bull Markets | Bear Markets |
|---|---|---|---|
| Average price change | -0.42% | -0.15% | -0.91% |
| Rank (of 48) | 43 | 47 | 33 |
|  |  |  |  |
| Per cent of time prices rise | 39% | 40% | 36% |
| Rank (of 48) | 48 | 48 | 31 |

*Source: Financial Times, Datastream/ICV*

Table 9.6: The second quarter is the weakest quarter of the year during bull markets. The bear market record is closer to average but investors still lose money in the average bear market year.

**14–15 September**

The last two days of the quarter, 14–15 September, rise about half of the time. But history also shows that the odds of a price rise are poor when either day lands on a Tuesday. Since records began in 1935, the 14th or 15th have landed on Tuesday 18 times. Prices rose just four times *(see Table 9.7)*.

**15 September**

15 September's record has been quite poor in recent years on all days of the week, not just Tuesday. Since 1976, prices have risen four times out of 15 tries. The record is even worse the following day, 16 September, which is discussed in the following section.

### INCREASE YOUR PROFIT ODDS

The only way to profit consistently in the second quarter is to bet against the market. To help you improve the odds of identifying periods when prices will decline, the market sends several useful signals.

Here is a newly-emerging trend that has been running

313

**PERCENTAGE OF TIME PRICES RISE EACH DAY OF WEEK IN SEPTEMBER'S SECOND QUARTER**

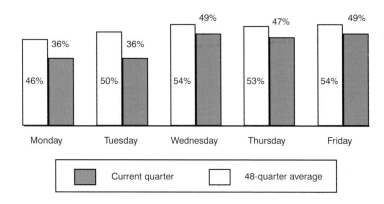

*Source: Financial Times, Datastream/ICV*

Figure 9.5: Monday and Tuesday rise much less often than the rest of the week. The chance of a rise on either day is well below average compared to other quarters.

First-quarter signal No.1

on the FTSE All Share Index since 1969. During this period, there have been six occasions when prices fell in the first quarter by -1.35% or more. Second-quarter prices continued to decline each time.

*Rose (0)*

*Fell (6)*

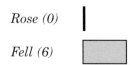

Second-quarter record after a first quarter fall of -1.35% or more (FTSE All Share Index since 1969)

A similar trend has been running on the FT Ordinary

## PERCENTAGE OF TIME PRICES RISE EACH TRADING DAY IN SEPTEMBER'S SECOND QUARTER

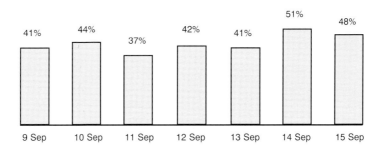

| 9 Sep | 10 Sep | 11 Sep | 12 Sep | 13 Sep | 14 Sep | 15 Sep |
|-------|--------|--------|--------|--------|--------|--------|
| 41% | 44% | 37% | 42% | 41% | 51% | 48% |

*Source: Financial Times, Datastream/ICV*

Figure 9.6: Prices rise less than half the time on most days. Unfortunately, the record on 15 September has grown steadily weaker in recent years.

**First-quarter signal No.2**

Share Index since 1935. During this period, there have been 11 occasions when first-quarter prices fell -1.35% or more. Second-quarter prices fell 10 times.

*Rose (1)*

*Fell (10)*

Second-quarter record after a first quarter fall of -1.35% or more (FT Ordinary Share Index since 1935)

**Prior two-quarters signal**

Another signal which helps to improve the odds of spotting a drop is the direction of prices in the preceding two quarters. If they shift in the fourth quarter of August on the FT Ordinary Share Index by -2.29% to +0.52% *and* rise in the first quarter of September by +0.69% to

315

## PERCENTAGE OF TIME PRICES RISE ON 14–15 SEPTEMBER: 1935–1996

|  | Prices rise |
|---|---|
| Total | 49% |
| Tuesday | 22% |
| Rest of week | 56% |

*Source: Financial Times, Datastream/ICV*

Table 9.7: Prices rise less than one in four times when 14–15 September land on a Tuesday. The chance of a rise is above 50:50 in the rest of the week.

+4.37%, it is quite probable that they will fall in the second quarter. Out of 11 occasions since 1957 when the price of the average share shifted in the preceding periods within the appropriate range, second-quarter prices declined each time.

IMPROVEMENT

*Rose (0)* |

*Fell (11)*

Second-quarter record after an August fourth-quarter shift of -2.29% to +0.52% and September first-quarter rise of +0.69% to +4.37% (FT Ordinary Share Index since 1957)

Prior four-quarters signal

On the FT-Non-Financial Index and its predecessor index, history shows that a rise in the previous four quarters of +2.78% or more is usually followed by a drop in the second quarter. Since 1959, prices rose by +2.78% or more on 14 occasions. Second-quarter prices fell in 13 of those years.

NEW

*Rose (1)*

*Fell (13)*

Second-quarter record after a price rise of +2.78% or more in the previous four quarters (FT-Non-Financial Index since 1959)

January signal

The odds of a second-quarter decline on the FT-Non-Financial Index are higher than normal if January's prices decline by up to -7.57%. We first called attention to this indicator in an earlier edition of the *Schwartz Stock Market Handbook*. Since then, prices fell in January 1995 and again in the second quarter of September. At present, there have been 16 years in which January prices declined by up to -7.57%. September second-quarter prices fell in 14 of those years.

UPDATE

*Rose (2)*

*Fell (14)*

Second-quarter record after a January fall of up to -7.57% (FT-Non-Financial Index since 1938)

317

# THIRD QUARTER OF SEPTEMBER – SEPTEMBER 16TH TO 23RD

---

Third-quarter prices have risen half the time over the long run but the recent trend has weakened.

Two of the worst days of the year land in this quarter, 16 and 23 September. Each rise just 32% of the time. There have been no signs of improvement for either day in recent years.

---

As in the second quarter, investors usually lose money by investing during the third quarter. Between 1935 and 1996, the stock market rose 52% of the time in the third quarter of September and generated an average loss of -0.23% per year.

**Recent trend poor**

A review of recent trends reveals more of the same. The average share price fell in both the 1970s and '80s. In the last seven years, prices have fallen five times. One of the two increases raised the value of the typical share by just +0.29%. The only large rise was an +8.78% increase in prices in 1992 in response to Britain's surprise withdrawal from the ERM.

**Bear market drops**

The odds of a price rise are 58% in bull market years and 41% in bear market years. Both figures are about average compared to other quarters of the year. But when prices fall in bear market years, the drop can be quite painful. About half of all bear market declines in the third quarter were in excess of 4% (see Table 9.8)

**18 September**

There are good odds of a price rise on several different days of this quarter including 18 September (up 60% of the time) and 21 September (up 61% of the time), tied with one another as the best day of the month. But the very first and last days of the quarter are a horror for investors. Both rise just 32% of the time, tied as the second-worst trading day of the entire year.

**16, 23 September**

The poor 16 September record has been running for many decades. There have been no signs of improvement

## SEPTEMBER THIRD QUARTER PERFORMANCE IN BULL/BEAR MARKETS: 1935–1996

|  | Total | Bull Markets | Bear Markets |
|---|---|---|---|
| Average price change | -0.23% | 0.37% | -1.31% |
| Rank (of 48) | 39 | 30 | 40 |
|  |  |  |  |
| Per cent of time prices rise | 52% | 58% | 41% |
| Rank (of 48) | 27 | 25 | 24 |

*Source: Financial Times, Datastream/ICV*

Table 9.8: Prices rise an average number of times in third-quarter bull and bear markets. However, when prices fall in bear market years, the decline is often a large one.

in the recent past. Since 1976, 16 September has fallen in 10 out of 12 years and both exceptions to the rule were small rises. A similar trend runs on 23 September which has fallen in 12 out of the most recent 16 years *(see Figure 9.7)*.

**Weak Friday**    Analysis of price trends by day of week reveals that prices rise most often in mid-week. The poorest day in this quarter is Friday which rises just 43% of the time, the third-weakest Friday of all 48 quarters *(see Figure 9.8)*.

### INCREASE YOUR PROFIT ODDS

Here are two signals that can help to increase the odds of spotting a decline in the third quarter.

**January signal**    Since 1939, a January decline on the FT-Non-Financial Index or its predecessor index of -2.25% to -6.99% is often followed with a poor third-quarter performance. Third-quarter prices declined in 10 of 11 years after January fell by the designated amount.

319

**PERCENTAGE OF TIME PRICES RISE EACH TRADING DAY IN SEPTEMBER'S THIRD QUARTER**

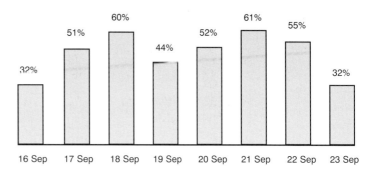

*Source: Financial Times, Datastream/ICV*

Figure 9.7:  Be careful. Two of the year's 10 worst days land in this quarter. There have been no signs of improvement on either 16 or 23 September in recent years.

IMPROVEMENT

*Rose (1)*

*Fell (10)*

Third-quarter record after a January decline of -2.25% to -6.99% (FT-Non-Financial Index since 1939)

First-half signal    A second useful signal worth monitoring is the direction of prices on the FT Ordinary Share Index in the first half of September. If they fall in both the first and second quarter, with a second-quarter decline no more than -2.17%, the odds of a third-quarter decline are higher. Since 1946, there have been 11 occasions when first-half prices fell within the designated range. In 10 of those years, the stock market continued to fall in the third quarter.

## PERCENTAGE OF TIME PRICES RISE EACH DAY OF WEEK IN SEPTEMBER'S THIRD QUARTER

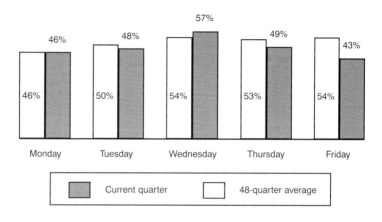

Source: Financial Times, Datastream/ICV

Figure 9.8: Friday is the worst day of the week for third-quarter investors. It is the third-worst Friday of all 48 quarters.

IMPROVEMENT

*Rose (1)*

*Fell (10)*

Third-quarter record after a first-quarter fall (any amount) and second-quarter fall of up to -2.17% (FT Ordinary Share Index since 1946)

Prior three-quarters signal We also find two signals that often tip third quarter up-moves. The first is newly emerging on the FT-Non-Financial Index. Since 1978, the past three quarters have risen within a range of +0.43% to +1.93% in eight different years. Prices rose in the third quarter each time.

321

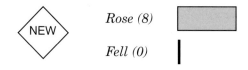

*Rose (8)*

*Fell (0)*

Third-quarter record after a price rise of +0.43% to +1.93% in the previous three quarters (FT-Non-Financial Index since 1978)

Second-quarter signal

If second-quarter prices rise on the FT Ordinary Share Index by no more than +1.40%, the odds are good that the third quarter will also rise. Since 1942, there have been 14 second-quarter rises within this range. Third-quarter prices rose in 13 of those years. The sole exception was back in 1954.

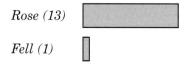

*Rose (13)*

*Fell (1)*

Third-quarter record after a second quarter price rise of up to +1.40% (FT Ordinary Share Index since 1942)

# FOURTH QUARTER OF SEPTEMBER – SEPTEMBER 24TH TO 30TH

Prices rise less than half the time during the fourth quarter. The trend is weak in bull and bear markets alike.

The profit odds are especially poor on Monday which rises just one-third of the time. Also note that 26 September, the worst day of the entire year, rises just 28% of the time over the long run.

**Another poor quarter**

The fourth quarter of September offers very poor investment potential. Investors lost money in every single decade on record. Prices rise just 44% of the time, one of the weakest quarters of the entire year.

The odds of a price rise are 50:50 during bull market years and 30% in bear markets. Both figures are well below-average compared with other years *(see Table 9.9)*.

**26 September**

Despite the poor trend, prices rise around 50% of the time on most days in the fourth quarter. One glaring exception is 26 September, the worst trading day of the entire year. Prices rise just 28% of the time on this date *(see Figure 9.9)*. The recent trend shows no significant sign of improvement. Since 1980, 26 September has risen four times in 11 attempts.

**Random walkers, please note**

There are four other days around this point in the month that are also among the 10 least profitable trading days of the year. 16 and 23 September both rise 32% of the time. 9 and 10 October rise just slightly more often. Given the proximity of these five days, we find it hard to believe Random Walk Theory supporters who claim all short-term fluctuations are completely random. As we see things, five of the worst days of the year in a four-week stretch is anything but random.

**Monday**

Analysis of fourth-quarter trends by day of week shows significant weakness throughout the week, especially on Mondays. Prices rise just 34% of the time, one of the worst Monday records of all 48 quarters *(see Figure 9.10)*.

## SEPTEMBER FOURTH QUARTER PERFORMANCE IN BULL/BEAR MARKETS: 1935–1996

|  | Total | Bull Markets | Bear Markets |
|---|---|---|---|
| Average price change | -0.34% | -0.25% | -0.54% |
| Rank (of 48) | 42 | 48 | 23 |
| | | | |
| Per cent of time prices rise | 44% | 50% | 30% |
| Rank (of 48) | 44 | 42 | 39 |

*Source: Financial Times, Datastream/ICV*

Table 9.9: The chance of a price rise is below average in bull markets and bear markets alike.

The single exception to this poor profit pattern is Tuesday which rises 57% of the time, well above average compared to the rest of the year.

28 September  The 28 September price trend provides another positive bit of news. Although shares rise exactly half the time on this day over the long run, the chance of a price rise is quite good when it lands in mid-week. Since 1935, 28 September landed on Tuesday or Wednesday on 18 occasions. Prices rose in 14 of those years. The likelihood of a price rise is much lower when 28 September lands on other days of the week *(see Table 9.10)*.

### INCREASE YOUR PROFIT ODDS

For investors seeking to avoid a drop, there are several indicators associated with an increased likelihood of a fourth-quarter fall.

Prior four-quarters signal  We start with a newly-discovered trend based upon the FTSE All Share Index. Since 1969, a decline in the previous four quarters of -1.45% or more occurred in nine

## PERCENTAGE OF TIME PRICES RISE EACH TRADING DAY IN SEPTEMBER'S FOURTH QUARTER

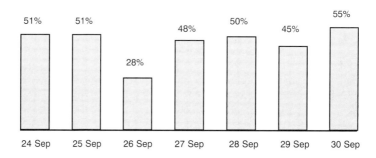

*Source: Financial Times, Datastream/ICV*

Figure 9.9: The 26th is the worst day of the entire year. Since 1980, the record for the 26th is four rises and seven declines.

different years. Fourth-quarter prices fell in eight of those years. In the remaining 18 years untouched by this trend, the fourth quarter rose nine times and fell nine times.

*Rose (1)*

*Fell (8)*

Fourth-quarter record after prices drop in four prior quarters by at least -1.45% (FTSE All Share Index since 1969)

January signal | Once again, January prices strongly correlate with a poor September performance. Since 1937, January prices fell on the FTSE All Share Index or its predecessor index by -1.23% to -7.57% in 12 different years. September's fourth quarter also declined in 11 of those years.

### PERCENTAGE OF TIME PRICES RISE EACH DAY OF WEEK IN SEPTEMBER'S FOURTH QUARTER

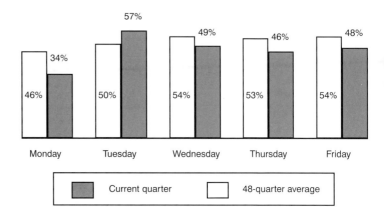

| | Monday | Tuesday | Wednesday | Thursday | Friday |
|---|---|---|---|---|---|
| 48-quarter average | 46% | 50% | 54% | 53% | 54% |
| Current quarter | 34% | 57% | 49% | 46% | 48% |

Current quarter     48-quarter average

*Source: Financial Times, Datastream/ICV*

Figure 9.10: The chance of a price rise is below average on most days. Be especially cautious on Monday which rises just 34% of the time, making it one of the worst Monday records of all 48 quarters.

UPDATE

*Rose (1)*

*Fell (11)*

Fourth-quarter record after a January decline of -1.23% to -7.57% (FTSE All Share Index since 1937)

Third-quarter signal

Since 1941, a small third-quarter price decline on the FT Ordinary Share Index has often tipped further stock market declines in the fourth quarter. Out of 13 third-quarter drops no greater than -1.37%, fourth-quarter prices fell 10 times.

## PERCENTAGE OF TIME PRICES RISE ON
## 28 SEPTEMBER: 1935–1996

|  | Prices rise |
|---|---|
| Total | 50% |
| Tuesday or Wednesday | 78% |
| Rest of week | 31% |

*Source: Financial Times, Datastream/ICV*

Table 9.10: Prices rise in three out of four years when 28 September lands on Tuesday or Wednesday but much less often when it lands on the other week days.

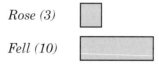

*Rose (3)*

*Fell (10)*

Fourth-quarter record after a third quarter decline of up to -1.37% (FT Ordinary Share Index since 1941)

**Prior three-quarters signal**

If prices fall on the FT Ordinary Share Index in September's first, second and third quarters, they are likely to fall in the fourth quarter as well. Since 1935, there have been 12 years in which prices fell in each of the three preceding quarters. They fell in the fourth quarter in nine of those years. The signal failed twice in a row in recent years. 1993 saw a price rise of just +0.26% after three consecutive quarterly declines. 1994 saw an even smaller rise of +0.12% after three consecutive falls.

Despite the two recent failures, we continue to track this signal. The reason is that even when it fails, the rise tends to be quite weak.

327

*Rose (3)*

*Fell (9)*

Fourth-quarter record after prices drop in all three prior
September quarters (FT Ordinary Share Index since 1935)

**August fourth-
quarter signal**

A final trend worth monitoring is based on price swings
during the fourth quarter of August. Since 1960, the FT
Ordinary Share Index has fallen in this quarter on 15
occasions. Prices also fell in the fourth quarter of
September in 13 of those years. One of the two exceptions
was a rise of just +0.16% in 1982. While we can not
explain why the correlation works, regardless of what
happens in the intervening quarters, there is no doubt
that it is a trend worth monitoring.

In the 22 years untouched by this trend since 1960, the
fourth-quarter record is 14 rises and eight declines.

*Rose (2)*

*Fell (13)*

Fourth-quarter record after prices drop in the fourth quarter of
August (FT Ordinary Share Index since 1960)

## LOOKING AHEAD

**Rising prices by next 28 February**

So much for the past. What of the future? Here is a useful trend that gives good insight into the five months ahead. Since 1927, a price rise on the FTSE All Share Index or its predecessor index of +6.44% to +17.86% in the first nine months of the year often signalled that prices will rise even higher by the end of next February.

Out of 21 times with a price rise within this range, prices rose in the next five months 19 times. Both exceptions to the rule were drops of under 2%. During the remaining 49 years, the 1 October to 28 February record was 29 increases and 20 decreases.

*Rose (19)*

*Fell (2)*

Trend to 28 February (next year) after a January–September price rise of +6.44% to +17.86% (FTSE All Share Index since 1927)

**Rising prices by next 30 April**

On the FT Ordinary Share Index, a May to September price swing of -7.13% to +6.28% has usually been followed by a stock market advance in the following seven months, to the end of next April.

Out of 22 occasions with a price swing within this range, prices rose in the next seven months 20 times. One of the two exceptions to the rule was a decline of just -0.16% following the 1955 signal.

*Rose (20)*

*Fell (2)*

Trend to 30 April (next year) after a May-September shift of -7.13% to +6.28% (FT Ordinary Share Index since 1952)

**Rising prices by next 30 September**

Another important clue is provided by the August/September price trend on the FT-Non-Financial Index or its predecessor index. Although it is not widely known, the direction that share prices move in this two-month stretch is an important tool with which to forecast the direction of share prices in the year ahead.

Since 1919, there have been 18 years with price shifts of -14% to +14% in the 12 months ending 31 July and a price rise of +3.86% or more between 1 August and 30 September. In 16 of those years, prices rose still further in the 12 months that followed. The average increase was almost 20%.

One of the two exceptions was the 1965 signal. Prices rose as expected in the next nine months through June 1966. The trend suddenly changed in July in response to Labour's surprise 'July Measures' which increased the Bank Rate to 7%, and added new hire-purchase restrictions, indirect taxes, an overseas travel allowance of £50 and price controls.

If July/August prices either rise by less than +3.86% or fall, it is strictly a 50/50 gamble that prices will rise in the year ahead, as far as this indicator is concerned.

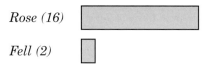

*Rose (16)*

*Fell (2)*

Trend to 30 September (next year) after a -14% to +14% price shift in the 12 months ending 31 July and an August/September rise of +3.86% or more (FT-Non-Financial Index since 1919)

**Rising prices by 31 December**

September also serves as an excellent contrarian predictor of fourth-quarter price trends. Since 1959, a price drop in September on the FT-Non-Financial Index has usually been followed with price increases in the final three months of the year.

330

During this period, there were 16 years when September prices fell by -0.67% or more. Shares rose in the next three months in 15 of those years (94%) at an average rate of +7.08%. The sole exception occurred in 1974 at the tail end of a vicious two-year-long bear market when prices fell in October to December by -13.07% after a September drop of -12.35%.

Rose (15)

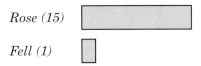

Fell (1)

Trend to 31 December after a September decline of at least -0.67% (FT-Non-Financial Index since 1959)

The signal last flashed in 1994 when a painful September decline of -7.38% was followed by a small up-move in the year's final three months.

During the other 22 years of this period, when September prices either fell slightly or rose by any amount, the record for the last three months of the year was 13 up and nine down.

There is a new twist to the September trend which first appeared in 1970. Although it is early days, we note that in the last 27 years, September has risen by +2.99% or more in eight different years. The stock market fell in the final quarter of the year in six of those years. The two exceptions were in 1982 and 1992. Both were near the start of lengthy bull market rallies.

These recent events suggest that if September prices rally strongly in the midst of a bull market that has been advancing for several years, the odds are higher than normal that prices will decline in the fourth quarter.

# CHAPTER 10 – OCTOBER

There is no getting away from it. As October arrives, many investors start thinking about October Crashes and wondering what the gods have in store for them in the month ahead.

In fact, there is a wide difference in October between perception and reality. The month's reputation is a poor one, heavily affected by the events of 1929 and 1987. But the truth of the matter is that October is profitable in most years and returns a healthy average annual profit over the long term.

October's bull market record is quite strong, with price rises in three out of four years. But the bear market trend has weakened in recent decades. The stock market used to rise half the time in bear market Octobers. More recently, it rose just three times in the last 13 bear market years.

The first quarter is the best segment of the month. Each of the remaining three quarters rise about half of the time. Be especially cautious in the final quarter. The trend has deteriorated in recent years, having risen just twice in the last 10 years.

**Image worse than reality**

Mention October to the average investor and the losses of 1929 and 1987 immediately come to mind. Is it any wonder that a poetic stock market commentator once said that 'Bull market bashes end with October crashes'? Happily, October's image is worse than its reality.

Over the long term, October investors do pretty well. Between 1919, when records first began, and 1996, October prices rose 62% of the time (see Table 10.1). The recent record continues to be largely positive. By way of example, the stock market has risen in seven of the last nine Octobers.

**Occasional stumble**

Analysis of share price trends decade-by-decade reveals an interesting point. Investors profited in most decades, and if shares happened to stumble in any single decade, it was usually due to a poor performance in just one or two years. A good example was in the 1920s when October investors lost a small amount of money in the typical year. The source of the problem was not 1929 as many would guess but 1921 when share prices fell by -9.76%.

Prices rose in six of the other nine years of the 1920s, and produced an average annual profit during these nine years, 1929's performance included. Incidentally, October 1929 fell by just -5.46%, much less than many modern-day investors would guess. It is what happened in the three following years that gives 1929 its notoriety, not its poor October performance.

Despite the Great Depression and the price weakness in the run-up to World War II, October investors made an average annual profit of +3.58% in the 1930s when it was the Number One-ranked month. The month continued to be profitable in the 1940s and through to the 1960s.

**Recent appearance deceptive**

The trend appears to have weakened in the recent past with average annual losses recorded in the 1970s and 1980s. But further analysis shows that two years accounted for each decade's poor results: 1976 and 1979 (down -11.17% and -6.78%), and 1987 and 1989 (down -26.59% and -7.59%). Without these four years, the 1970s

## OCTOBER PRICE RISES AND DECLINES: 1919–1996

|  | Average October price change | Up | Down/ No change |
|---|---|---|---|
| 1920–29 | -0.11% | 6 | 4 |
| 1930–39 | 3.58% | 7 | 3 |
| 1940–49 | 0.78% | 6 | 4 |
| 1950–59 | 2.87% | 7 | 3 |
| 1960–69 | 0.35% | 5 | 5 |
| 1970–79 | -1.32% | 4 | 6 |
| 1980–89 | -1.00% | 7 | 3 |
| 1990–96 | 1.59% | 6 | 1 |
| Average October change: 1919–96 | 0.75% | 62% | 38% |
| Rank (of 12) | 5 | 4 | |

Source: BZW, Datastream/ICV

Table 10.1: Despite its poor reputation, October is profitable in most years. Investors lost money in the average year during the 1970s and '80s but losses were largely due to two poor years in each decade. The average annual return in the rest of the 1970s and 1980s was positive.

Good long-term record

and 1980s would have been profitable.

Even with each poor year included in the computations, prices rise in the average October by +0.75%, equal to 30 points on an FTSE 100 in the area of 4000. Historically, October is the fifth-best month in which to invest in shares. A hypothetical investor who invested only in October from 1919 to 1996, and switched to cash for the rest of the year, would have run up his £1,000 to £1,568.

Analysis of price trends during bull markets shows a

## OCTOBER PERFORMANCE IN BULL/BEAR MARKETS: 1919–1996

|  | Bull Markets | Bear Markets |
|---|---|---|
| Average per cent price change | 2.14% | *-2.02% |
| Rank (of 12) | 4 | 6 |
|  |  |  |
| Per cent of time prices rise | 75% | 35% |
| Rank (of 12) | 4 | 7 |
|  |  |  |
| Average per cent price change in: |  |  |
| Rising years | 3.63% | 5.20% |
| Declining years | -2.32% | **-5.85% |

\*   -1.04% if not for 1987
\*\*  -4.55% if not for 1987

*Source: BZW, Datastream/ICV*

Table 10.2: Prices rise in three out of four bull market years. The odds of a rise are much lower in bear market years but close to average compared to other months. Unfortunately, October's bear market record has weakened in recent decades.

**Bull and bear market record**

high likelihood of profit. Prices rise 75% of the time and increase at an average rate of +2.14%, making October fourth-ranked on both dimensions *(see Table 10.2)*.

The typical decline in bear market years is -2.02% which places October in sixth position on the monthly league tables for bear markets, on this dimension. But one year, 1987, played a major role in depressing October's bear market performance. If not for 1987, the typical bear market October would decline by just -1.04%, placing this month in third place on the monthly performance rankings.

Unfortunately, October's bear market record is changing

## ODDS OF BULL/BEAR MARKET TIPPED BY AUGUST'S TREND

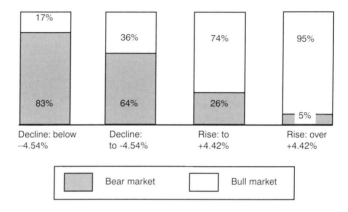

Source: BZW, Datastream/ICV

Figure 10.1: An August decline greater than -4.54% is usually associated with a bear market at the start of October. A rise over +4.42% in August is usually linked with an October bull market.

**Spotting bear markets**

for the worse. Up to 1951, prices rose six times and fell seven times. Since then, October's record for bear markets has been very poor, three up and 10 down.

Given the pain associated with an October investment during bear markets, the historical relationships illustrated in Figure 10.1 are worth noting. Over the long run, August drops greater than -4.54% are associated with bear market Octobers 83% of the time, regardless of what happens in September.

Remember that these figures do not tell you when the bear market started or will end. It is conceivable that the following month will see the start of a new bull market. Also, it is possible for a bear market to be in progress without being flagged by this indicator. Still, as a bear market warning signal, a large August price drop should not be ignored.

**Spotting bull markets**

At the other end of the scale, big price increases in August, +4.43% or more, are virtually always associated with bull markets in October, regardless of what happens in September.

**First quarter is best**

Analysis of October profit trends by segment of the month finds that prices rise most often during the first quarter. The odds of a first-quarter price rise are 63%, well above average compared to the other 47 quarters of the year. From then on, the likelihood of profit steadily slips with the third and fourth quarters rising at a below-average rate, compared with other quarters of the year *(see Figure 10.2)*.

### INCREASE YOUR PROFIT ODDS

Investors can increase October profits by identifying specific years when prices are especially likely to rise or fall. There are several historical correlations which have done a good job of anticipating the direction of the October trend.

**July signal**

We start with a trend which correlates the direction of prices in July, the first month of the third quarter, with October, the first month of the fourth quarter.

Since 1922, there have been 17 occasions when the FTSE All Share Index or its predecessor index shifted by a small amount in July, no more than -1.49% on the down-side, and no more than +1.15% on the up-side. In each of those years, October prices rose.

| UPDATE |

*Rose (17)*

*Fell (0)*

October record after a July price shift of -1.49% to +1.15% (FTSE All Share Index since 1922)

## QUARTERLY ODDS OF PRICE RISE IN OCTOBER

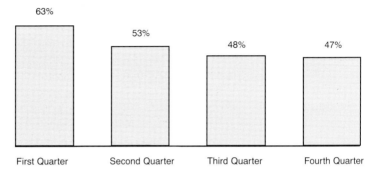

Source: *Financial Times, Datastream/ICV*

Figure 10.2: The first quarter is the month's most profitable segment. The third and fourth quarters both rise slightly less than half the time, below average compared to the rest of the year.

**Prior 12-months signal**

The direction in which prices[1] have shifted in the past 12 months is also a good October price signal. Since 1922, there have been 15 years in which the FTSE All Share Index or its predecessor index rose in the past 12 months by +12.19% to +21.66%. The stock market rose each time in October.

*Rose (15)*

IMPROVEMENT

*Fell (0)*

October record after a price rise of +12.19% to +21.66% in past 12 months (FTSE All Share Index since 1922)

---

[1]We will provide closing price trends on key indices for the last 12 months at no cost (see page 9).

Prior eight-
months signal

Since 1963, there have been 13 occasions when the FTSE All Share Index or its predecessor index shifted between -3.63% to +10.42% from February to September. October prices rose 12 times.

*Rose (12)*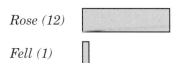

*Fell (1)*

October's record after previous eight-month price shift of -3.63% to +10.42% (FTSE All Share Index since 1963)

August/
September
signal No.1

If August prices rise by at least +3.57%, and are followed by a September price increase under +4.33%, or a September fall of any amount, October prices tend to rise. Since 1952, there have been 17 years with August and September price shifts on the FT-Non-Financial Index or its predecessor index in the correct range. October prices rose each time.

*Rose (17)*

IMPROVEMENT

*Fell (0)*

October record after an August price rise of at least +3.57% and a September rise of less than +4.33% or a September fall (FT-Non-Financial Index since 1952)

August/
September
signal No.2

Here is another variation of the August/September trend to monitor. Since 1922, there have been 17 years when the FTSE All Share Index or its predecessor index rose in the preceding two months by +2.82% to +5.88%. October prices rose in 16 of those years. The single exception was back in 1949, in the midst of a serious post-war balance of payments crisis.

340

IMPROVEMENT

*Rose (16)*

*Fell (1)*

October record after an August/September price rise of +2.82% to +5.88% (FTSE All Share Index since 1922)

**September signal**

Focusing on bull market years alone, there have been 15 occasions since 1945 when the FTSE All Share Index or its predecessor index rose in September between +0.53% to +5.70%. The stock market rose in October each time. October's record in the remaining 20 bull market years of this period was 12 up and eight down.

*Rose (15)*

*Fell (0)*

October's record during bull markets after a September price rise of +0.53% to +5.70% (FTSE All Share Index since 1945)

**Prior seven-months signal**

Each of the signals discussed so far are associated with price rises. Here is a trend to help spot when a decline is more likely. Since 1943, there have been nine occasions when prices rose on the FT Ordinary Share Index in the preceding seven months (March to September) by +9.85% to +15.87%. October prices fell in eight of those years. The single exception was a rise of just +0.07% in 1983.

*Rose (1)*

*Fell (8)*

October's record after previous seven-month price rise of +9.85% to +15.87% (FT Ordinary Share Index since 1943)

341

# FIRST QUARTER OF OCTOBER – OCTOBER 1ST TO 8TH

Here comes the best quarter of the month. Prices often rise in bull and bear markets alike.

If you plan to buy shares during October, history suggests the best time to do so is near the beginning of the month.

As in other months, there are widely different profit potentials associated with each segment of October.

**Best quarter**

The best segment of the month, by far, is the first quarter. It has risen 63% of the time and produced an average annual profit in every single decade on record. Between 1935 and 1996, the average first-quarter profit was +0.81% per year, fifth-best quarter for the entire year (*see Table 10.3*).

Prices rise more than half the time in bull and bear markets alike. They rise 66% of the time in bull markets and 57% in bear markets. Both figures are well above average compared to other quarters of the year (*see Table 10.4*).

**1–3 October**

The chance of a price rise is quite good throughout the quarter. Shares rise more than half the time from 1 October to 7 October with the most profitable point of the quarter near the beginning. Prices rise 58–60% of the time on 1–3 October. (*see Figure 10.3*). The recent trend for 1 October is improving. Since 1980, prices have risen in nine out of 11 occasions that the stock market was open on this day.

**8 October**

The trend weakens on 8 October which rises a little less than half the time, a prelude to horrible conditions on the following two days which are discussed in fuller detail in the following section.

Analysis of price trends by day of week shows a familiar pattern, good odds of a price rise throughout the week, except for Monday which rises a little less than half the time (*see Figure 10.4*).

## PERCENTAGE PRICE CHANGE: OCTOBER 1935–96

| | Oct 1–8 | Oct 9–15 | Oct 16–23 | Oct 24–31 |
|---|---|---|---|---|
| Annual average | | | | |
| 1935–39 | 0.46% | 0.24% | 1.56% | 0.47% |
| 1940–49 | 0.70% | -0.74% | 0.42% | 0.76% |
| 1950–59 | 0.31% | 1.10% | 0.65% | -0.42% |
| 1960–69 | 0.87% | -0.40% | -1.34% | 1.23% |
| 1970–79 | 0.68% | -0.42% | 0.17% | -1.74% |
| 1980–89 | 1.06% | -0.38% | -2.07% | 0.24% |
| 1990–96 | 1.68% | -0.07% | 0.62% | -0.54% |
| | | | | |
| Average quarterly price change | 0.81% | -0.12% | -0.15% | -0.01% |
| | | | | |
| Per cent of time prices rise | 63% | 53% | 48% | 47% |

*Source: Financial Times, Datastream/ICV*

Table 10.3: The first quarter has been steadily profitable since our records began. In contrast, the second quarter has been a frequent loser since the 1950s. But prices have risen the last five years in a row. A trend change, perhaps?

**2 October**

The chance of a price rise on 2 October is especially good when it lands on a Thursday or Friday. Since our records began, 2 October landed on Thursday or Friday on 17 occasions. Prices rose in 13 of those years. On other days of the week, the odds of a price rise are just 50:50 *(see Table 10.5).*

**3 October**

Another example of mid-week strength appears on 3 October. Since 1935, it has landed on Tuesday or Wednesday on 17 occasions. Prices rose 13 times. On other days of the week, the profit odds are much lower *(see Table 10.6).*

### OCTOBER FIRST-QUARTER PERFORMANCE IN BULL/BEAR MARKETS: 1935–1996

|  | Total | Bull Markets | Bear Markets |
|---|---|---|---|
| Average price change | 0.81% | 1.35% | -0.24% |
| Rank (of 48) | 5 | 3 | 15 |
| | | | |
| Per cent of time prices rise | 63% | 66% | 57% |
| Rank (of 48) | 11 | 16 | 9 |

*Source: Financial Times, Datastream/ICV*

Table 10.4: Prices rise with a frequency that is well above average in bull and bear markets alike.

### INCREASE YOUR PROFIT ODDS

Prior four-quarters signal No.1

Although a 63% chance of profit over the long run is nothing to complain about, it is possible to do better than that by investing selectively. We start with a newly emerging trend that has run since 1969 on the FTSE All Share Index.

During this period, a rise in the preceding four quarters within a range of +2.66% to +8.67% has often proven to be a promising sign for the first quarter. There have been nine moves of this magnitude in the past three decades and the first quarter rose in eight of those years. The single exception to the rule was a tiny decline of just -0.01% in 1984.

*Rose (8)*

*Fell (1)*

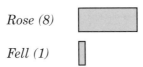

First-quarter record after a rise in the preceding four quarters of +2.66% to +8.67% (FTSE All Share Index since 1969)

## PERCENTAGE OF TIME PRICES RISE EACH TRADING DAY IN OCTOBER'S FIRST QUARTER

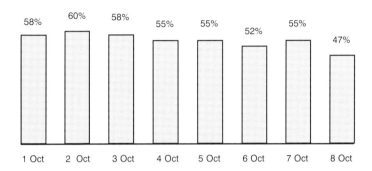

*Source: Financial Times, Datastream/ICV*

Figure 10.3: Prices rise more than half the time on most days in this quarter. The trend on 1 October is improving. Prices have risen in nine of the last 11 tries.

During the remaining 19 years of this period that were untouched by this signal, the first-quarter record was 11 rises and eight declines.

Prior four-quarters signal No.2

A related trend runs on the FT Ordinary Share Index. Since 1948, a moderate shift in September is often followed by a rally in the first quarter of October. During the period under study, there have been 17 occasions when September prices shifted -1.43% to +1.34%. October's first quarter rose in 15 of those years.

*Rose (15)*

*Fell (2)*

First-quarter record after a September price shift of -1.43% to +1.34% (FT Ordinary Share Index since 1948)

**PERCENTAGE OF TIME PRICES RISE EACH DAY OF WEEK IN OCTOBER'S FIRST QUARTER**

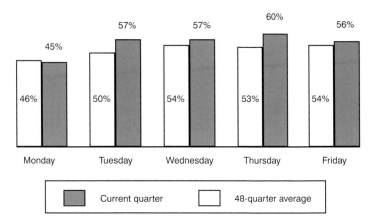

Source: *Financial Times, Datastream/ICV*

Figure 10.4: Prices rise at an above-average rate from Tuesday to Friday.

September
second-half
signal No.1

The FT Ordinary Share Index also tends to rise in years with either a small loss or a rise in September's second half. Since 1947, there have been 19 years in which September's third quarter either fell by up to -1.74% or rose by any amount, and the fourth quarter fell by up to -0.09% or rose by any amount. Prices rose in October's first quarter in 17 of those years.

*Rose (17)*

*Fell (2)*

First-quarter record after a September third-quarter price decline of up to -1.74% or a rise, and a fourth-quarter price decline of up to -0.09% or a rise (FT Ordinary Share Index since 1947)

346

**PERCENTAGE OF TIME PRICES RISE ON 2 OCTOBER: 1935–1996**

| | Prices rise |
|---|---|
| Total | 60% |
| Thursday and Friday | 76% |
| Rest of week | 50% |

*Source: Financial Times, Datastream/ICV*

Table 10.5: The chance of a price rise is quite good when 2 October lands on Thursday or Friday.

**PERCENTAGE OF TIME PRICES RISE ON 3 OCTOBER: 1935–1996**

| | Prices rise |
|---|---|
| Total | 58% |
| Tuesday and Wednesday | 76% |
| Rest of week | 46% |

*Source: Financial Times, Datastream/ICV*

Table 10.6: The chance of a price rise is above average when 3 October lands on Tuesday or Wednesday.

September fourth quarter

You can also out-perform the averages by watching the direction of prices on the FT Ordinary Share Index in September's fourth quarter. Since 1949, if fourth-quarter prices fell by -1.50% to -5.66%, the odds of a rise in October's first quarter was quite high. Out of 16 years with a fourth-quarter fall of this magnitude, first-quarter prices rose 14 times (88%). The average price rise was

+1.46% in those 16 years.

*Rose (14)*

*Fell (2)*

First quarter record after a September fourth-quarter price decline of -1.50% to -5.66% (FT Ordinary Share Index since 1949)

September
second-half
signal No.2

A new trend is in the process of developing on the FT-Non-Financial Index. Since 1971, the second half of September has fallen by -3.21% or more in seven different years. Prices rose in the first quarter in each of those years. We shall watch further developments with great interest.

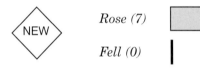

NEW

*Rose (7)*

*Fell (0)*

First-quarter record after a September second-half price decline of -3.21% or more (FT-Non-Financial Index since 1971)

## SECOND QUARTER OF OCTOBER – OCTOBER 9TH TO 15TH

> The second quarter has lost money in the average year from the 1950s to the 1980s. However, prices have risen in the last five years in a row. It is a promising sign but it is too early to tell if a major trend change has occurred.
>
> Trend change or not, be careful on 9–10 October. Both rise about one-third of the time and are among the 10 worst days of the entire year.

The second quarter rose 53% of the time between 1935 and 1996 and fell -0.12% in the average year. This record is much weaker than that of the first quarter.

**Bull market weak**

History shows that the chance of a price rise is about 50:50 in bull and bear markets alike. Compared to other quarters of the year, the second quarter's bull market record is poor *(see Table 10.7)*.

**'60s to '80s poor**

The last profitable decade for the second quarter was the 1950s. Since then, the second-quarter investor has lost money in the 1960s, '70s and '80s. The trend in the 1990s is also in the red, largely due to a drop of -4.15% in 1990. But prices have been rising steadily in recent years – five ups in a row since 1992. We don't yet know if this is a random event or the start of a major trend change. We shall watch the future with great interest *(see Table 10.8)*.

**9–10 October**

Analysis of price trends on a day-by-day basis reveals lots of red ink at the beginning of the quarter. In fact, most of the losses that occur during the second quarter happen in its first half when stock market conditions are often atrocious. 9 October is the worst day of the month and sixth-worst of the entire year. Prices rise just 33% of the time. 10 October is not much better with price increases in just 35% of all years, second-worst day of the month and ninth-worst in the year. These two days, back-to-back, are the worst two-day stretch of the entire year *(see Figure 10.5)*.

## OCTOBER SECOND-QUARTER PERFORMANCE IN BULL/BEAR MARKETS: 1935–1996

|  | Total | Bull Markets | Bear Markets |
|---|---|---|---|
| Average price change | -0.12% | 0.05% | 0.46% |
| Rank (of 48) | 33 | 41 | 20 |
|  |  |  |  |
| Per cent of time prices rise | 53% | 54% | 52% |
| Rank (of 48) | 24 | 35 | 15 |

*Source: Financial Times, Datastream/ICV*

Table 10.7: Prices rise 53% of the time, precisely average. But the bull market record is poor compared to other bull market quarters.

Nothing has changed in recent years. Prices have fallen on these two days two-thirds of the time since 1980. In other words, second-quarter prices have risen in recent years despite these two days, not because of them.

More bad news    History shows that if prices have fallen during the preceding five days, 9 and 10 October are even more likely to fall. Out of 41 times with a price decline in the previous five trading days, 9 and 10 October rose four times between them. Three of the increases were in the area of +0.10%, about four points on an FTSE 100 in the area of 4000.

*Rose (4)*

*Fell (35)*

*No change (2)*

Trend on October 9–10 if prices fell in preceding five trading days.

## PERCENTAGE PRICE CHANGE: OCTOBER 1985–96

|  | October 1–8 | October 9–15 | October 16–23 | October 24–31 |
|---|---|---|---|---|
| 1985 | 1.16% | 1.49% | 1.85% | 2.41% |
| 1986 | 1.73% | 1.58% | -1.55% | 3.22% |
| 1987 | 0.81% | -2.36% | -21.81% | -4.62% |
| 1988 | 1.06% | -0.06% | 1.29% | -0.26% |
| 1989 | -1.40% | -2.48% | -1.98% | -1.95% |
| 1990 | 10.01% | -4.15% | 1.10% | -3.22% |
| 1991 | -0.91% | -0.99% | -0.52% | 0.26% |
| 1992 | -0.55% | 0.10% | 4.88% | -0.21% |
| 1993 | 2.02% | 0.32% | 2.28% | -0.75% |
| 1994 | -1.11% | 3.27% | -2.00% | 1.59% |
| 1995 | 0.56% | 0.62% | -0.93% | -0.21% |
| 1996 | 1.74% | 0.37% | -0.50% | -1.23% |
| Average quarterly price change | 1.26% | -0.19% | -1.49% | -0.41% |
| Number of years in which prices | | | | |
| Rose | 8 | 7 | 5 | 4 |
| Fell | 4 | 5 | 7 | 8 |

*Source: Datastream/ICV*

Table 10.8: The second to fourth quarters have been weak in recent years. But second-quarter prices have just risen five times in a row. There are no signs of comparable improvement in the third and fourth quarters.

11–12 October    The stock market's poor track record during this quarter of the month is not limited solely to 9–10 October. Although the trend soon improves, the odds of a price rise for the next two days, 11 and 12 October, are also less

## PERCENTAGE OF TIME PRICES RISE EACH TRADING DAY IN OCTOBER'S SECOND QUARTER

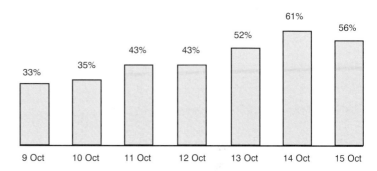

*Source: Financial Times, Datastream/ICV*

Figure 10.5: 9 October is the worst day of the month and sixth-worst of the year. 10 October is not much better. 9 and 10 October comprise the worst two-day stretch of the year.

than 50:50.

**13–15 October**

Happily, the chance of a price rise improves still further as the end of the second quarter approaches. 13–15 October are strong performers, especially the 14th which rises 61% of the time, the second-best performance of the month.

**Poor weekday trend**

Analysis of trading conditions by day of week shows that poor trading conditions are not associated with any specific weekday. Each rises less than half of the time *(see Figure 10.6)*. However, there are some interesting trends that affect specific weekdays in this quarter. Take 9 October, for example. It is hard to imagine that trading conditions could be worse on 9 October than the top line figure. But in some circumstances, they can be worse. Since 1935, 9 October has landed on a Monday or Tuesday on 17 occasions. The stock market rose just 3 times *(see Table 10.9)*.

## PERCENTAGE OF TIME PRICES RISE EACH DAY OF WEEK IN OCTOBER'S SECOND QUARTER

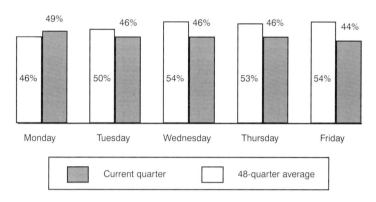

Source: Financial Times, Datastream/ICV

Figure 10.6: Prices rise less than half of the time on every week day in the second quarter.

On the up-side, prices are quite likely to rise on 13–14 October when either lands on a Monday *(see Table 10.10)*. Since 1935, there have been 17 occasions when the stock market landed on Monday on 13 or 14 October. Prices rose 14 times.

### INCREASE YOUR PROFIT ODDS

We find two signals that are associated with a second-quarter price rise.

October first-quarter signal

Since 1942, there have been 15 occasions when the FTSE All Share Index or its predecessor index has risen in the first quarter of this month within a range of +1.16% to +2.53%. Prices rose in the second quarter in 13 of those years.

### PERCENTAGE OF TIME PRICES RISE ON 9 OCTOBER: 1935–1996

|  | Prices rise |
|---|---|
| Total | 33% |
| | |
| Monday or Tuesday | 18% |
| Rest of week | 42% |

*Source: Financial Times, Datastream/ICV*

Table 10.9: 9 October is a poor day in the long run. But the odds are especially poor when it lands on Monday or Tuesday. Prices rise just one time in five when 9 October lands on the first two days of the week.

NEW

*Rose (13)*

*Fell (2)*

Second-quarter record after a price rise of +1.16% to +2.53% in October's first quarter (FTSE All Share Index since 1942)

Prior four-quarters signal

Also on the FTSE All Share Index and its predecessor index, there have been 17 years since 1937 when prices have risen in the last four quarters within a range of +1.16% to +4.80%. Second-quarter prices rose in 14 of those years.

NEW

*Rose (14)*

*Fell (3)*

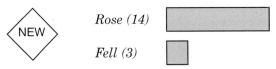

Second-quarter record after a price rise of +1.16% to +4.80% in the preceding four quarters (FTSE All Share Index since 1937)

354

## PERCENTAGE OF TIME PRICES RISE ON 13–14 OCTOBER: 1935–1996

|  | Prices rise |
|---|---|
| Total | 57% |
| Monday | 82% |
| Rest of week | 51% |

*Source: Financial Times, Datastream/ICV*

Table 10.10: The odds of a price rise on 13–14 October are high if either lands on a Monday.

There have been 31 additional years since 1942 not flagged by either of the previous two indicators. Prices rose in the second quarter in 11 of those years and fell 20 times.

**Prior five-quarters signal**     For readers interested in a short-term bet against the market, watch the trend in the preceding five quarters. If prices decline in September and continue to show signs of weakness in October's first quarter, they are likely to decline in the second quarter. Since 1937, there have been 11 years in which prices fell in September on the FTSE All Share Index or its predecessor index, and either bounced up in the first quarter – by no more than +0.90% – or fell to -3.48%. The stock market dropped in October's second quarter in 10 of those years.

*Rose (1)*

*Fell (10)*

Second-quarter record after a decline in September and a shift in October's first quarter of +0.90% to -3.48% (FTSE All Share Index since 1937)

September
second-half
signal

On the FT Ordinary Share Index, if prices fall in the second half of September within a range of -2.18% to -3.90%, the odds are high that October's second quarter will fall, regardless of what happens in the first quarter. Since 1946, prices fell to the required degree in September's second half on 11 occasions. They continued to fall in October's second quarter in nine of those years.

*Rose (2)*

*Fell (9)*

Second-quarter record after a drop in September's second half of -2.18% to -3.90% (FT Ordinary Share Index since 1946)

## THIRD QUARTER OF OCTOBER – OCTOBER 16TH TO 23RD

> The third-quarter long-term trend is heavily affected by the 1987 Crash. If 1987 is eliminated from the computations, some analysts would classify the third quarter as an average performer.
>
> Unfortunately, many of the so-called good years occurred several decades ago. The recent trend has weakened. Shares have risen a little better than one-third of the time since 1958.
>
> The odds of a price rise are especially low in bull market years. In fact, the third quarter has one of the worst bull market records of the entire year. In contrast, the bear market record is quite good if 1987 is excluded.

At first glance, the third quarter is not a particularly good time to be in the stock market. Since 1935, it has produced an average annual loss of -0.15%.

If not for 1987

But the problem was caused by 1987's crash which

dropped third quarter prices by -21.81%. If 1987 were eliminated from the computations, a small profit of +0.20% was produced in the remaining 61 years of our historical record. This would have placed the third quarter in 20th place on the quarterly profit rankings, right in the middle of the average range.

**Recent weakness**

Unfortunately, the record has weakened in recent years. From 1935–57, third-quarter prices rose 17 times out of 23 attempts, a 74% success rate. Since then, prices have risen just 38% of the time, a very poor showing.

**Bull and bear markets**

Another point of concern is its below-average performance during bull market years. Third-quarter prices rise just 46% of the time during bull markets, the 45th-ranked quarter of the year. In contrast, the bear market trend is quite strong if 1987's (hopefully) once-in-a-lifetime crash is subtracted from the figures. Without 1987, the typical third-quarter bear market performance is a small loss of just -0.05%, which places the third quarter in 12th position on the quarterly bear market performance rankings *(see Table 10.11)*.

Here is a final point of concern. Even in promising years, don't be too quick to buy shares during this point in the year unless you are a very short-term trader. The quarter to follow is one of the year's worst. Over the long run, the best advice for long term investors contemplating a purchase of shares is to wait for the next few weeks to pass.

**18 October**

Happily, the news is not all bleak. Despite the overall pessimism, history also reveals a small pocket of mid-quarter strength. While shares rise on the opening day of the quarter just 40% of the time, making it the weakest day of the quarter, the trend quickly improves. By 18 October, prices rise 64% of the time, the best day of the entire month *(see Figure 10.7)*.

**Wednesday**

Another recurring trend of interest is for prices to be quite strong in the middle of the week. Over the long run, they rise 61% of the time on third-quarter Wednesdays,

## OCTOBER THIRD-QUARTER PERFORMANCE IN
## BULL/BEAR MARKETS: 1935–1996

|  | Total | Bull Markets | Bear Markets |
|---|---|---|---|
| Average price change | -0.15%* | 0.32% | -1.09%** |
| Rank (of 48) | 35 | 32 | 36 |
| Per cent of time prices rise | 48% | 46% | 52% |
| Rank (of 48) | 34 | 45 | 15 |

\* Without 1987's loss, the average price change would be +0.20%, ranked 20th.

\*\* Without 1987's loss, the average price change would be -0.05%, ranked 12th.

*Source: Financial Times, Datastream/ICV*

Table 10.11: 1987 had a major effect on the long-term third-quarter trend. Without 1987, the third quarter would have been profitable over the long run.

the fifth-best Wednesday of all 48 quarters *(see Figure 10.8).*

### INCREASE YOUR PROFIT ODDS

Prior four-quarters signal

Here is a newly discovered trend that does a good job of flagging third-quarter declines. If the FTSE All Share Index declines in the preceding four quarters by -0.44% to -9.49%, the odds are high that the third quarter will fall as well.

Since 1969, prices fell within the target range on 12 occasions and third-quarter prices continued to fall in 11 of those years. During the remaining 16 years of this period, the third quarter rose two-thirds of the time.

## PERCENTAGE OF TIME PRICES RISE EACH TRADING DAY IN OCTOBER'S THIRD QUARTER

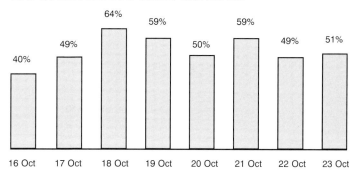

*Source: Financial Times, Datastream/ICV*

Figure 10.7: The odds of making a profit are comfortably above average in the middle of the quarter. 18 October is the best day of the month.

*Rose (1)*

*Fell (11)*

Third-quarter record after a price decline in preceding four quarters of -0.44% to -9.49% (FTSE All Share Index since 1969)

**Second-quarter signal**

Another good down-side indicator seems to be developing on the FT-Non-Financial Index.

Since 1978, a small decline in October's second quarter has often been followed by a third-quarter loss. During the designated period, second-quarter prices fell by up to -2.55% on seven different occasions. Third-quarter prices fell still further in six of those years.

## PERCENTAGE OF TIME PRICES RISE EACH DAY OF WEEK IN OCTOBER'S THIRD QUARTER

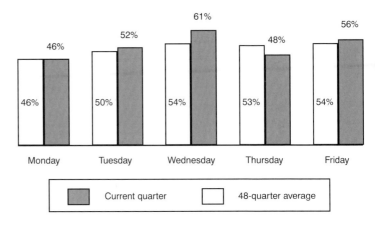

*Source: Financial Times, Datastream/ICV*

Figure 10.8: Third-quarter Wednesdays are the fifth-best of all 48 quarters.

NEW

*Rose (1)*

*Fell (6)*

Third-quarter record after a price fall of up to -2.55% in the second quarter (FT-Non-Financial Index since 1978)

First-half signal No.1

The final down-side trend worth monitoring is the direction of prices on the FT Ordinary Share Index during the previous two quarters. Since 1964, there have been 10 years when prices dropped on the FT Ordinary Share Index in October's first half by no more than -2.49%. They continued to decline in the third quarter in nine of those years.

Rose (1)

Fell (9)

Third-quarter record after a first-half price decline of up to -2.49% (FT Ordinary Share Index since 1964)

**First-half signal No.2**

Despite the weak overall trend during this quarter, price shifts on the FT Ordinary Share Index during the first half of the month occasionally flag a third-quarter profit opportunity.

Since 1936, there have been 15 years when the FT Ordinary Share Index rose in October's first half between +1.55% to +4.02%. They continued to rise in the third quarter in 12 of those years (80%).

Rose (12)

Fell (3)

Third-quarter record after a first-half price rise of +1.55% to +4.02% (FT Ordinary Share Index since 1936)

# Fourth quarter of October – October 24th to 31st

The fourth-quarter record is weak over the long term and has steadily worsened in recent years. Prices rose in just two of the last 10 years.

Be especially careful on 26 October. It has a poor record over the long run and prices have risen just once in the last 10 tries.

**Weak trend**

The fourth quarter of October is a poor time to hold shares. Between 1935 and 1996, this quarter has risen just 47% of the time.

If anything, the record has worsened in recent years. Shares rose just two times in the last 10 years.

**Poor bear market record**

During bull markets, shares rise a little over half of the time and produce a +0.47% average annual profit. Both figures are comfortably in the average range compared with other quarters of the year. In contrast, the bear market record is poor and getting worse. Over the long run, prices rise three times out of 10. But since 1965, the fourth quarter has fallen in eight out of nine bear market years *(see Table 10.12)*.

**26 October**

Despite the poor overall record, prices tend to rise about half the time on most days throughout the quarter. However, the odds of a price rise on 26 October are a notable exception. Prices rise just 39% of the time. The recent record for this day is even worse than the long-term average suggests. Since 1984, prices have risen just once out of 10 attempts *(see Figure 10.9)*.

No one can explain why, but both 26 and 27 October are often slammed when they land on Friday. Since 1935, these two days have risen on Friday in just three out of 17 attempts *(see Table 10.13)*.

**30 October**

Another recent trend change has occurred on 30 October which rises slightly more than half of the time over the long run. Since 1980, prices have risen in 10 out of 11 attempts. Even better news, eight of the 10

## OCTOBER FOURTH-QUARTER PERFORMANCE IN BULL/BEAR MARKETS: 1935–1996

|  | Total | Bull Markets | Bear Markets |
|---|---|---|---|
| Average price change | -0.01% | 0.47% | -0.95% |
| Rank (of 48) | 29 | 26 | 34 |
|  |  |  |  |
| Per cent of time prices rise | 47% | 56% | 29% |
| Rank (of 48) | 39 | 29 | 42 |

*Source: Financial Times, Datastream/ICV*

Table 10.12: Prices rise at a below-average rate during the fourth quarter. The trend has weakened in recent years with a rise in just two of the last 10 years. Be especially cautious during bear markets. The trend is poor and getting worse.

advances were greater than one-half of one percent, the equivalent of at least 20 points on an FTSE 100 in the area of 4000.

**Poor Friday**

Prices rise about half of the time on most days of the week. The single exception is Friday which rises just 43% of the time, the fifth-worst Friday of all 48 quarters *(see Figure 10.10)*. The problem is entirely caused by 26–27 October. Friday prices rise 56% of the time during the rest of the quarter, stronger than the Monday–Thursday record.

### INCREASE YOUR PROFIT ODDS

**Third-quarter signal**

Fourth-quarter price drops are often anticipated by the direction of prices during the third quarter.

Since 1951, there have been 11 occasions when third-quarter prices shifted on the FT Ordinary Share Index within a range of -0.80% to +0.51%. The fourth quarter

**PERCENTAGE OF TIME PRICES RISE EACH TRADING DAY IN OCTOBER'S FOURTH QUARTER**

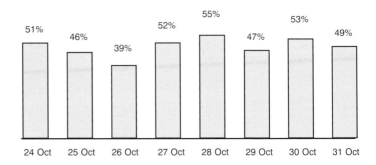

Source: Financial Times, Datastream/ICV

Figure 10.9: Prices rise about half of the time on most days in the quarter. 26 October is an exception. Since 1984, it has risen just once out of 10 attempts.

fell in 10 of those years.

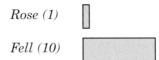

IMPROVEMENT

Fourth-quarter record after a third-quarter price shift of -0.80% to +0.51% (FT Ordinary Share Index since 1951)

**PERCENTAGE OF TIME PRICES RISE ON 26–27 OCTOBER: 1935–1996**

| | Prices rise |
|---|---|
| Total | 45% |
| Friday | 18% |
| Rest of week | 52% |

*Source: Financial Times, Datastream/ICV*

Table 10.13: Investing on Friday is a poor option in most years on 26 or 27 October.

## Looking Ahead

Here are four useful signals that can help to forecast where shares are heading in the months ahead.

Rising prices by next 31 January

A price rise of +2.27% to +18.21% on the FTSE All Share Index in the past 10 months is usually a good signal that prices will rise even higher in the next three months, that is, to the end of next January.

Since 1941, there have been 26 occasions when the FTSE All Share Index or its predecessor index rose within the designated range. Prices continued to rise in the next three months 24 times.

NEW

Trend to 31 January (next year) after a January-October price rise of +2.27% to +18.21% (FTSE All Share Index since 1941)

Here is another newly discovered trend, also based upon

## PERCENTAGE OF TIME PRICES RISE EACH DAY OF WEEK IN OCTOBER'S FOURTH QUARTER

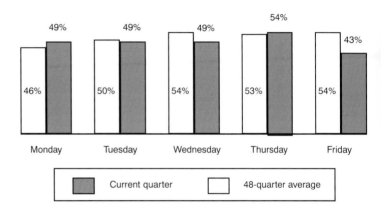

*Source: Financial Times, Datastream/ICV*

Figure 10.10: Fourth-quarter Fridays often disappoint investors with the fifth-worst Friday record of all 48 quarters.

Rising prices by next 31 July

the FTSE All Share Index. Since 1924, there have been 26 years with a price rise of at least +6.54% in the May–October period. Prices continued to rise in the next nine months 24 times. One of the two exceptions was a drop of less than -2%.

*Rose (24)*

*Fell (2)*

Trend to 31 July (next year) after a May to October price rise of at least +6.54% (FTSE All Share Index since 1924)

If prices shift during September and October on the FT-

**Rising prices by next 31 March**

Non-Financial Index or its predecessor index within a range of -3.03% to +3.47%, a price rise in the next five months, that is, to the end of next March, is very likely.

Since 1939, September/October prices have shifted within this range 21 times. Prices rose in the five months that followed in 20 of those years.

*Rose (20)*

*Fell (1)*

Trend to 31 March (next year) after a September/October shift of -3.03% to +3.47% (FT-Non-Financial Index since 1939)

**Rising prices by next 31 August**

Also on the FT-Non-Financial Index, if prices rise strongly from August to October by +4.03% to +20.13%, there is a good chance they will rise still higher 10 months later. Out of 19 occasions since 1952 with a price rise within this range, prices rose still higher by the following 31 August in 18 of those years.

The single exception occurred in 1965. Once the signal flashed, prices rose steadily as expected until July, 1966. But a series of July Measures which included higher Base Rates, increased taxes, price and income freezes, and overseas travel allowances caught the markets by surprise. Shares fell sharply.

*Rose (18)*

IMPROVEMENT

*Fell (1)*

Trend to 31 August (next year) after a August to October rise of +4.03% to +20.13% (FT-Non-Financial Index since 1952)

367

# CHAPTER 11 – NOVEMBER

It is hard to know what is the best course of action during bull market Novembers. Although prices rise about two-thirds of the time, the typical annual profit is quite small.

The heart of the problem is the fact that stock market shifts tend to be smaller than average during bull market up years and larger than average in bull market down years.

On balance, there does not seem to be a compelling reason to buy shares during the average bull market November.

The November bear market record is better than in many other months but is still a money-loser in most years. And when prices do fall in a bear market November, the fall is often a very large one.

The odds of a November price rise are good. Between 1919 and 1996, November prices rose 59% of the time, fifth-best of all 12 months on this dimension.

**Disappointing profits**

Unfortunately, the average price increase was smaller than normal in profitable years, and the average price drop larger than normal in money-losing years. As a result, the average price rise over the 78 years studied was just +0.21% per year, a lowly ninth-ranked, and much less than the risk-free return provided by a neighbourhood building society *(see Table 11.1)*.

A hypothetical £1,000 November investment, started in 1919, with money moved into cash for the other 11 months each year, would be worth just £1,076 in 1996.

**Strong second quarter**

Over the long run, the second quarter has produced most of the month's profits *(see Figure 11.1)*. Up until 1992, the other three quarters typically disappointed investors with profits in some years but red ink over the long run.

Things changed in 1993–6, following the government's switch to a late-November Budget. The fourth quarter began to deliver steady profits and shifted a small average annual loss over the long term into positive territory. But with the government's recent decision to shift budgets (at least temporarily) back to the spring, this important profit crutch to share prices has been removed. We expect a return to past, profitless fourth-quarter trading trends.

**Bull market record weak**

History shows that November has been a weak performer in bull markets as well as bear markets. During bull markets, it has the eighth-best record in terms of the number of rises over the long term but is eleventh-best in terms of the size of the average monthly price rise. This is because the typical rise during bull market up years is below average and the average decline in down years is higher than average. Some temporary improvement to this pattern were noted in 1993–6, coinciding with the late-November Budget. With no budget to help

## NOVEMBER PRICE RISES AND DECLINES: 1919–1996

|  | Average November price change | Up | Down/ No change |
|---|---|---|---|
| 1920–29 | -0.87% | 4 | 6 |
| 1930–39 | -0.98% | 5 | 5 |
| 1940–49 | 2.90% | 8 | 2 |
| 1950–59 | -1.38% | 5 | 5 |
| 1960–69 | 1.92% | 7 | 3 |
| 1970–79 | -2.20% | 5 | 5 |
| 1980–89 | 1.73% | 8 | 2 |
| 1990–96 | 0.94% | 4 | 3 |
| | | | |
| Average November change: 1919–96 | 0.21% | 59% | 41% |
| | | | |
| Rank (of 12) | 9 | 5 | |

*Source: BZW, Datastream/ICV*

Table 11.1: November is the fifth-best month in terms of the number of times prices have risen, but only ninth-best in terms of the size of the increase. Over time, investors would have made more profit with their money in a risk-free building society savings account.

the future November trend, we forecast a return to the historical bull market pattern.

**Bear markets can be painful**     During bear markets, November rises 45% of the time which is quite good compared to the bear market record of other months. Unfortunately, November has a distressing habit of suffering very large price declines during some bear market down years. Putting it in other terms, when things go bad in bear market Novembers, they often go very bad. Since our records began, a bear market has been running in 22 different Novembers.

371

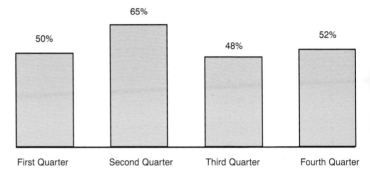

**QUARTERLY ODDS OF PRICE RISE IN NOVEMBER**

| First Quarter | Second Quarter | Third Quarter | Fourth Quarter |
| --- | --- | --- | --- |
| 50% | 65% | 48% | 52% |

*Source: Financial Times, Datastream/ICV*

Figure 11.1: The second quarter has long been the month's most profitable segment. The fourth quarter was helped in recent years by the late-November budget. Without the benefit of an Autumn Budget, prices are expected to return to past patterns of price rises slightly less than half the time.

Prices fell in 12 of those years. The average drop in those 12 down-years was -6.30%, the weakest result of all 12 months. Even worse, many of the smaller falls occurred before 1931. Since then, there have been eight bear market down-years. Shares fell by over five percent in six of the eight years *(see Table 11.2)*.

**Spotting bull markets**

Given the drastically different profit potential in bull versus bear market Novembers, it is useful for investors to know whether or not we are in a bull market. To help make this forecast, the following historical trend is worth monitoring.

Since our records began, an October price rise of +3.79% or more has been associated with a bull market in 17 out of 20 different years. Unfortunately, history provides no useful bear market signal as it does in other months *(see Figure 11.2)*.

## NOVEMBER PERFORMANCE IN BULL/BEAR MARKETS: 1919–1996

|  | Bull Markets | Bear Markets |
|---|---|---|
| Average per cent price change | 1.04% | -1.92% |
| Rank (of 12) | 11 | 4 |
|  |  |  |
| Per cent of time prices rise | 64% | 45% |
| Rank (of 12) | 8 | 3 |
|  |  |  |
| Average per cent price change in: |  |  |
| Rising years | 3.10% | 3.33% |
| Declining years | -2.66% | -6.30% |

*Source: BZW, Datastream/ICV*

Table 11.2: Prices tend to rise at a below-average rate in bull markets. In contrast, November's bear market record is above average in many respects. However, when prices fall in bear market years, the fall is often a very large one.

### INCREASE YOUR PROFIT ODDS[1]

History provides several trends to help investors significantly to improve upon the odds of making a profitable November investment.

Prior nine-months signal

One useful trend correlates November price shifts with the direction of prices in the nine preceding months. Since 1940, there have been 12 years when prices fell on the FT Ordinary Share Index in February to October from -7.22% to -33.71%. November prices rose in 11 of those years.

---

[1]We will provide closing price trends on key indices for the last 12 months at no cost (see page 9).

## ODDS OF BULL/BEAR MARKET TIPPED BY OCTOBER'S TREND

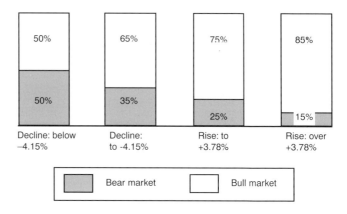

Source: BZW, Datastream/ICV

Figure 11.2: Large October rises are usually a signal that a bull market is in place at the start of November.

November trend after a February-to-October price drop of -7.22% to -33.71% (FT Ordinary Share Index since 1940)

**Prior 10-months signal**

Another trend which, historically, has done a good job of anticipating the direction of November price shifts is the direction of prices in the first 10 months of the year. Since 1958, there have been 15 years when prices on the FT-Non-Financial Index or its predecessor index rose between 2 January and 31 October within a range of +11.76% to

+42.89%. November prices rose in 14 of those years.

*Rose (14)*

*Fell (1)*

November trend after a price rise in the preceding 10 months of +11.76% to +42.89% (FT-Non-Financial Index since 1958)

Prior six-months signal

Also on the FT-Non-Financial Index and its predecessor index, there have been 14 years since 1934 when prices shifted slightly in the last six months, within a range of -3.91% to +1.53%. November share prices rose in 12 of those years.

UPDATE

*Rose (12)*

*Fell (2)*

November trend after a price shift in the preceding six months of -3.91% to +1.53% (FT-Non-Financial Index since 1934)

September – October signal No.1

The direction of prices over the past two months often flags which way November prices will shift. Since 1934, there have been 19 occasions in which prices shifted on the FTSE All Share Index or its predecessor index in the last two months within a range of -0.88% to +4.42%. November rose 17 times.

NEW

*Rose (17)*

*Fell (2)*

November's record after a previous two-month price shift of -0.88% to +4.42% (FTSE All Share Index since 1934)

September/
October signal
No.2

On the down-side, there have been 10 years since 1925 when share prices increased on the FTSE All Share Index or its predecessor index in September/ October by +4.45% to +6.50%. November prices fell each time.

IMPROVEMENT

*Rose (0)*

*Fell (10)*

November trend after a price rise in the preceding two months of +4.45% to +6.50% (FTSE All Share Index since 1925)

# FIRST QUARTER OF NOVEMBER – NOVEMBER 1ST TO 8TH

Over the long run, prices rise about half the time during the first quarter. But since 1950, the trend has worsened.

Not all the news is poor. The odds of a mid-week price rise are well above average.

Poor long-term
record

While no one can predict what will happen in any single year, the overall trend is quite clear – no profits over the long run. Between 1935 and 1996, prices have risen exactly half the time and produced a small average loss of -0.02% per year *(see Table 11.3)*.

Unfortunately, a profit was more likely in the first half of the century when prices rose in two out of three years. Since then, shares have fallen 55% of the time and produced an average annual loss in most recent decades.

Bull and bear
markets

Prices rise a little over half the time in bull market years and provide a small average annual profit. During bear markets, prices rise 43% of the time over the long run, about average compared to other bear market

## PERCENTAGE PRICE CHANGE: NOVEMBER 1935–96

| | Nov 1–8 | Nov 9–15 | Nov 16–23 | Nov 24–30 |
|---|---|---|---|---|
| Annual average | | | | |
| 1935–39 | 0.70% | 0.22% | -2.02% | 0.27% |
| 1940–49 | 0.70% | 0.83% | 0.74% | -0.05% |
| 1950–59 | -0.10% | 0.16% | -0.43% | -0.20% |
| 1960–69 | -0.47% | 1.96% | -1.41% | -0.03% |
| 1970–79 | -0.69% | -1.03% | -0.60% | 0.00% |
| 1980–89 | 0.48% | 1.20% | 0.06% | -0.05% |
| 1990–96 | -0.54% | 0.61% | 0.07% | 0.81% |
| | | | | |
| Average quarterly price change | -0.02% | 0.59% | -0.42% | 0.06% |
| | | | | |
| Per cent of time prices rise | 50% | 65% | 48% | 52% |

*Source: Financial Times, Datastream/ICV*

Table 11.3: Prices rise about half of the time in most segments of November. A notable exception is the second quarter which rises two-thirds of the time and is profitable in most decades.

quarters and typically produce a loss *(see Table 11.4)*. Unfortunately, the bear market trend has weakened recently. Prices have risen just 28% of the time in recent decades.

**Mid-week strength** Bull or bear market, history shows that profits are easiest to come by in mid-week. Prices rise 57% of the time on Tuesday and 59% on Wednesday. Both figures are well above average compared with other quarters of the year. The weakest point is on Monday which rises at a substandard 40% of the time *(see Figure 11.3)*.

**3 November** The stock market rises near to half the time on most days of the quarter. A notable exception is 3 November

### NOVEMBER FIRST-QUARTER PERFORMANCE IN BULL/BEAR MARKETS: 1935–1996

|                           | Total  | Bull Markets | Bear Markets |
|---------------------------|--------|--------------|--------------|
| Average price change      | -0.02% | 0.46%        | 0.95%        |
| Rank (of 48)              | 30     | 27           | 34           |
|                           |        |              |              |
| Per cent of time prices rise | 50% | 54%          | 43%          |
| Rank (of 48)              | 29     | 35           | 22           |

Source: Financial Times, Datastream/ICV

Table 11.4: Shares tend to rise just over half of the time in bull market years and produce an average annual profit. The bear market record is about average compared with other bear market quarters, but has weakened recently.

which rise 59% of the time, the best trading day of the quarter *(see Figure 11.4)*.

4–5 November     The chance of a rise is quite poor when 4 or 5 November lands on Friday. Since 1935, one of them landed on Friday 18 times. Prices rose just three times *(see Table 11.5)*. Both days have experienced a trend change in recent years. 4 November has fallen in seven out of eight attempts since 1985. Its poor Friday track record now seems to be affecting other days of the week as well.

In contrast, the odds of a price rise on 5 November have improved in recent years. Since 1980, prices have risen in eight out of 11 years. Note though that the Friday jinx continues to operate. Two of the three declines were on a Friday.

### INCREASE YOUR PROFIT ODDS

It is possible to increase the odds of anticipating a

## PERCENTAGE OF TIME PRICES RISE EACH DAY OF WEEK IN NOVEMBER'S FIRST QUARTER

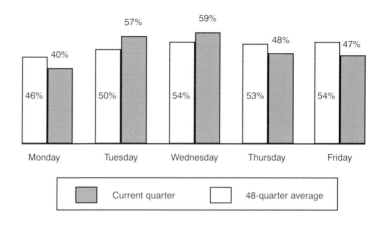

Source: Financial Times, Datastream/ICV

Figure 11.3: Prices rise more than half of the time on Tuesday and Wednesday. The trend is much weaker on other weekdays, especially Monday.

**October second-half signal No.1**

decline in some years by watching the direction of prices in the second half of October. Since 1935, there have been 16 years in which prices fell in October's second half by -1.16% to -4.03%. In 15 of those years, prices continued to fall in the first quarter of November. The average price drop was -1.31%.

*Rose (1)*

*Fell (15)*

First-quarter trend after a price drop in October's second half of -1.16% to -4.03% (FT Ordinary Share Index since 1935)

379

**PERCENTAGE OF TIME PRICES RISE EACH TRADING DAY IN NOVEMBER'S FIRST QUARTER**

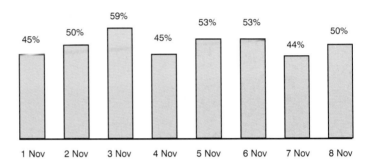

*Source: Financial Times, Datastream/ICV*

Figure 11.4: The trend on 5 November has improved since 1980. But no improvement has been noted on 1 or 7 November.

Prior three-quarters signal

Another good down-side indicator worth monitoring is a decline in the preceding three quarters. The FTSE All Share Index or its predecessor index fell by -2.39% to -6.22% on 11 occasions since 1949. First-quarter prices fell still further in 10 of those years.

*Rose (1)*    ▐

*Fell (10)*   ▭

First-quarter record after a price fall of -2.39% to -6.22% in the preceding three quarters (FTSE All Share Index since 1949)

October second-half signal No.2

On the up-side, prices have shifted in the two previous quarters on the FT-Non-Financial Index and its predecessor index within a range of -0.29% to +1.07% in 13

## PERCENTAGE OF TIME PRICES RISE ON 4–5
## NOVEMBER: 1935–1996

|  | Prices rise |
|---|---|
| Total | 49% |
| Friday | 17% |
| Rest of week | 57% |

*Source: Financial Times, Datastream/ICV*

Table 11.5: The chance of a rise is quite poor when 4 or 5 November lands on a Friday.

different years since 1935. First-quarter prices rose in 12 of those years.

*Rose (12)*

*Fell (1)*

First-quarter record after a price shift of -0.29% to +1.07% in the previous two quarters (FT-Non-Financial Index since 1935)

# SECOND QUARTER OF NOVEMBER – NOVEMBER 9TH TO 15TH

Here comes the best quarter of the month and one of the best of the year. Prices rise in two out of three years.

Most days rise more than half of the time. Two of them, 10 and 15 November, are tied as the best performers of the month.

Over the long term, Tuesday has turned in a particularly good performance, providing investors with the best Tuesday record of all 48 quarters.

Month's best quarter

Second-quarter prices rose 65% of the time between 1935 and 1996, the best performance of the month and seventh-best of the entire year. They rose at an average annual rate of +0.59%.

The second-quarter was November's Number One-ranked quarter in the 1940s, '50s, '60s, and '80s. Investors made money in every complete decade on record except for the 1970s and the losses of that decade were due to drops in the bear market years of 1973–4. The recent record continues to be a strong one. In the current decade, prices have risen in six of the last seven years *(see Table 11.6)*.

Bull and bear markets

The record is even better in bull market years. Prices rise 73% of the time, the sixth-best bull market quarter of the year. During bear markets, prices rise 44% of the time, about average compared to other bear market quarters *(see Table 11.7)*.

10 and 15 November

Analysis of daily price shifts shows generally good trading conditions throughout the quarter *(see Figure 11.5)*. Aside from the opening day which goes up 45% of the time, all other days rise more than 50% of the time. Several of them increase more than 60% of the time including 10 November and 15 November, both rising 68% of the time, a tie for the best performance of the month.

## PERCENTAGE PRICE CHANGE: NOVEMBER 1985–96

|  | November 1–8 | November 9–15 | November 16–23 | November 24–30 |
|---|---|---|---|---|
| 1985 | 0.81% | 0.88% | 2.58% | -0.44% |
| 1986 | 1.86% | -0.75% | -1.03% | 0.95% |
| 1987 | -8.07% | 3.02% | -1.27% | -4.02% |
| 1988 | -0.47% | -1.98% | 1.66% | -2.52% |
| 1989 | 2.69% | -0.24% | 0.53% | 2.31% |
| 1990 | -0.92% | 0.95% | 5.01% | -1.00% |
| 1991 | -0.18% | -0.62% | -3.76% | -1.15% |
| 1992 | 1.78% | 0.10% | 0.85% | 1.68% |
| 1993 | -2.76% | 0.17% | -0.51% | 2.60% |
| 1994 | -0.77% | 1.93% | -2.97% | 1.36% |
| 1995 | 0.22% | 0.78% | 0.74% | 1.37% |
| 1996 | -1.15% | 0.97% | 1.11% | 0.78% |
| Average quarterly price change | -0.58% | 0.43% | 0.24% | 0.16% |
| Number of years in which prices | | | | |
| Rose | 5 | 8 | 7 | 7 |
| Fell | 7 | 4 | 5 | 5 |

*Source: Datastream/ICV*

Table 11.6: Prices have frequently risen in the second and fourth quarters in recent years. Keep in mind that the fourth-quarter trend was helped by the late-November Budget in 1993–6.

12 November

Close behind is 12 November which rises 65% of the time. The odds of a price rise on 12 November are especially high on Tuesdays and Wednesdays. Since our records began in 1935, 12 November rose in 15 out of 17 times on these two days of the week *(see Table 11.8)*.

**NOVEMBER SECOND-QUARTER PERFORMANCE IN BULL/BEAR MARKETS: 1935–1996**

| | Total | Bull Markets | Bear Markets |
|---|---|---|---|
| Average price change | 0.59% | 0.95% | -0.29% |
| Rank (of 48) | 12 | 8 | 17 |
| Per cent of time prices rise | 65% | 73% | 44% |
| Rank (of 48) | 7 | 6 | 20 |

*Source: Financial Times, Datastream/ICV*

Table 11.7: The second quarter is the month's best performer over the long term, especially in bull markets.

Tuesday

Tuesday is a good profit-maker on most other days in the second quarter as well. Shares rise 72% of the time on second-quarter Tuesdays, the best Tuesday performance of all 48 quarters *(see Figure 11.6)*.

### INCREASE YOUR PROFIT ODDS

There are several price trends that have done a good job of tipping second quarter price increases.

November first-quarter signal

Since 1946, the FTSE All Share Index or its predecessor index has shifted within a range of -0.17% to +1.78% in the previous quarter in 16 different years. Prices rose in the second quarter in 15 of those years.

NEW

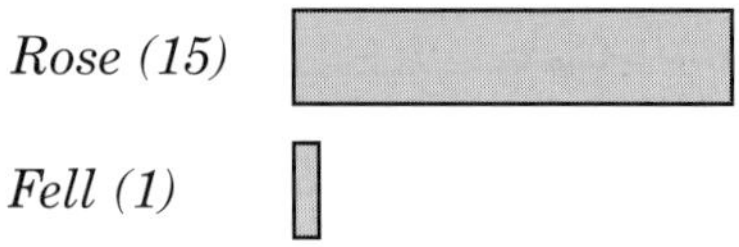


Second-quarter record after a price shift of -0.17% to +1.78% in November's first quarter (FTSE All Share Index since 1946)

**PERCENTAGE OF TIME PRICES RISE EACH TRADING DAY IN NOVEMBER'S SECOND QUARTER**

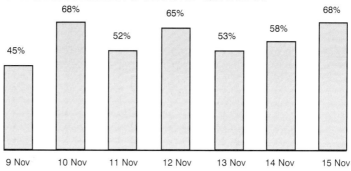

*Source: Financial Times, Datastream/ICV*

Figure 11.5: This is the best quarter of the month. Prices rise more than half of the time on most days.

**Prior four-quarters signal**

Here is another newly discovered trend involving the FTSE All Share Index or its predecessor index. Since 1938, a price rise of +0.77% to +3.26% in the preceding four quarters has usually been followed by a price increase in the second quarter. There have been 15 shifts of this magnitude and second-quarter prices rose in 14 of those years.

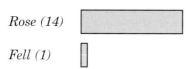

*Rose (14)*

*Fell (1)*

Second-quarter trend after price rise in the preceding four quarters of +0.77% to + 3.26% (FTSE All Share Index since 1938)

There have been 26 years since 1938 touched by one or both of the two previous signals. The second-quarter

## PERCENTAGE OF TIME PRICES RISE ON 12 NOVEMBER: 1935–1996

|  | Prices rise |
|---|---|
| Total | 65% |
| Tuesday and Wednesday | 88% |
| Rest of week | 50% |

Source: Financial Times, Datastream/ICV

Table 11.8: The chance of a price rise is quite high when 12 November lands on a Tuesday or Wednesday.

record in those years is 24 up and two down. In the remaining 33 years untouched by either signal, the second-quarter record is just a little better than 50:50, 18 up and 15 down.

October fourth-quarter signal

If prices rise on the FT Ordinary Share Index in October's final quarter by +0.59% to +4.90%, they are very likely to rise in the second quarter, no matter what happens in the first quarter. Since 1935, there have been 24 years in which prices rose by the appropriate amount. Shares continued to rise in November's second quarter in 22 of those years (92%).

Rose (22)

Fell (2)

Second-quarter trend after a price rise in October's fourth quarter of +0.59% to +4.90% (FT Ordinary Share Index since 1935)

No one knows why the fourth quarter of October affects the second quarter of November, regardless of what

## PERCENTAGE OF TIME PRICES RISE EACH DAY OF WEEK IN NOVEMBER'S SECOND QUARTER

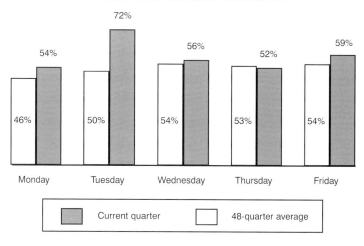

*Source: Financial Times, Datastream/ICV*

Figure 11.6: Prices rise on second-quarter Tuesdays in almost three out of four years, the best Tuesday record of all 48 quarters.

happens in the first quarter which sits between the two. Whatever the reason, it is a strong signal. And in the 38 years that it did not flash, the second quarter (November's best segment) rose 19 times and fell 19 times.

# THIRD QUARTER OF NOVEMBER – NOVEMBER 16TH TO 23RD

> Prices rise about half the time in bull market years and four years out of 10 in bear markets.
>
> Despite the weak overall record, the trend is strong in the first four days of the quarter, a continuation of strong second-quarter trading conditions. Profit odds weaken from then on.

**Weakest quarter**

Historically, the third quarter is the month's worst performer, averaging an annual loss of -0.42%. Prices rose 48% of the time since our records began.

The third-quarter investor lost money in the 1950s, '60s, and '70s. An exception to the trend occurred in the bull market 1980s when the quarter managed to turn a tiny profit.

**Bull and bear markets**

Over the long run, prices rise 52% of the time during bull markets, well below average compared to other quarters of the year *(see Table 11.9)*. In bear market years, prices rise 39% of the time, which is about average. However, the average price change is -1.82%, the second-worst bear market performance of the year. The reason for this apparent inconsistency is that when prices drop during bear markets, they tend to drop a lot. In fact, the typical bear market decline in down years is a whopping -3.56%, almost 150 points on an FTSE 100 of 4000.

**23 November**

The daily price trend is strong in the first four days of the quarter, a continuation of good second-quarter trading conditions. Unfortunately, the profit odds slip dramatically from 20 November onwards. The worst-performer is 23 November (whose prices go up just 32% of the time), the worst day of the entire month and tied with several others as the second-worst of the year *(see Figure 11.7)*. There have been no recent signs of change. Prices have risen on this day in just four of the last 15 years.

## NOVEMBER THIRD-QUARTER PERFORMANCE IN BULL/BEAR MARKETS: 1935–1996

|  | Total | Bull Markets | Bear Markets |
|---|---|---|---|
| Average price change | -0.42% | 0.15% | -1.82% |
| Rank (of 48) | 43 | 38 | 47 |
| Per cent of time prices rise | 48% | 52% | 39% |
| Rank (of 48) | 34 | 40 | 27 |

*Source: Financial Times, Datastream/ICV*

Table 11.9: Prices rise about half the time in bull market years which is below average compared with other quarters. The odds of a price rise in bear market years are about average. But be cautious because when prices drop, the decline is often a very large one.

20 and 21 November

History also shows that profitability trends are even weaker than usual when 20 or 21 November land on Tuesday. Since records began, one of these two days landed on Tuesday 17 times. Prices rose just three times *(see Table 11.10)*.

Monday

For the quarter as a whole, the odds of a price rise are low at the beginning of the week, especially Monday which rises just 36% of the time *(see Figure 11.8)*.

### INCREASE YOUR PROFIT ODDS

Here are two signals that often precede a third-quarter price rise.

November second-quarter signal

Since 1948, the FT Ordinary Share Index has shifted within a range of -0.38% to +0.81% during the second quarter in 10 different years. Prices rose in the third quarter in nine of those years.

## PERCENTAGE OF TIME PRICES RISE EACH TRADING DAY IN NOVEMBER'S THIRD QUARTER

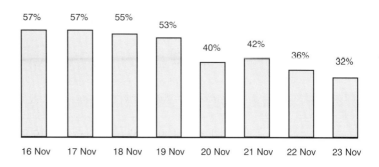

*Source: Financial Times, Datastream/ICV*

Figure 11.7: Second-quarter strength carries over to the first four days of this quarter. Prices rise more than half the time on each of these days. The likelihood of a price rise then weakens dramatically. The next four days rise at a substandard rate, especially 23 November, the month's worst day and second-worst of the year (tied with several others).

NEW

*Rose (9)*

*Fell (1)*

Third-quarter record after a price shift of -0.38% to +0.81% in the second quarter (FT Ordinary Share Index since 1948)

Prior three-quarters signal No.1

Since 1952, the FT-Non-Financial Index or its predecessor index has shifted within a range of -0.38% to +2.40% in the last three quarters in 11 different years. The stock market rose in the third quarter in 10 of those years.

## PERCENTAGE OF TIME PRICES RISE ON 20–21 NOVEMBER: 1935–1996

|  | Prices rise |
|---|---|
| Total | 41% |
| | |
| Tuesday | 18% |
| Rest of week | 47% |

*Source: Financial Times, Datastream/ICV*

Table 11.10: The odds of a price rise are poor when 20 or 21 November land on Tuesday. Prices rise less than one in five times.

NEW

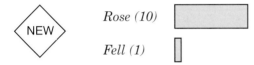

*Rose (10)*

*Fell (1)*

Third-quarter record after a price shift of -0.38% to +2.40% in the previous three quarters (FT-Non-Financial Index since 1952)

**Prior three-quarters signal No.2**

A good down-side indicator is a strong rise in the previous three quarters on the FTSE All Share Index or its predecessor index. Prices rose by +4.34% or more on 10 occasions since 1935. Third-quarter prices fell in nine of those years. The single exception was a tiny +0.17% rise in 1962.

NEW

*Rose (1)*

*Fell (9)*

Third-quarter record after a price rise of +4.34% or more in the previous three quarters (FTSE All Share Index since 1935)

391

## PERCENTAGE OF TIME PRICES RISE EACH DAY OF WEEK IN NOVEMBER'S THIRD QUARTER

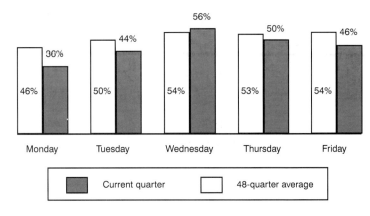

Source: Financial Times, Datastream/ICV

Figure 11.8: The chance of a price rise on Monday is quite low compared to Monday's record during other quarters of the year.

November first-half signal

Out of 11 years when the FT Ordinary Share Index dropped in November's first half by -2.79% or worse, they continued to decline in the third quarter nine times (82%). The average annual decrease was -2.56%.

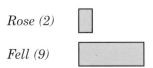

*Rose (2)*

*Fell (9)*

Third-quarter trend after price drop of -2.79% or more in November's first half (FT Ordinary Share Index since 1937)

# FOURTH QUARTER OF NOVEMBER – NOVEMBER 24TH TO 30TH

> Over the long run, prices rise about half the time. Aside from a short-lived window of profitability in 1993–6 after the Spring Budget was switched to late-November, the long term fourth-quarter trend was a money-loser.
>
> Now that the budget has been switched once again, we expect a return to weaker trading conditions.

The long term profit trend in fourth quarter of November is close to average. Between 1935 and 1996, prices rose a little over half of the time (52%) at an average annual rate of +0.06%.

**Long-term loser**    Despite the neutral overall record, fourth-quarter investors failed to profit in every complete decade for which we have records, from the 1940s to the 1980s. The same old familiar reason explains why – smaller than average rises in up-years and larger than average losses in down-years. Big profits were seen in 1993–6 after the Spring Budget was switched to late-November. Given that the budget has recently been switched back to the spring, we look for a return to weaker fourth-quarter trading conditions.

**Bull and bear markets**    The trend is weak during bull markets. Prices rise 51% of the time, well below average, and have produced a small average annual loss over the long run. As we have shown throughout this book, the bull market trend is usually stronger than the bear market trend, but not this time. Prices rise 53% of the time during bear markets, making this quarter the eleventh-best of all 48 quarters during bear markets *(see Table 11.11)*.

**27 November**    Shares often rise in mid-quarter, especially 27 November which rises 63% of the time, the best day of the quarter *(see Figure 11.9)*.

Over the long term, prices tend to rise most often on

## NOVEMBER FOURTH-QUARTER PERFORMANCE IN BULL/BEAR MARKETS: 1935–1996

|  | Total | Bull Markets | Bear Markets |
|---|---|---|---|
| Average price change | 0.06% | -0.09% | 0.45% |
| Rank (of 48) | 27 | 45 | 3 |
| Per cent of time prices rise | 52% | 51% | 53% |
| Rank (of 48) | 27 | 41 | 11 |

*Source: Financial Times, Datastream/ICV*

Table 11.11: Prices rise about half the time in bull and bear markets alike. This is a strong showing for bear markets compared with other quarters of the year.

**Wednesday and Friday**

Wednesday and Friday. The odds of a price rise are close to 50:50 for the remaining days of the week *(see Figure 11.10).*

### INCREASE YOUR PROFIT ODDS

Here are several historical correlations that have helped investors in the past.

**Prior three-quarters signal No.1**

Since 1948, the FTSE All Share Index or its predecessor index has shifted within a range of -0.25% to +1.85% in the past three quarters in 12 different years. Prices rose in the fourth quarter in 11 of those years.

*Rose (11)*

*Fell (1)*

Fourth-quarter record after a price shift of -0.25% to +1.85% in the past three quarters (FTSE All Share Index since 1948)

## PERCENTAGE OF TIME PRICES RISE EACH TRADING DAY IN NOVEMBER'S FOURTH QUARTER

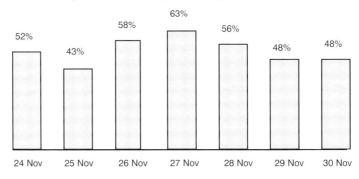

*Source: Financial Times, Datastream/ICV*

Figure 11.9: The most profitable segment of the fourth quarter is the middle portion, especially 27 November which rises almost two-thirds of the time.

November third-quarter signal No.1

During bull market periods, a small shift on the FTSE All Share Index in the preceding quarter within a range of -1.10% to +0.85% has often been associated with a fourth-quarter rise. Since 1969, there have been 10 bull market years with a third-quarter price shift within the target range. Shares rose in the fourth quarter in nine of those years.

*Rose (9)*

*Fell (1)*

Fourth-quarter trend after a third quarter price shift of -1.10% to +0.85% in bull market years (FTSE All Share Index since 1969)

Since 1952, the FT-Non-Financial Index or its predecessor

395

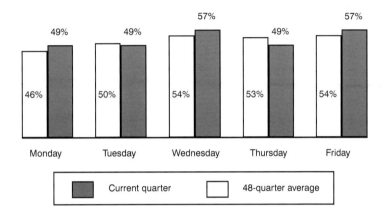

## PERCENTAGE OF TIME PRICES RISE EACH DAY OF WEEK IN NOVEMBER'S FOURTH QUARTER

*Source: Financial Times, Datastream/ICV*

Figure 11.10: The odds of a price rise for each day are close to their respective averages. However, Wednesday and Friday both rise more often than the other three days.

Prior three-quarters signal No.2

index has risen within a range of +0.23% to +2.67% in the previous three quarters in 13 different years. Prices rose in the fourth quarter each time.

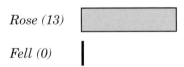

Fourth-quarter record after a price rise of +0.23% to +2.67% in the past three quarters (FT-Non-Financial Index since 1952)

Here is still another trend that monitors the direction of prices in the first three quarters of November, this time

**Prior three-quarters signal No.3**

based upon the FT Ordinary Share Index. Since 1935, there have been eight occasions when prices rose in each of the first three quarters of November. Fourth-quarter prices continued to rise in seven of them (88%). The average yearly increase was +0.91%.

*Rose (7)*

*Fell (1)*

Fourth-quarter trend after prices rose in the past three quarters (FT Ordinary Share Index since 1935)

**November third-quarter signal No.2**

Also on the FT Ordinary Share Index, there have been 10 years since 1972 when third-quarter prices shifted slightly, within a range of -0.40% to +1.25%. Fourth-quarter prices rose in each of those years.

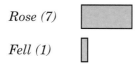

IMPROVEMENT

*Rose (10)*

*Fell (0)*

Fourth-quarter trend after third-quarter prices shifted by -0.40% to +1.25% (FT Ordinary Share Index since 1972)

## LOOKING AHEAD

For a glimpse of what the year ahead has to offer, November offers several price signals worth following.

**Rising prices by next 30 April**

A price rise of +7.07% to +22.85% in the last seven months is usually a good signal that prices will rise even further in the next five months, that is, to the end of next April.

Out of 22 times since 1922 when the FTSE All Share Index or its predecessor index rose within this range, shares continued to rise in the next five months 20 times. One of the two exceptions to the rule was in 1962–3 when prices fell just -0.10%.

*Rose (20)*

*Fell (2)*

Trend to April (next year) after a May to November price rise of +7.07% to +22.85% (FTSE All Share Index since 1922)

**Rising prices by next 28 February**

Over to the FT Ordinary Share Index, there have been 22 occasions since 1944 when shares shifted within a range of -1.50% to +5.78% in the past three months. The index rose in the next three months 20 times. In the remaining 31 years since 1944 that were untouched by this signal, December–February prices rose 18 times and fell 13 times.

*Rose (20)*

*Fell (2)*

Trend to February (next year) after a September to November price shift of -1.50% to +5.78% (FT Ordinary Share Index since 1944)

**Rising prices by next 31 July – signal No.1**

On the FT-Non-Financial Index and its predecessor index, November shares rose from +0.49% to +4.84% in 29 different years since 1926. Prices continued to rise in the next eight months, to 31 July of the following year, in 28 of those years.

*Rose (28)*

IMPROVEMENT

*Fell (1)*

Trend to 31 July (next year) after a November rise of +0.49% to +4.84% (FT-Non-Financial Index since 1926)

**Rising prices by next 31 July – signal No.2**

Here is a second signal based on the FT-Non-Financial Index that has a good track record of tipping where prices will stand by next 31 July. Since 1922, the first 11 months of the year rose by +15.54% or more in 22 different years. Prices continued to rise in the eight months that followed in 21 of those years.

*Rose (21)*

*Fell (1)*

Trend to 31 July (next year) after a January to November rise of +15.54% or more (FT-Non-Financial Index since 1922)

There have been 36 occasions since 1926 when one or both of these FT-Non-Financial Index price signals flashed. The record on 31 July of the following year was 34 up and two down. In the remaining 35 years untouched by either signal, the record for the next eight months was a disappointing 17 up and 18 down.

# CHAPTER 12 – DECEMBER

Investors often profit in December, a steady money-maker which has grown even more profitable in recent decades.

But there are wide differences in profitability between the different quarters of the month. Losses often appear in the first half of the month. In contrast, the third quarter is the year's second-best quarter. The fourth quarter is the year's best quarter. Five of the year's 10 best days land in this month.

Even better, the month to follow is the year's best month over the long-run, making December the start of the best two-month period of the year.

If you are thinking of buying shares, this is the month in which to do it.

Investors usually make money in December. Between 1919 and 1996, December prices rose 59% of the time. The average price rise was +1.13%, equal to 45 points on an FTSE 100 in the area of 4000. Over the long run, December is fourth-best in terms of monthly profitability, surpassed only by January, April and August.

**Steady profits** The constant December investor made an average annual profit in every decade on record, with the exception of the 1930s *(see Table 12.1)*. And even in that troubled decade, the record was five up and five down. A sharp fall of over 7% in 1931 during the heart of the 1928–32 bear market caused much of that decade's average annual loss.

To put things into context, a £1,000 December investment in 1919 would have grown to £2,277 by 1996 even with the 1930s included.

**Recent improvement** December's record is getting better. Since 1980, prices have risen in 12 out of 17 years, with an average monthly price rise of +2.01%, the third-best month of the year during this recent period.

**Infrequent bear markets** One reason for December's strong performance in recent decades is the below-average chance that a bear market down-turn will be in progress as the year draws to a close. As Table 12.2 reveals, bear markets more frequently occur in mid-year months. November, December and January suffered them less often. December is especially fortunate, having participated in just three bear markets since 1970, the best month of the year on this dimension.

**Small declines** And when a bear market is in progress as December rolls around, the pain is relatively small. The typical price change during December bear markets is -0.56%, the number one-ranked month on this dimension. Even when prices fall during December bear markets, the typical decline is -3.59%. While a drop of this size is nothing to sneer at, most other months are associated with much larger falls during bear market down-months. In fact,

## DECEMBER PRICE RISES AND DECLINES: 1919–1996

|  | Average December price change | Up | Down/ No change |
|---|---|---|---|
| 1920–29 | 0.57% | 7 | 3 |
| 1930–39 | -0.85% | 5 | 5 |
| 1940–49 | 0.66% | 4 | 6 |
| 1950–59 | 1.60% | 7 | 3 |
| 1960–69 | 0.94% | 5 | 5 |
| 1970–79 | 2.50% | 6 | 4 |
| 1980–89 | 1.88% | 6 | 4 |
| 1990–96 | 2.19% | 6 | 1 |
| Average December change: 1919–96 | 1.13% | 59% | 41% |
| Rank (of 12) | 4 | 5 | |

*Source: BZW, Datastream/ICV*

Table 12.1: The only loss-making decade was back in the 1930s. Since then, December has been consistently profitable.

December bear market drops are the most moderate of all 12 months *(see Table 12.3).*

Incidentally, small drops are not limited to bear markets. When prices fall in bull market Decembers, the size of the fall also tends to be lower than average. The typical December bull market decline is just -1.30%. In other words, you are unlikely to lose a great deal of money during down-months in bull market Decembers.

**Spotting bull markets** History shows that a small decline in November, no greater than -1.57%, or a rise of up to +4.86%, is usually associated with December bull markets. Keep in mind that these figures do not tell you when the bull market will end. It is conceivable that the following month will

403

## NUMBER OF BEAR MARKET MONTHS SINCE 1970

| | |
|---|---|
| January | 5 |
| February | 7 |
| March | 6 |
| April | 6 |
| May | 9 |
| June | 8 |
| July | 7 |
| August | 8 |
| September | 8 |
| October | 6 |
| November | 5 |
| December | 3 |

*Source: Datastream/ICV*

Table 12.2: The odds are low that the stock market will be engulfed in a bear market at year-end. December has participated in a bear market just three times since 1970, much less often than most other months.

see the start of a major trend change. Still, as a bull market announcement signal, a mild November price drop or gain cannot be beaten.

Unfortunately, we find no trend that is strongly associated with December bear markets. History does provide one note of caution however. As Figure 12.1 reveals, a November fall of -1.72% or more is associated with a bear market more than half the time. This is hardly conclusive evidence of course but if November is hit by a sizeable loss, it pays to invest with extreme caution until the situation is clarified.

First-half weakness

In bull markets and bear markets alike, there are differences in profitability between quarters. The month often starts off slowly with frequent losses near the

## DECEMBER PERFORMANCE IN BULL/BEAR MARKETS: 1919–1996

|  | Bull Markets | Bear Markets |
|---|---|---|
| Average per cent price change | 1.73% | -0.56% |
| Rank (of 12) | 7 | 1 |
|  |  |  |
| Per cent of time prices rise | 63% | 45% |
| Rank (of 12) | 9 | 3 |
|  |  |  |
| Average per cent price change in: |  |  |
| Rising years | 3.49% | 3.14% |
| Declining years | -1.30% | -3.59% |

*Source: BZW, Datastream/ICV*

Table 12.3: The average price change during bear markets is the best of all 12 months. Even during the average bear market down-month, prices drop -3.59%. While this represents a healthy decline, it is the best record of all 12 months.

beginning. But things soon start to sizzle. The third and fourth quarters are usually profitable and are ranked, respectively, in second and first place for the entire year *(see Figure 12.2)*. Investors should also recall that Number One-ranked January is just around the corner. The mid-December to January period is one of the most profitable stretches of the entire year.

### INCREASE YOUR PROFIT ODDS[1]

Although the overall December 'story' is a good one, there are several historical price trends that help investors to

---

[1]We will provide closing price trends on key indices for the last 12 months at no cost (see page 9).

## ODDS OF BULL/BEAR MARKET TIPPED BY NOVEMBER'S TREND

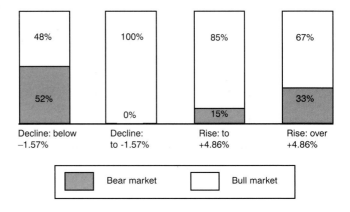

| 48% | 100% | 85% | 67% |
| 52% | 0% | 15% | 33% |

| Decline: below | Decline: | Rise: to | Rise: over |
| −1.57% | to -1.57% | +4.86% | +4.86% |

Bear market ☐ Bull market

*Source: BZW, Datastream/ICV*

Figure 12.1: Small November price swings, up or down, are usually associated with a bull market at the beginning of December.

**Prior 12-months signal**

improve significantly the odds of making a profitable December investment. Here is one of the best.

There have been 22 years in which share prices rose on the FT-Non-Financial Index or its predecessor index in the previous 12 months by at least +8.74% and in the previous two months by +0.96% to +7.94%. December prices rose in 21 of those years. The single losing month was December 1941 when prices fell in the aftermath of Japan's 7 December surprise attacks and Britain's Declaration of War on Japan on 8 December.

In the recent past, this signal flashed in 1995 and 1996. Stock market prices rose in December in both years.

## QUARTERLY ODDS OF PRICE RISE IN DECEMBER

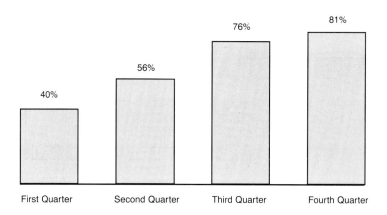

*Source: Financial Times, Datastream/ICV*

Figure 12.2: The trend steadily improves as the month progresses. The final quarter of the year rises 81% of the time, the year's best record. The third-quarter record is almost as good.

UPDATE

*Rose (21)*

*Fell (1)*

December's record after a previous 12 month price rise of at least +8.74% and previous two-month rise of +0.96% to +7.94% (FT-Non-Financial Index since 1922)

Prior three-months signal

The price trend in the three months that precede December often provides good clues for the December investor. There have been 16 years when the FT-Non-Financial Index or its predecessor index shifted between -1.74% to +5.96% in the preceding three months and rose by +0.61% to +5.58% in November. December share prices rose in every one of those years.

UPDATE

*Rose (16)*

*Fell (0)* |

December's record after a previous three-month shift of -1.74% to +5.96% and a November rise of +0.61% to +5.58% (FT-Non-Financial Index since 1922)

If we eliminate duplication within these two trends, there are 29 years that are flagged by at least one of them since 1922. The December record during these years is 28 up and one down. In years untouched by either one of these two up-trend signals, December's record has been simply terrible – 17 up and 29 down.

October/
November
signal

Here are two more trends to help improve the odds of identifying a declining December. In years untouched by either of the two up-trend forecasts just discussed, an October/November price rise on the FT-Non-Financial Index or its predecessor index within a range of +0.90% to +14.51% is an important red flag danger signal. Out of 20 occasions with a price rise within this range since 1933, December prices fell 17 times.

*Rose (3)*

*Fell (17)*

December's record after an October/November price rise of +0.90% to +14.51% in years untouched by either up-trend forecast (FT-Non-Financial Index since 1933)

Prior seven-
months signal

If prices are weak in the seven months preceding December, there is a reasonably high likelihood that shares will also fall in December. Since 1931, there have been 11 declines on the FTSE All Share Index or its predecessor index between 1 May and 30 November within a range of -1.06% to -6.71%. Shares fell further in December in nine of those years. One of the exceptions was a rise of just +0.10% in 1990. The most recent May to November decline occurred in 1994 and December prices fell as expected.

IMPROVEMENT

*Rose (2)*

*Fell (9)*

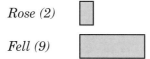

December's record after a May to November price drop of -1.06% to -6.71% in years untouched by either up-trend forecast (FTSE All Share Index since 1931)

**Prior six-months signal**

Here is a useful down-side indicator based upon the price trend on the FT Ordinary Share Index over the past six months. Since 1948, there have been 10 occasions when prices shifted moderately in the preceding six months by -2.19% to +1.26%. December prices fell in nine of those years.

NEW

*Rose (1)*

*Fell (9)*

December's record after a previous six-month price shift of -2.19% to +1.26% (FT Ordinary Share Index since 1948)

**November signal**

Also on the FT Ordinary Share Index, there have been 11 occasions since 1958 when the stock market rose in November by +1.74% to +6.25%. December rose 10 times out of the 11.

409

Rose (10)

Fell (1)

December's record after a November price rise of +1.74% to +6.25% (FT Ordinary Share Index since 1958)

There have been 28 additional years since 1958 untouched by this signal. The December record on the FT Ordinary Share Index was quite poor, 12 increases and 16 declines.

## FIRST QUARTER OF DECEMBER – DECEMBER 1ST TO 8TH

Prices rise just 40% of the time, the year's second-worst quarter. The chance of a price rise is below average in bull and bear markets alike. It is a funny way to start what will turn out to be a profitable month in most years.

Given this weak record and the fact that the beginning of December's second quarter is also often weak, the best strategy to follow is to invest cautiously during this part of the month.

Be especially careful on 4 December, the worst day of the quarter.

Poor record

December may be a good month in which to invest – but not its first quarter. Prices rise just 40% of the time, making the first quarter the worst performer of the month and the 47th-ranked out of 48 quarters (*see Table 12.4*).

Prices fell in the average year in most decades. Two exceptions were in the 1950s and 1970s. Further investigation finds a record of three up and seven down in the

## PERCENTAGE PRICE CHANGE: DECEMBER 1935–96

|  | Dec 1–8 | Dec 9–15 | Dec 16–23 | Dec 24–31 |
|---|---|---|---|---|
| Annual average |  |  |  |  |
| 1935–39 | -0.63% | 0.12% | 0.40% | 0.73% |
| 1940–49 | -0.04% | 0.29% | 0.54% | 0.67% |
| 1950–59 | 0.18% | 1.20% | 0.36% | 1.23% |
| 1960–69 | -0.61% | 0.69% | -0.18% | 0.92% |
| 1970–79 | 0.31% | -1.07% | 1.93% | 1.36% |
| 1980–89 | -0.30% | 0.06% | 1.16% | 0.94% |
| 1990–96 | -0.23% | -0.01% | 1.41% | 1.07% |
| Average quarterly price change | -0.15% | 0.20% | 0.80% | 1.00% |
| Per cent of time prices rise | 40% | 56% | 76% | 81% |

*Source: Financial Times, Datastream/ICV*

Table 12.4: Despite the profitable record for the month, the first quarter is a money-loser in most years. The second-quarter trend has taken a turn for the worse with a poor performance in recent decades. But things soon change. The second half of the month is usually quite profitable.

1950s. Strong profits in 1955 and 1956 were responsible for all of that decade's profit. A similar pattern unfolded in the 1970s with a record of five up and five down. However, a single rise of +7.63% in 1976 accounted for most of that decade's profit.

Recent weakness

The recent record has brought more of the same. Since 1990, the record was three up and four down.

During bull market years, prices rise 44% of the time, well below average. It is the second-worst bull market quarter of the year. The bear market trend is also poor

411

## DECEMBER FIRST-QUARTER PERFORMANCE IN BULL/BEAR MARKETS: 1935–1996

|  | Total | Bull Markets | Bear Markets |
|---|---|---|---|
| Average price change | -0.15% | 0.10% | -0.82% |
| Rank (of 48) | 35 | 39 | 31 |
| Per cent of time prices rise | 40% | 44% | 29% |
| Rank (of 48) | 47 | 47 | 40 |

*Source: Financial Times, Datastream/ICV*

Table 12.5: The first quarter is the second-worst segment of the year, quite surprising for a month with such a strong overall record. The odds of a price rise are disappointing in bull and bear markets alike.

with the chance of a price rise just 29%, the 40th-ranked quarter of the year during bear markets *(see Table 12.5)*.

4 December

Despite the poor overall record, prices rise about half the time on most days. A notable exception is 4 December, the worst day of the quarter. Prices rise just 35% of the time, one of the worst trading days of the year.

In recent editions of the *Schwartz Stock Market Handbook*, we warned investors that there has been no sign of a trend change on this day in recent years. This warning continues to hold true.

Since 1984, the 4 December record is one up and eight down. The single exception was a rise of just +0.03% in 1990 – an exception that proves the rule *(see Figure 12.3)*.

Weak Monday

Prices tend to rise at a below-average rate on most days of the week, with Monday having the worst record of all *(see Figure 12.4)*. The only day of the week that rises more than half the time is Friday.

## PERCENTAGE OF TIME PRICES RISE EACH TRADING DAY IN DECEMBER'S FIRST QUARTER

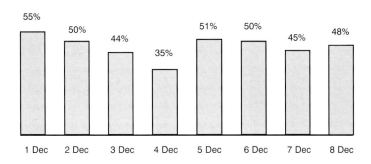

*Source: Financial Times, Datastream/ICV*

Figure 12.3: Stock market prices often fall on 4 December, a trend that has been in progress for many decades. Nothing has changed in recent years. Since 1984, the record is one up and eight down. The single exception was a gain of just +0.03% in 1990.

### INCREASE YOUR PROFIT ODDS

If you are thinking about betting on a first-quarter price drop, one word of caution. Be prepared to move fast. Even if the second quarter continues to be weak, a trend that has been apparent in recent years, the year-end rally is likely to begin soon.

We start with a trend that has frequently been associated with price drops in the first quarter in recent decades.

November fourth-quarter signal

Since 1971, a swing on the FT-Non-Financial Index in the preceding quarter within a range of -2.82% to +1.32% has occurred 14 times. First-quarter prices fell in 12 of those years. In the remaining 12 years of this period, prices rose nine times and fell three times.

413

## PERCENTAGE OF TIME PRICES RISE EACH DAY OF WEEK IN DECEMBER'S FIRST QUARTER

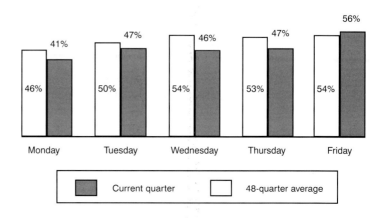

*Source: Financial Times, Datastream/ICV*

Figure 12.4: The odds of a price rise are low for most week days except Friday.

<NEW>

*Rose (2)*

*Fell (12)*

First-quarter record after a price shift of -2.82% to +1.32% in November's fourth quarter (FT-Non-Financial Index since 1971)

November
second-half
signal

A similar trend runs on the FTSE All Share Index within in a range of -3.00% to +1.37%.

Turning to the FT Ordinary Share Index, there have been 10 years since 1942 with a small price shift in November's second half, no more than -0.48% on the down-side and no more than +0.58% on the up-side.

First-quarter prices fell in nine of those years at an average of -1.19% per year. The single exception occurred back in 1944.

*Rose (1)*

*Fell (9)*

First-quarter record after a price shift of -0.48% to +0.58% in November's second half (FT Ordinary Share Index since 1942)

## SECOND QUARTER OF DECEMBER – DECEMBER 9TH TO 15TH

> Invest with caution in the second quarter which has risen less than half of the time in recent years.
>
> History shows that much of the weakness occurs in the first half of the quarter, especially 9 December which falls in two out of three years.

**Recent weakness**

Over the long term, the second quarter rose 56% of the time and produced an average annual profit of +0.20%. Unfortunately, the trend has weakened in recent years. Up until 1970, prices rose 66% of the time. Since 1970, the odds of a price rise have slipped to less than 50:50. There has been no sign of recovery since the 1987 crash. Prices have risen five times and fallen five times in the last 10 years. Clearly, the year-end rally that investors enjoy in most years is often not yet in progress during the second quarter *(see Table 12.6)*.

**Bull markets weak**

During bull markets, the odds of a price rise are about average compared with other bull market quarters of the year. But as we have just seen, the trend slipped in recent decades. Since 1975, the second quarter has risen

415

## PERCENTAGE PRICE CHANGE: DECEMBER 1985–96

| | December 1–8 | December 9–15 | December 16–23 | December 24–31 |
|---|---|---|---|---|
| 1985 | -2.50% | -1.37% | 0.38% | 1.58% |
| 1986 | -0.40% | 0.75% | 1.09% | 1.02% |
| 1987 | 2.41% | 3.28% | 6.32% | -2.82% |
| 1988 | -2.53% | -0.16% | 0.79% | 1.21% |
| 1989 | 3.36% | -0.61% | 0.63% | 2.34% |
| 1990 | 1.80% | -0.74% | -0.33% | -0.69% |
| 1991 | -1.75% | 2.30% | -4.16% | 5.47% |
| 1992 | 0.12% | -1.42% | 4.52% | 0.69% |
| 1993 | 3.29% | 0.30% | 3.57% | 0.73% |
| 1994 | -2.08% | -1.12% | 3.16% | -0.32% |
| 1995 | -0.85% | 0.39% | 0.41% | 0.83% |
| 1996 | -2.16% | 0.20% | 2.67% | 0.78% |
| Average quarterly price change | -0.11% | 0.15% | 1.59% | 0.90% |
| Number of years in which prices | | | | |
| Rose | 5 | 6 | 10 | 9 |
| Fell | 7 | 6 | 2 | 3 |

*Source: Datastream/ICV*

Table 12.6: A price rise in the first half of December has not been the norm in recent years. But shares usually rise in the second half of the month. It is a long-running trend that shows no signs of weakening recently.

**Good bear market record**

in just nine of 21 bull market years, a 43% success rate. The chance of a price rise in bear markets appears to be quite good. Over the long run, shares rise 59% of the time, the seventh-best bear market quarter of the year.

## DECEMBER SECOND-QUARTER PERFORMANCE IN BULL/BEAR MARKETS: 1935–1996

|  | Total | Bull Markets | Bear Markets |
|---|---|---|---|
| Average price change | 0.20% | 0.50% | -0.61% |
| Rank (of 48) | 20 | 24 | 26 |
|  |  |  |  |
| Per cent of time prices rise | 56% | 56% | 59% |
| Rank (of 48) | 20 | 32 | 7 |

*Source: Financial Times, Datastream/ICV*

Table 12.7:  Prices have risen more than half the time in bull market years over the long term. But the trend has weakened in recent years. Since 1975, prices have risen 43% of the time in bull markets. There have been few bear markets in recent years so we cannot tell if the bear market trend is changing as well.

But keep in mind that there have been few bear markets in this quarter in recent years and we don't know the degree to which recent weakness will affect bear markets during this part of the year *(see Table 12.7)*.

**First-half damage**

Bull or bear market, history shows that much of the damage often occurs near the beginning of the quarter. The quarter's worst day is its opener, 9 December. Prices rise just 36% of the time. This is a long-running pattern that continues right to the present. In recent years, prices have fallen in nine of the last 12 years.

**10 and 11 December**

It also pays to be watchful on 10–11 December, two other potentially dangerous days near the beginning of the quarter. Although the long-term record for each day is profitable, the record has weakened in recent years. Since 1984, prices rose once and fell seven times on each day *(see Figure 12.5)*.

**13 December**

The record is good for the remaining days of this

417

## PERCENTAGE OF TIME PRICES RISE EACH TRADING DAY IN DECEMBER'S SECOND QUARTER

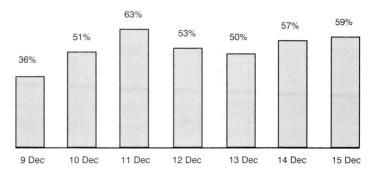

*Source: Financial Times, Datastream/ICV*

Figure 12.5: The worst day of the quarter is 9 December. It is a long-running trend that has shown no sign of improvement in recent years. Be careful on 11–12 December as well. Prices have been very weak in recent years.

quarter with no signs of recent weakness. In fact, 13 December has risen in eight out of nine attempts since 1984.

Analysis of profit trends by day of week shows that Tuesday and Thursday are generally the best days in the second quarter *(see Figure 12.6)*.

Don't jump in too soon

Considering all the evidence, our historical review sends an exceedingly clear message. If you are thinking about buying shares, the time to do it is fast approaching. (More information will be provided in the next section.) But don't be too quick to jump into shares at the very start of the second quarter.

### INCREASE YOUR PROFIT ODDS

Although the profit odds have weakened in recent years,

## PERCENTAGE OF TIME PRICES RISE EACH DAY OF WEEK IN DECEMBER'S SECOND QUARTER

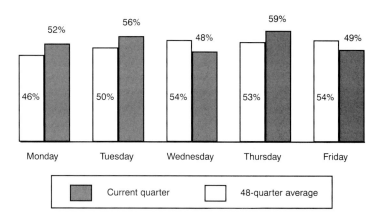

Source: Financial Times, Datastream/ICV

Figure 12.6: The chance of profiting is best on second-quarter Tuesdays and Thursdays.

**First-quarter signal**

prices do rise in some years. Here are three trends that have done a good job of forecasting rising second-quarter prices.

Since 1941, there have been 15 occasions in which the FTSE All Share Index or its predecessor index fell between -0.15% to -0.96% in the preceding quarter. The stock market rose in the second quarter in 14 of those years.

*Rose (14)*

*Fell (1)*

Second-quarter record after a price drop in the first quarter of -0.15% to -0.96% (FTSE All Share Index since 1941)

Prior two-
quarters signal
No.1

There have been 12 occasions since 1958 in which prices on the FTSE All Share Index or its predecessor index shifted between -0.62% to +1.13% in the preceding two quarters. Second-quarter prices rose in 11 of those years.

*Rose (11)*

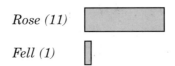

*Fell (1)*

Second-quarter record after a price shift in the preceding two quarters of -0.62% to +1.13% (FTSE All Share Index since 1958)

Prior two-
quarters signal
No.2

Turning to the FT Ordinary Share Index, if shares shift within a narrow range of -1.00% to +2.96% in November's fourth quarter, and -1.54% to +0.39% in December's first quarter, they will probably rise in the second quarter. There have been 21 years with price shifts within these ranges. Second-quarter prices rose in 19 of them.

UPDATE

*Rose (19)*

*Fell (2)*

Second-quarter record after a price shift of -1.00% to +2.96% in November's fourth quarter and -1.54% to +0.39% in December's first quarter (FT Ordinary Share Index since 1936)

We called attention to this indicator in a previous edition of the *Schwartz Stock Market Handbook*. Since then, the necessary conditions occurred in 1995 and second-quarter prices rose as expected.

# THIRD QUARTER OF DECEMBER – DECEMBER 16TH TO 23RD

> Here comes the start of a very profitable stretch. Prices rise in three out of four years. Good trading conditions often run through to the end of January.
> Several of the year's most profitable days land in this quarter including 22 and 23 December.

**Good profit opportunity**

December's third quarter has been a nice little money-earner during the past six decades. Even more important, it marks the beginning of a profitable stretch that runs through to early February. While you would not have profited in every single quarter nor in every single year, the record shows that between 1935 to 1996, the average share price rose sharply during this seven-quarter stretch.

**Second-best quarter**

A year-by-year study of December's third quarter trend reveals that prices have risen 76% of the time. The only segment of the year that rose more often was December's fourth quarter which rose 81% of the time. Third-quarter share prices have increased by an average annual rate of +0.80%.

The worst-ever decade for the third quarter was in the 1960s when investors lost at an average rate of -0.18% per year. But even then, the record was six up and four down. Many of the price moves of that decade were small. As a result, the biggest decline of that decade, a relatively small -3.84% in 1967, had a much larger effect on the overall average than similar-sized declines usually have.

**Good recent trend**

The recent trend is as strong as ever. Prices rose in the 1980s 10 times in a row. They fell in 1990 and 1991, and were immediately followed by five more advances in a row.

**Bull and bear markets**

Broad stock market conditions have little affect on the third-quarter record. During bull markets, prices rise

## DECEMBER THIRD-QUARTER PERFORMANCE IN BULL/BEAR MARKETS: 1935–1996

|  | Total | Bull Markets | Bear Markets |
|---|---|---|---|
| Average price change | 0.80% | 0.95% | 0.37% |
| Rank (of 48) | 6 | 8 | 4 |
| Per cent of time prices rise | 76% | 80% | 63% |
| Rank (of 48) | 2 | 1 | 4 |

*Source: Financial Times, Datastream/ICV*

Table 12.8: Prices rise in three out of four years, the second-best record of the year. The chance of profit is high in bull and bear markets alike.

80% of the time, the best bull market quarter of the year. During bear markets, prices rise 63% of the time, the fourth-best quarter of the year *(see Table 12.8)*.

**22 and 23 December**

Analysis of share price trends on a day-by-day basis finds several weak days near the beginning of the quarter. But things soon improve. Prices rise 75% of the time on 22 December, and 70% of the time on 23 December, each one being among the year's top 10 days *(see Figure 12.7)*.

**Friday**

The odds of a price rise are also quite good on third-quarter Fridays. Prices rise 73% of the time, the best Friday performance of all 48 quarters *(see Figure 12.8)*.

We have previously warned *Schwartz Stock Market Handbook* readers of above-average third-quarter volatility. Nothing has changed in recent years. Prices have shifted by over 2.50% (down as well as up) in five of the six most recent years. It is great news in up years but could be painful when the trend is down. We shall continue to watch this new trend with great interest.

## PERCENTAGE OF TIME PRICES RISE EACH TRADING DAY IN DECEMBER'S THIRD QUARTER

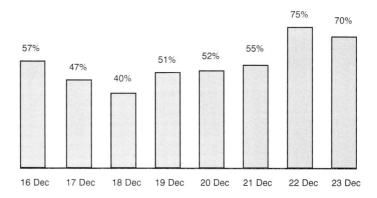

Source: Financial Times, Datastream/ICV

Figure 12.7: The week before Christmas has a secret weapon. 22 December rises 75% of the time, and 23 December rises 70% of the time. Both are among the year's best performers.

### Increase Your Profit Odds

There have been just five declines on the FTSE All Share Index during this quarter since 1969, so there is not much point in trying to spot occasions when the likelihood of a price rise is better than normal. After all, it is hard to improve upon perfection.

Prior two-quarters signal No.1

However, one recent development is worth noting. Each of the five recent falls occurred when the previous two quarters rose by +0.21% to +1.54%. Since 1969, there have been eight up-moves within this range. The third-quarter record was three rises and five declines. It does not mean prices will automatically drop following this signal but it does suggest a need for caution.

During the remaining 20 years untouched by this trend, the third quarter rose each time.

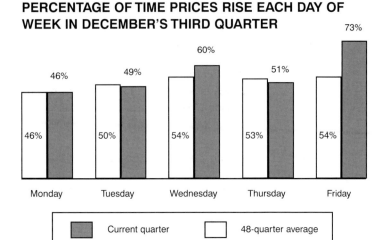

**PERCENTAGE OF TIME PRICES RISE EACH DAY OF WEEK IN DECEMBER'S THIRD QUARTER**

*Source: Financial Times, Datastream/ICV*

Figure 12.8: Fridays rise 73% of the time, the best Friday record of all 48 quarters.

NEW

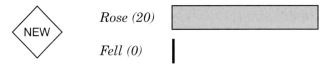

*Rose (20)*

*Fell (0)*

Third-quarter record if prices did not rise within a range of +0.21% to +1.54% in the first and second quarter of December (FTSE All Share Index since 1969)

**Prior two-quarters signal No.2**

A similar trend has run on the FT-Non-Financial Index in recent decades. Since 1969, there have been seven occasions with a swing in the preceding two quarters of -0.02% to +0.99%. Third-quarter prices fell in five of those years. In the remaining 21 years, third-quarter prices rose each time.

*Rose (21)*

*Fell (0)*

Third-quarter record if prices did not shift within a range of
-0.02% to +0.99% in the first and second quarter of December
(FT-Non-Financial Index since 1969)

Second-quarter
signal

It also helps to monitor the FT Ordinary Share Index.
History shows that if prices shift moderately in the
second quarter, the odds of a third-quarter increase are
quite good. Since 1939, there have been 26 years with
second-quarter price shifts in the range of -1.14% to
+0.61%. Third-quarter prices rose in 25 of those years.
The single exception was back in 1957.

*Rose (25)*

*Fell (1)*

Third-quarter record after a price shift in the second quarter of
-1.14% to +0.61% (FT Ordinary Share Index since 1939)

425

# Fourth Quarter of December – December 24th to 31st

Historically, this is the best quarter of the year. Prices rise, unbelievably, 81% of the time. Three of the year's best days land in this segment of the month.

Year's Number
One quarter

Investors frequently profit during the fourth quarter of December. It is the very best quarter of the entire year. Three of the 10 best days of the year are in this segment of December.

Unbelievably
good record

Between 1936 and 1996, prices rose, unbelievably, 81% of the time. The average annual gain was +1.00%. Both figures are the best of all 48 quarters of the year. There are no guarantees for any single year of course. By definition, an 81% likelihood of profit means that shares will fall in one out of five years as well. Still, an 81% likelihood of profit is an impressive record.

The fourth segment of the month has produced an average annual profit in every decade on record. The 'worst' decade was the 1940s when the average annual profit was just +0.67%, equivalent to 27 points on an FTSE 100 in the area of 4000.

Recent trend
good

The recent trend remains strong. The record for the bull market 1980s was nine up, one down, and an average annual profit of +0.94%. Since 1990, the fourth quarter has risen in five of the past seven years.

Prices rise in four out of five years in bull and bear markets alike, the number one-ranked quarter in both cases *(see Table 12.9)*.

Happy
Christmas

In the period covering the final three trading days before Christmas and all trading days between Christmas and New Year's Day, share prices fell just nine times in the 62 years between 1935 and 1996 (15%). It is the closest thing to a guaranteed profit that the stock market will ever offer.

## DECEMBER FOURTH-QUARTER PERFORMANCE IN BULL/BEAR MARKETS: 1935–1996

|  | Total | Bull Markets | Bear Markets |
|---|---|---|---|
| Average price change | 1.00% | 0.91% | 1.27% |
| Rank (of 48) | 1 | 11 | 1 |
|  |  |  |  |
| Per cent of time prices rise | 81% | 80% | 81% |
| Rank (of 48) | 1 | 1 | 1 |

*Source: Financial Times, Datastream/ICV*

Table 12.9: During bull and bear markets alike, the chance of a price rise is high.

**24, 27 and 29 December**

Analysis of share price trends on a daily basis shows above-average strength throughout this quarter. 24, 27 and 29 December are each among the 10 most profitable days of the entire year *(see Figure 12.9)*. The recent record shows no sign of weakness for any day in this quarter.

The odds of a price rise on each day of the week are also quite high. Each day turns in one of the best records of all 48 quarters *(see Figure 12.10)*.

### INCREASE YOUR PROFIT ODDS

Given that there have been just six declines on the FTSE All Share Index during the fourth quarter since 1969, it is difficult to spot occasions when the profit odds are better than average.

**Prior four-quarters signal**

But one development is worth noting. Five of the six recent falls occurred when the previous four quarters shifted within a range of -0.30% to +2.77%. Since 1969, there have been 10 shifts within this range. The fourth-

427

## PERCENTAGE OF TIME PRICES RISE EACH TRADING DAY IN DECEMBER'S FOURTH QUARTER

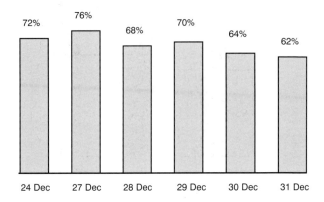

*Source: Financial Times, Datastream/ICV*

Figure 12.9: The fourth quarter may be shortened by holidays, but prices tend to rise on the few days that trading does occur. 24, 27 and 29 December are among the year's best days. The odds of a profit on the remaining days are also quite good.

quarter record was five rises and five declines.

During the remaining 18 years untouched by this trend, the second quarter rose virtually every time.

*Rose (17)*

*Fell (1)*

Fourth-quarter record if the previous four quarters fell by more than -0.30% or rose by more than +2.77% (FTSE All Share Index since 1969)

Here is another useful trend to help spot when a fourth-

## PERCENTAGE OF TIME PRICES RISE EACH DAY OF WEEK IN DECEMBER'S FOURTH QUARTER

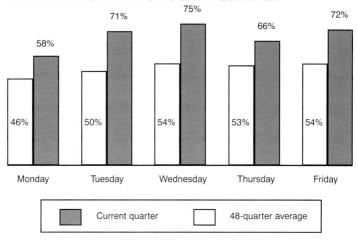

*Source: Financial Times, Datastream/ICV*

Figure 12.10: Price rises are likely to occur on each weekday of the quarter.

**Third-quarter signal No.1**

quarter drop is most likely. Since 1969, third-quarter prices fell by at least -0.12% on the FT-Non-Financial Index five times. Fourth-quarter prices fell still further in four of those years.

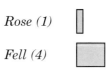

*Rose (1)*

*Fell (4)*

Fourth-quarter record after a price fall in the third quarter of at least -0.12% (FT-Non-Financial Index since 1969)

On the FT Ordinary Share Index, the size of the third-

Third-quarter
signal No.2

quarter price shift also does a fine job of helping investors to increase the odds of catching a profitable fourth quarter. There have been 29 third quarters with small price shifts, within a range of -0.19% to +0.89%. Fourth-quarter prices fell in just one of those years, a -0.09% fall (equal to four points on a 4000 FTSE 100) back in 1950.

*Rose (28)*

*Fell (1)*

Fourth-quarter record after a price shift in the third quarter of -0.19% to +0.89% (FT Ordinary Share Index since 1935)

Prior three-
quarters signal

Although the odds of losing money on shares like those in the FT Ordinary Share Index are low, most fourth-quarter declines occur when prices in the first three quarters of the month shift by a small amount. Since 1946, there have been 12 occasions when prices shifted by -0.45% to +1.30% in the first three quarters. Fourth-quarter prices fell in eight of those years. In two of the four exceptional years, fourth-quarter profits were tiny, +0.35% in 1977 and +0.26% in 1963.

*Rose (4)*

UPDATE

*Fell (8)*

Fourth-quarter record after a price shift of -0.45% to +1.30% in the first three quarters of December

In the remaining 39 years since 1946, the fourth-quarter record was 37 up and two down.

## LOOKING AHEAD

For a preview of what the first three months of 1997 have in store for you, the price trend over the past 12 months provides a useful clue.

**Rising prices by next 31 March**

Since 1956, there have been 16 years when prices shifted on the FTSE All Share Index or its predecessor index within a range of -14.31% to +7.24% in the year ending 31 December. On each occasion, prices rose in the next three months (to 31 March of the year ahead).

IMPROVEMENT

*Rose (16)*

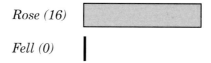

*Fell (0)*

Trend to March 31 (next year) after a January to December price shift of -14.31% to +7.24% (FTSE All Share Index since 1956)

In the remaining 25 years of this period, the odds of a first-quarter profit were much lower – 15 up and 10 down.

**Rising prices by next 30 June**

A price shift on the FTSE All Share Index or its predecessor index in the past six months of -0.27% to +8.48% is usually a good signal that prices will rise in the next six months, that is, to the end of June of next year. Out of 24 times with a price shift within this range, prices rose in the next six months 21 times.

*Rose (21)*

*Fell (3)*

Trend to 30 June (next year) after a price shift of -0.27% to +8.48% (FTSE All Share Index since 1926)

And on the down-side, a price decline on the FTSE All

**Falling prices
by next 30 June**

Share Index or its predecessor index in the preceding six months of -3.86% to -11.60% is a useful signal that prices are likely to decline still further in the next six months.

Since 1920, there have been 12 occasions with price drops within this range in the preceding six months. Prices fell still further in the following six months 11 times.

*Rose (1)*

*Fell (11)*

Trend to 30 June (next year) after a price decline in the last six months of -3.86% to -11.60% (FTSE All Share Index since 1920)

**Rising prices by
next 30 April**

The FT Ordinary Share Index also does a good job of tipping where shares are heading in the months ahead.

Since 1943, there have been 18 years on record with a September to December price swing of -2.24% to +2.88%. Prices rose by 30 April of the following year in 17 of those years.

*Rose (17)*

*Fell (1)*

Trend to 30 April (next year) after a September to December price swing of -2.24% to +2.88% (FT Ordinary Share Index since 1943)